C000297983

MUSIC
CONNECTIONS

Practical Music for all Primary Class Teachers
Key Stages 1 and 2

KATE BUCHANAN & STEPHEN CHADWICK

CRAMER MUSIC

This Book Belongs to
Estelle Furnell
8 The Pightle
Burnham Thorpe, King's Lynn
Norfolk PE31 8HT
01328 730574 or 07779 205705

CONTENTS

THREE SEEDS

Music: Traditional
Words: Kate Buchanan

Play last 2 bars for introduction

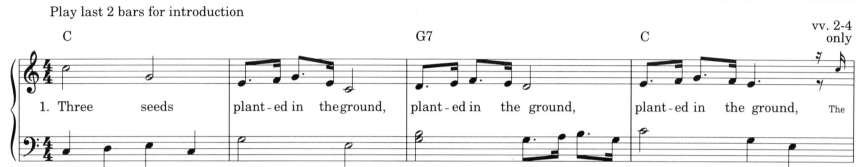

© 1995 Middle Eight Music Ltd. Published by Cramer Music Ltd.

C.M. Ltd. 2173

HIDDEN IN THE JUNGLE

Words and music: Stephen Chadwick

© 1995 Middle Eight Music Ltd. Published by Cramer Music Ltd.

WHAT TIME IS IT ON THE CLOCK?

Words and music: Stephen Chadwick

Fine last time

© 1995 Middle Eight Music Ltd. Published by Cramer Music Ltd. C.M. Ltd. 2173

ROOF TOP CAT

Words and music: Stephen Chadwick

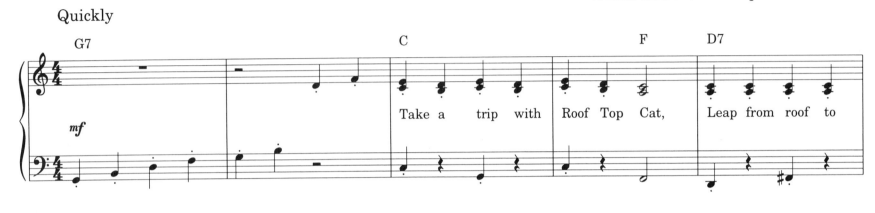

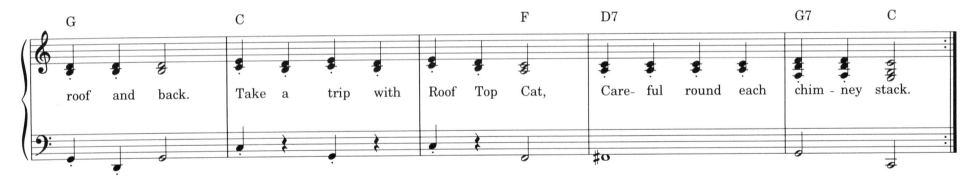

© 1995 Middle Eight Music Ltd. Published by Cramer Music Ltd.

C.M. Ltd. 2173

WASH DAY

Music: Traditional
Words: Stephen Chadwick

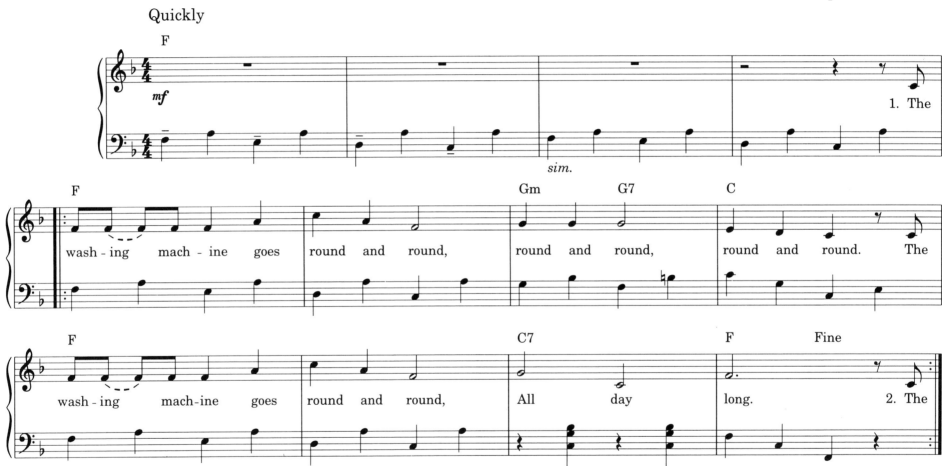

Verse 2   The water down the pipe goes
glug glug glug etc.

Verse 3   The clothes on the line go
flap flap flap etc.

Verse 3   The iron on the board goes
left and right etc.

© 1995 Middle Eight Music Ltd. Published by Cramer Music Ltd.

C.M. Ltd. 2173

NOISY TRAFFIC

Words and music: Kate Buchanan

Reggae style

© 1995 Middle Eight Music Ltd. Published by Cramer Music Ltd.

C.M. Ltd. 2173

Counting section

D.C. Verses 2 & 3

(One two three four five six seven) Lis-ten to the roar!

Verse 2   Noisy traffic, clogging up our town,
           Buses, vans, don't they make you frown?
           Fumes all around us, we want no more.
           Noisy traffic, listen to the roar!

Counting Section
           (One two three four five six seven)
           Listen to the roar!

Verse 3   Noisy traffic, what a dreadful din!
           Motorbikes, throw them in the bin.
           Fumes all around us, we want no more
           Noisy traffic, listen to the roar!

Counting Section
           (One two three four five six seven)
           Listen to the roar!

© 1995 Middle Eight Music Ltd. Published by Cramer Music Ltd.

C.M. Ltd. 2173

TOP ATHLETE

Music: Traditional
Words: Stephen Chadwick

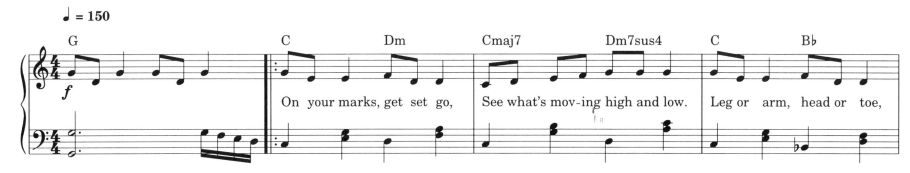

On your marks, get set go, See what's mov-ing high and low. Leg or arm, head or toe,

Is it fast or slow? Heart beat pound-ing like a drum, Mus-cle pops up like a plum. Top ath-lete, fit-ness freak,

last time to Coda **Counting or Grid Score section**   **Coda**

TRAIN-ING at your peak (One Two Three Four Five Six Seven GET READY)

© 1995 Middle Eight Music Ltd. Published by Cramer Music Ltd.

C.M. Ltd. 2173

WEATHER WITCH

Words and music: Stephen Chadwick

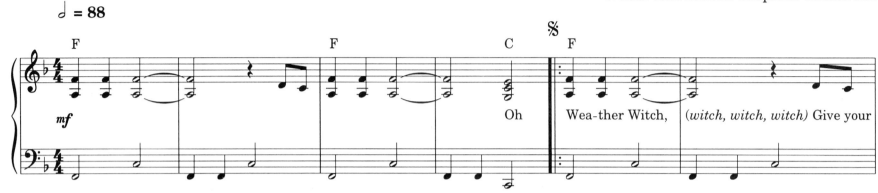

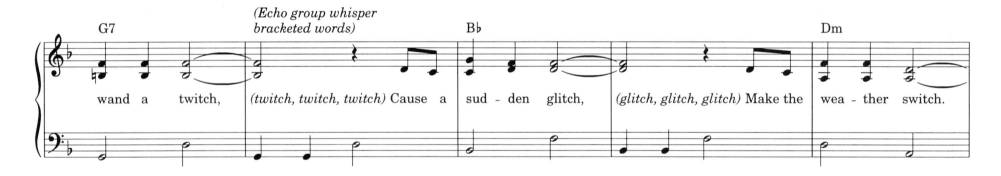

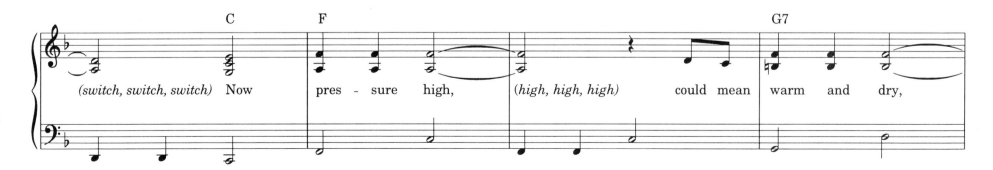

© 1995 Middle Eight Music Ltd. Published by Cramer Music Ltd.

C.M. Ltd. 2173

DINOSAUR

Words and music: Stephen Chadwick

© 1995 Middle Eight Music Ltd. Published by Cramer Music Ltd.

C.M. Ltd. 2173

force was hurled. Dust and smoke blot out the sun, For di-no-saurs their time had come, But some sur-vive and

cresc.

stay a-live, I'm sure.

mf

Coda

gone.

dim.

rit.

pp

Verse 2   Fossilised within a rock,
A skeleton we tap and knock.
Skull or thigh or tooth or toe,
It's all we've got to put on show,
But some survive and stay alive, I'm sure.

Chorus

Verse 3   In my sleep I thought I saw
A very large pink dinosaur.
Dreamt of things pre-history,
That when I woke could no more see,
But some survive and stay alive, I'm sure.

Chorus

CHATTER WITH THE ANGELS

Words and Music: Traditional

© 1995 Middle Eight Music Ltd. Published by Cramer Music Ltd.

C.M. Ltd. 2173

THE CARNIVAL OF ANIMAL LIFE

Words and music: Stephen Chadwick
based on music by Saint-Saëns

© 1995 Middle Eight Music Ltd. Published by Cramer Music Ltd.

C.M. Ltd. 2173

Chorus

In the wa-ter plank-ton soup will set the food chain on its loop. From the co-ral to the whale, they all ex-ist on
E - vo - lu -tion star-ted here, it's where the world got in-to gear. From a - moe-ba to man-kind, a bil-lion spe-cies

D.C. (Introduction) for Verses 2 & 3
3rd time carry on to coda

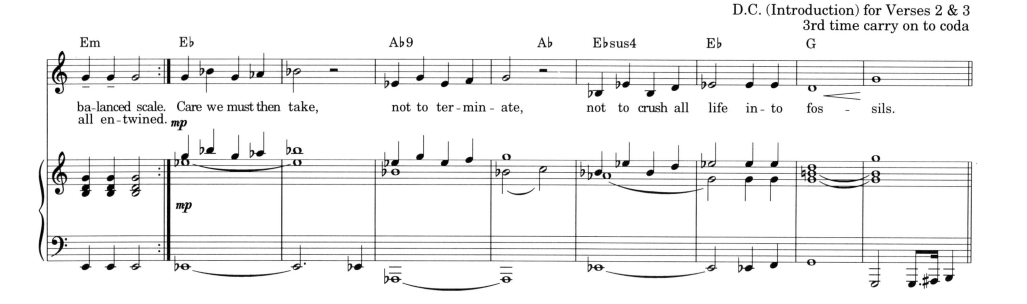

ba-lanced scale. Care we must then take, not to ter-min - ate, not to crush all life in-to fos - sils.
all en-twined.

Chorus: In the water.....

C.M. Ltd. 2173

Coda from chorus 3rd time

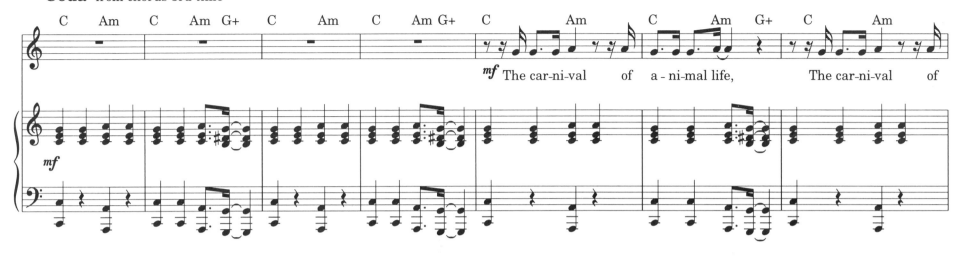

mf The car-ni-val of a-ni-mal life, The car-ni-val of

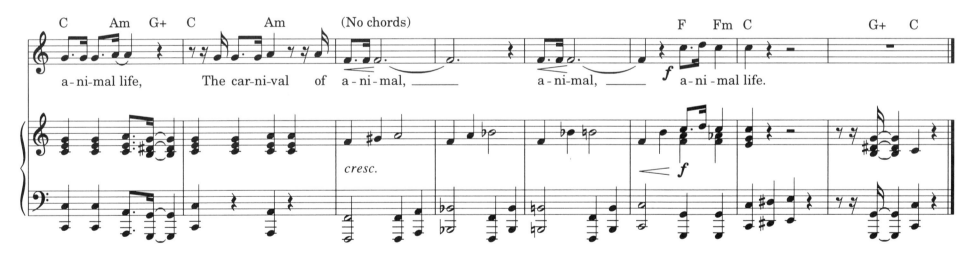

a-ni-mal life, The car-ni-val of a-ni-mal, a-ni-mal, a-ni-mal life.

Verse 2 The carnival of animal tone,
         Parade of signals in full colour shown.
         Colours warn, colours hide,
         Colours say will you be my bride.
         The carnival of animal sound,
         Primeval music to tell all around.
         Tell of love, tell of fear,
         Tell the world freedom you hold dear.

Chorus

Verse 3 The carnival of animal shape,
         Processional from the ant to the ape.
         Shaped for strength, shaped for speed,
         Shaped to suit every single need.
         The carnival of animal skill,
         Astounding movement is set to thrill.
         Skill of the limb, skill of eye,
         Skills in life needed to get by.

Chorus

Coda: The carnival of animal life,
       The carnival of animal life,
       The carnival of animal,
           animal, animal life.

C.M. Ltd. 2173

SATELLITE

Words and music: Stephen Chadwick

© 1995 Middle Eight Music Ltd. Published by Cramer Music Ltd.

C.M. Ltd. 2173

Chorus

One day soon you'll fall to earth, but 'til that time my Sa - tel - lite _____

spins the world, once a day, comes your way. Sat - tel - lite in out - er space. _____

last time

Verse 2	Folding out to left and right, Solar panels capture light. Turn it into energy, Powering the circuitry.
Chorus	

Verse 3	Electronic wizardry, Eating signals we can't see. Pictures, words and numbers too, Processed all inside of you.
Chorus	

WELCOME TO THE PARTY

Words and music: Kate Buchanan

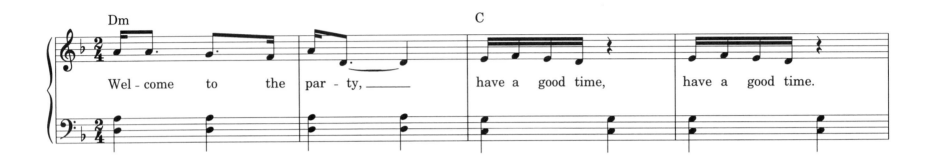

Wel - come to the par - ty, _____ have a good time, have a good time.

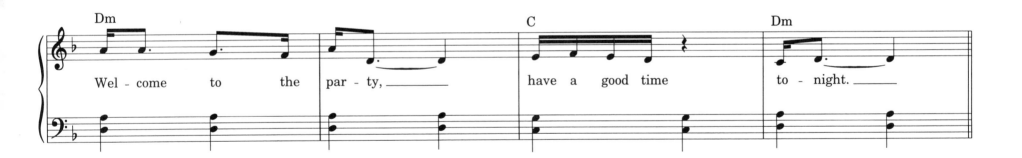

Wel - come to the par - ty, _____ have a good time to - night. _____

© 1995 Middle Eight Music Ltd. Published by Cramer Music Ltd. C.M. Ltd. 2173

COTOPAXI

Words and music: Stephen Chadwick

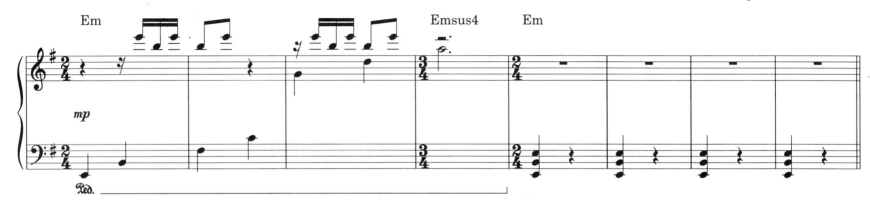

Verse

1. Co - to - pax - i, I feel your tre - mor, Warn-ing of the force with-in you soon to a - wake.

Co - to - pax - i I see your form change, Wrench-ing up the ground a - round you, mak-ing earth quake.

© 1995 Middle Eight Music Ltd. Published by Cramer Music Ltd.   C.M. Ltd. 2173

Chorus

I have wor-shipped you all my life, made the peo-ple sac-ri-fice.

3rd time to Coda

No one knows or can un-der-stand, what more from us you de-mand.

Coda

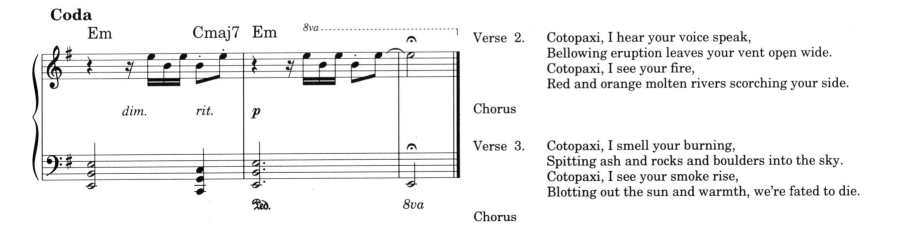

Verse 2. Cotopaxi, I hear your voice speak,
Bellowing eruption leaves your vent open wide.
Cotopaxi, I see your fire,
Red and orange molten rivers scorching your side.

Chorus

Verse 3. Cotopaxi, I smell your burning,
Spitting ash and rocks and boulders into the sky.
Cotopaxi, I see your smoke rise,
Blotting out the sun and warmth, we're fated to die.

Chorus

© 1995 Middle Eight Music Ltd. Published by Cramer Music Ltd.

C.M. Ltd. 2173

PEOPLE OF THE ANDES

Words and music: Stephen Chadwick

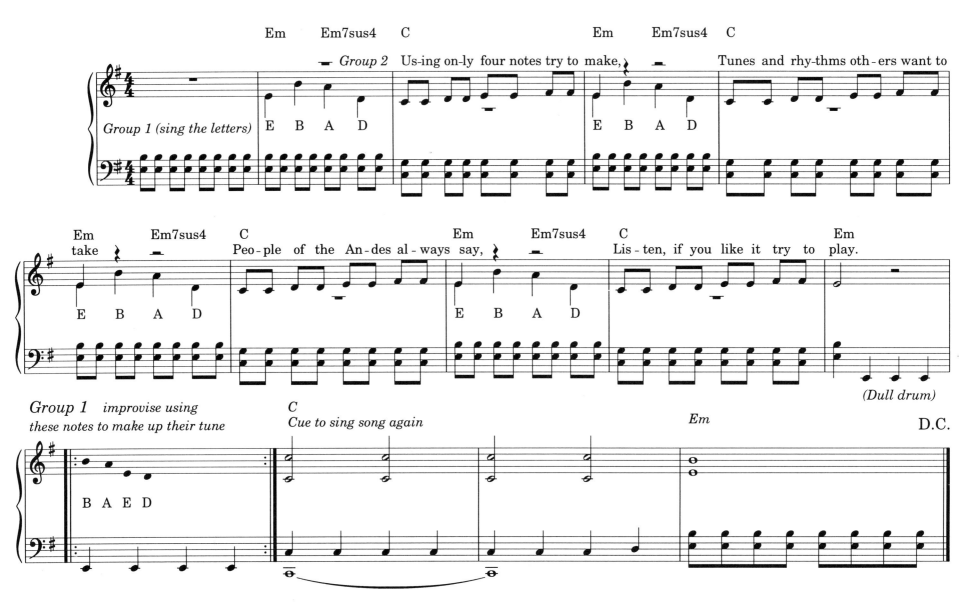

© 1995 Middle Eight Music Ltd. Published by Cramer Music Ltd.

C.M. Ltd. 2173

PAN GU

Words and music: Stephen Clark

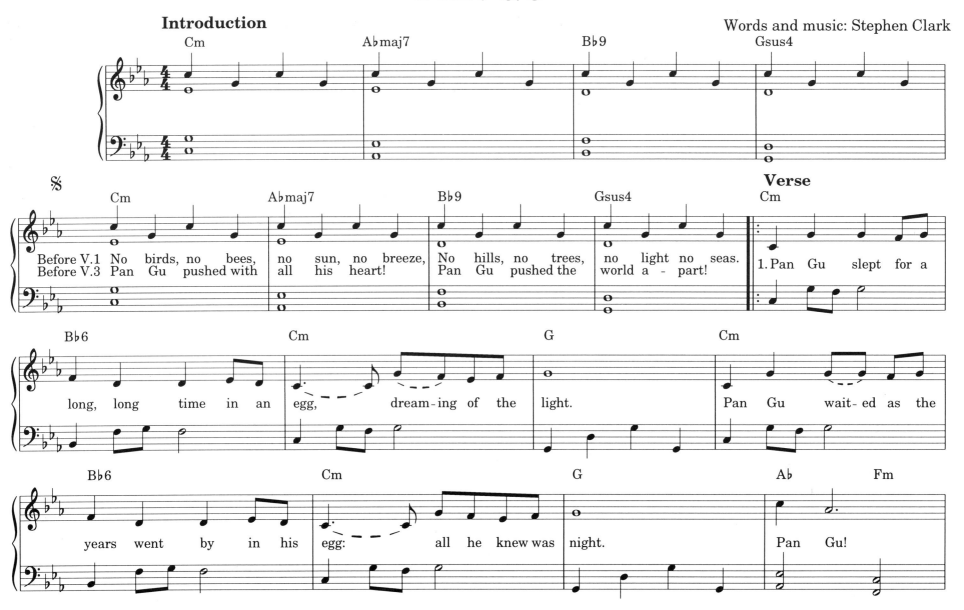

© 1995 Middle Eight Music Ltd. Published by Cramer Music Ltd.

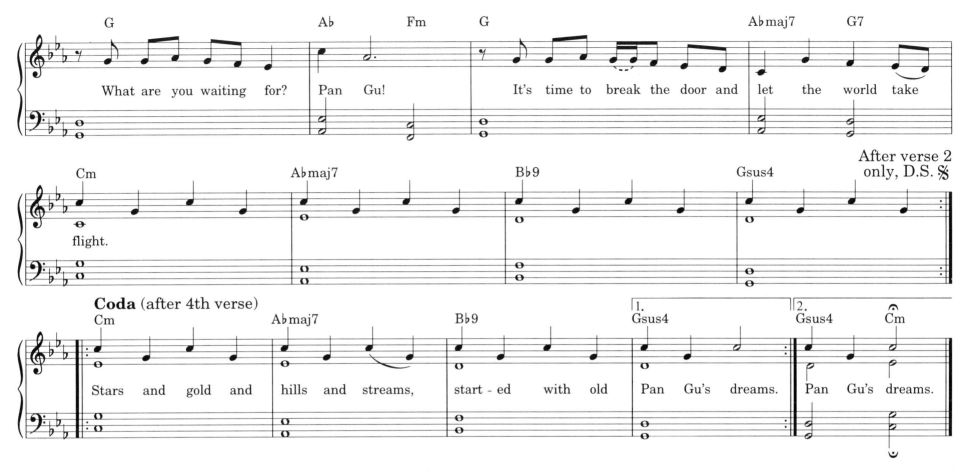

2. Pan Gu woke from his deep, deep sleep
   In his egg and couldn't see the light.
   Pan Gu shouted but no one heard
   In his egg, so he began to fight.
       Pan Gu!
   It's time to break the shell!
       Pan Gu!
   It's time to leave your cell
   And let the world take flight!

   Pan Gu pushed with all his heart!
   Pan Gu pushed the world apart!

3. Pan Gu stopped when his job was done
   And the land was miles from the sky.
   Pan Gu knew he could do no more
   Then he fell, knowing he would die.
       Pan Gu!
   Now you have done your task.
       Pan Gu!
   What more could anyone ask?
   It's time to say goodbye!

4. Pan Gu's breath gave us wind and clouds
   And his blood flowed into the seas.
   Pan Gu died, but he gave us life
   And his gair grew into the trees.
       Pan Gu!
   He died for everyone.
       Pan Gu!
   His eyes became the sun
   That shines upon the breeze.

Coda   Stars and gold and hills and streams
       Started with old Pan Gu's dreams.

C.M. Ltd. 2173

ON THE SKI SLOPE (Troika)

Music: Prokofiev
Words and arr: Stephen Chadwick

(NB voice sing octave higher)

© 1995 Middle Eight Music Ltd. Published by Cramer Music Ltd.   C.M. Ltd. 2173

Verse 2   Somehow I've got on to the ski jumping track,
          I think, in flight, I'm really much too young - for a heart attack.

Rap:

Chorus:

Verse 3   I am magnetic'lly attracted to trees,
          They say, it's all, because I like to drink - many 'Jaeger'* teas.

Rap:

Chorus:

Coda:

* Alpine alcoholic drink (Yager - 'a' as in 'say')

C.M. Ltd. 2173

MUSIC
CONNECTIONS

Practical Music for all Primary Class Teachers
Key Stages 1 and 2

KATE BUCHANAN & STEPHEN CHADWICK

CRAMER MUSIC

Estelle Furnell
8 The Pightle
Burnham Thorpe, King's Lynn
Norfolk PE31 8HT
01328 730574 or 07779 205705

Acknowledgements

Elizabeth Brown, Margaret Burton, Christine Hall, Liz Glasser, Helen MacGregor, Julia McCarthy, Jackie Mitchell, Evelyne Precieux. Bromley Road Infant School, Beckenham; Squirrels Heath Junior School, Romford; Suttons Primary School, Hornchurch.

CD acknowledgements:
Flute – Kate Buchanan
Guitar – Phil Fentiman
Harp – Rachel Masters
Keyboards – Stephen Chadwick
Panpipes/flutes – Incantation (Tony Hinnigan, Michael Taylor)
Percussion – Rachel Gledhill
Saxophone/Clarinet – Philip Tarlton
Strings – Priory String Trio (Violin – Fiona Brett,
  Viola – Josephine St.Leon, Cello – Philip Taylor)
Trumpet – Denis Curlett
Vocals – Angela Dixon, Rosamund Chadwick, Havering Sixth Form College Choir (94/95)

Produced and recorded by Stephen Chadwick
Sound effects by Bits & Pieces
Mastering by Simon Kahn

The Publishers would like to express their gratitude to the following for permission to use copyright material:

Tongoyo from Adzido Pan African Dance Ensemble-Siye Goli (EUCD 1223) by kind permission of ARC Music International Productions Ltd.

Ravel & Saint-Saëns recordings used by courtesy of Sound Ideas.

Prokofieff recording used by permission of EMI Records UK

Ravel *Prelude à la Nuit* © Editions Durand S.A.

Prokofieff *On the Ski Slope* © Copyright 1936 by Hawkes & Son (London) Ltd. This arrangement © Copyright 1996 by Hawkes & Son (London) Ltd. Reproduced by permission of Boosey & Hawkes Music Publishers Ltd.

Cramer Music Limited, 23 Garrick Street, London, WC2E 9AX.

About the Authors

Kate Buchanan is Communication and Teaching Skills Co-ordinator at Trinity College of Music. As music education consultant to The London Philharmonic, Kate leads workshops with orchestral players, teachers and pupils in London schools linked to concerts for which she also writes and edits Teachers' Packs. For a number of years Kate co-ordinated a programme of In-Service music courses for teachers at Goldsmiths' College, University of London and taught on the PGCE Primary and BA (Ed) courses. She is Chair of the Orff Society U.K. and was Course Director of their Summer School at the School of Education, Exeter University. She has written a series of articles in magazines on Primary Music Education.

Stephen Chadwick works throughout the whole music educational sector as a teacher, composer, author, workshop leader and music education consultant. He contributes to both BBC TV and Radio music education programmes. For The London Philharmonic he writes Teachers' Packs and leads workshops and has received various commissions for songs and music. He was a lecturer in composition at Goldsmiths' College, University of London. For seven years Stephen was Composer in Residence of Bromley LEA for INSET, working alongside teachers in the classroom to develop practical music activities for the non-specialist.

Catalogue number: 90559
ISBN: 0 902577 03 4

© 1996 Middle Eight Music Limited. Published by Cramer Music Limited. No part of this publication may be reproduced, stored in a retrieval system, or transmitted, in any form or by any means, electronic, mechanical, photocopying, recording or otherwise, outside of the permission given within this publication, without the prior written permission of the publishers:
Cramer Music Limited, 23 Garrick Street, London, WC2E 9AX.

With special thanks to:
Helen MacGregor for the *Keep Fit* and *Train Game* ideas.
Stephen Clark for the song *Pan Gu*.

Editor: Nicholas Hare
Cover Illustration: © Linda Dacey (Garden Studio)
Inside Illustrations: Roger Goslyn
Designers: Martin Lovelock and John Round
Music Setting: Spartan Press Music Publishers
Printed by Halstan & Co. Ltd., Amersham, Bucks., England

CONTENTS

Piano accompaniments to the songs are printed separately.

HOW TO USE THE BOOK

The book is in three chapters, but you can dip in anywhere or use a more structured approach (see **Planning Schemes of Work** on page 291):

- **Games** are short, easy-to-organise activities for use in any spare five minutes or as warm-ups for a **Project**. (Several games are recommended at the beginning of each **Project**). The games are grouped in two sections: *Games I* (starters) and *Games II* (more demanding).

- **Basics** makes the connection to music from very familiar starting points. The chapter is organised under the following headings: *Sorting & Matching, Words, Numbers, Pictures & Symbols* and *Dots, Lines & Spaces*. Each section of **Basics** can be used as a progressive programme of study for several weeks. Alternatively, individual parts of each section can be used to focus on a specific element in one lesson. The example themes (where given) establish basic frameworks for creative work and can be adapted for use with other themes.

- **Projects** generally develop a topic (e.g. transport, animals, etc.) over several weeks. Each project covers a number of the musical elements presented in **Games** and **Basics** as well as introducing additional knowledge about music.

Musical Elements:

The musical elements indicated in the focuses throughout the book are central to all musical activities. One or two focuses contain enough material to last approximately one lesson (apart from those in the **Games** chapter which are somewhat shorter). To find out which parts of the book focus on which musical elements see the **National Curriculum Cross Reference Tables** on pages 293-300 or the **Focus (musical element) index** on page 301.

Key Stages and Year Groups:

The Key Stages for **Games** and **Basics** are shown with each focus. They incorporate the following year groups:

KS1:	suitable for Reception – Year 2
KS1–2:	suitable for Years 1 – 6
KS2:	suitable for Years 3 – 6

Projects are labelled by Year Groups (instead of Key Stages) which are shown alongside each project title. This is, however, only a guide and much of the material could be adapted depending on the age and experience of the children. To find out which parts of the book are suitable for each Key Stage or Year Group see the contents page or **National Curriculum Cross Reference Tables**.

CDs 💿:

The songs, chants, musical examples and listening exercises are given on the two CDs . Most songs are followed by an instrumental version for use in assemblies, etc.

Resources and Instruments:

The resources (worksheets, etc.) and instruments required for each focus are shown in the margin of the corresponding page. If the same set of resources and instruments are used for all focuses they are stated once only at the beginning.

Worksheets:

Photocopiable worksheets are given throughout the book which include lyrics, music and pictorial stimuli as well as instructions and graphics:

* Worksheet 📋 = for use as a chart:
  The A4 size chart may be large enough to point at directly from the book (especially when children are gathered around in a group), but with less intimate situations, larger groups, special needs, etc. the chart may need to be enlarged to A3 or more.

* Worksheet 👀 = to look at:
  These are intended for distribution to individual or groups of children. Alternatively, one copy could be enlarged or transferred on to an OHP transparency.

* Worksheet ✏️ = to write on:
  These are intended for distribution to individual or groups of children as indicated under Resources.

Worksheets containing the music notation of a song (vocal line only) are optional to hand out. However, children can benefit from following the staff notation, even if they do not read music.

Songs and Chants:

The songs and chants in the book are an integral part of the related activities. Where the phrase 'sing the song' is used, time must be given to allow the children to become familiar with the song and sing it with confidence. The following tips are given as a guide (which are especially helpful if using the CD recordings):

1. Listen to the song.
2. Ask the children to read the words aloud.
3. Play one section of the song (verse, chorus, etc.), then on a second playing ask the children to join in.
4. Repeat the same procedure for other sections of the song.
5. Ask the children to sing several sections one after another before singing the song complete.
6. Encourage the children to breathe at the end of a phrase and not in the middle of a phrase.

Piano Accompaniments:

The piano accompaniments of the songs are given together in a separate book.

Key to Symbols:

Focus: relating to musical elements (pitch, rhythm, etc.).

Information in the margin contains the resources, instruments or method of organisation required for the activity.

The following symbols appear in the **Basics** and **Projects** chapters only:

Worksheet 📋 = for use as a chart

Worksheet 👀 = to look at

Worksheet ✏️ = to write on

Shaded text = class talking point

🎲 = creative/composing/improvising activity

♪ = performing activity

👂 = specific listening activity

💿 = CD reference

General Considerations for Music Making:

Instruments and Beaters:
A broad selection of tuned and untuned instruments to beat, tap, shake and blow will make music making a richer experience. A comprehensive list of common classroom instruments is given in the instrument glossary. 'Junk' instruments (e.g. old car hub caps, tin or wood boxes, plastic bottles) can also produce sounds of equal interest at no cost. A variety of hard and soft beaters multiply the different sound qualities that can be produced on the same instrument.

Playing Technique:
When playing instruments that are not hand held, a child should be encouraged to use two beaters (one in each hand) to develop co-ordination. The bars of tuned percussion instruments (e.g. xylophone) should be struck in the centre:

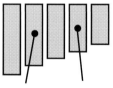

Music Friendly Environments:
Large echoing halls or glass walled classrooms are not always the most suitable places to make music. Rooms with soft furnishings, curtains and carpets help to dampen the sound and reduce noise level. When the children are working in groups place them as far apart as possible, taking advantage of 'natural' classroom screens, e.g. a rack of library books or desks. Other strategies for coping with noise level are built into the activities throughout the book.

Games

COPY ME

ORGANISATION
Circle

INSTRUMENTS
None

Focus: Timbre   KS1–2

Invent and copy vocal sounds:

- Starting with the leader make up cartoon type vocal
  sounds in turn round the circle
  (see picture opposite for ideas).
- Repeat the activity, but this time everyone copies
  each child's sound.
- Next, the children make up a movement or gesture
  to go with the sound effect and go round the circle
  again.
- Repeat the activity, but this time the leader passes a
  cartoon type vocal sound to the next child who
  must copy the sound and then add on a new sound.
- The next child copies the second sound and then
  adds on a new sound, and so on. For example:

Child 1	Child 2	Child 3, etc.
E E E K **AAAAARGH**	**AAAAARGH** *BOING*	wha wha wha *BOING*

HIGH OR LOW?

Focus 1: Pitch   KS1–2

Distinguish between notes of different pitch:

- With the listeners' eyes closed, play two different notes one after another on the xylophone:

low 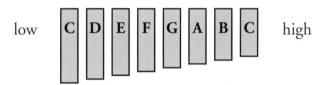 high

- Ask the children which was the higher or lower note – the first or second?
- Play notes wide apart to make it easier to tell the difference and closer together to make it harder.
- Make the game more difficult by asking which was the highest or lowest out of a sequence of three, four, or even five notes.

Focus 2: Pitch and timbre   KS2

Repeat the game comparing the pitch of different types of tuned and untuned instruments. For example: compare a woodblock sound to that of a tambour and ask which makes the lower sound. (Make sure the children are identifying the pitch and not the volume of the sounds).

ORGANISATION
Group

INSTRUMENTS
Focus 1
One xylophone or other tuned instrument
Focus 2
A selection of tuned and untuned

JOIN IN

ORGANISATION
Circle

INSTRUMENTS
None

Focus 1: Timbre   KS1–2

Invent and communicate body and vocal sounds:

● The leader makes a series of body or vocal sounds and everyone joins in. For example:

Pat knees; everyone joins in.
Clap hands; everyone joins in.
Tap shoulders; everyone joins in.

● The leader ends with the first sound, e.g. pat knees.
● Now ask the children to make body sounds in turn round the circle. For example:

Child 1 stamps; everyone joins in.
Child 2 pats tummy; everyone joins in.

● Use actions instead of sounds or as well as sounds (e.g. swing one arm making a swooshing sound) and repeat the game.

Focus 2: Dynamics   KS1–2

Repeat the game making the body sounds at different dynamic levels.

Focus 3: Rhythm   KS1–2

Repeat the game using a short rhythm played on different parts of the body.

KEEP FIT

Focus 1: Pulse and timbre – body sounds   KS1

As a class keep fit with the following exercises using different body sounds and movements. For each exercise keep a steady beat:

Exercise	Musical exercise
Bounce 1	Count up to 10 keeping a steady beat.
Bounce 2	Bounce both hands on knees while counting up to 10.
Walk	Pat knees with one hand at a time – left, right, left, right – up to 10.
Jog	Pat knees with both hands and then clap them in the air – pat clap pat clap.
Climb 1	Clap hands together to a count of 10 but this time start very quietly and get a little louder each time.
Climb 2	Clap to 10 again. This time start loudly and get quieter.
Slide 1	Slide one hand on top of the other to make a swishing noise to a count of 10.
Slide 2	Rub both hands together. Try to do this at different speeds, still keeping a steady beat.

Focus 2: Pulse and timbre – instrumental sounds   KS1

Keep fit to a steady beat using untuned percussion, e.g. drum, woodblock, maracas, bells, etc. (see table on page 6):

- Hand held instruments need to be played with a hand or one beater, e.g. tambour or woodblock. When the players have both hands free, play with two beaters.
- Choose several children to play each keep fit exercise.
- Those children not playing instruments copy the movements made by the players.

ORGANISATION
Group

INSTRUMENTS
Focus 1
None
Focus 2
A selection of untuned

ORGANISATION
Group

INSTRUMENTS
Focus 3
Xylophones
metallophones
and
glockenspiels

Exercise	Musical exercise
Bounce 1	Without beaters, bounce fingers gently on the instrument while counting up to 10.
Bounce 2	Tap gently with finger-tips or a beater while counting up to 10.
Walk	Hand held: with hand or beater, tap the instrument in two different places – left right left right – up to 10. Players with two beaters: tap – left right left right – up to 10.
Jog	Hand held: with hand or beater tap the instrument then tap the air – bounce tap bounce tap. Players with two beaters: tap beaters on the instrument then tap them in the air – bounce tap bounce tap.
Climb 1	Bounce on the instrument with one hand (or beater) Start quietly and get louder with each count.
Climb 2	Bounce on the instrument with one hand (or beater) This time start loudly and get quieter on each count.
Slide 1	Make a long sound by fast tapping to a count of 10.
Slide 2	Make a long sound by fast tapping but then gradually tap slower and slower.

Focus 3: Pulse and pitch   KS1

Keep fit to a steady beat using tuned percussion:
- Choose several children at a time to play each keep fit exercise. Each player needs 2 beaters.
- Those children not playing instruments copy the movements made by the players.

Exercise	Musical exercise
Bounce 1	Play 1 note and bounce 10 times in the middle of the bar with 1 beater.
Bounce 2	Play 1 note and bounce 10 times in the middle of the bar with the other hand.
Walk	With both beaters walk on the spot keeping in the middle of 1 bar – left right left right up to 10.
Jog	Play 2 notes and bounce with both hands at the same time. Then tap the beaters together in the air – bounce tap bounce tap up to 10.
Climb 1	Start on the lowest note and climb up step by step (one note at a time), then back down again. Use 1 hand.
Climb 2	Climb up and down step by step using both hands – left right left right.
Slide 1	Start on the lowest note and slide up to the top and down again with one beater. One slide is one count.
Slide 2	Starting in the middle of the instrument, with 2 beaters slide them in and out, towards and away from each other 10 times.

LEFT AND RIGHT

Focus 1: Pitch – up and down   KS1–2

Play 'leap frog' patterns on tuned percussion:

- Divide the class into pairs or a maximum group of 4 and give each group a tuned instrument.
- In each group choose one child to be the player. The players hold two beaters (one in each hand) and hide their strong hand behind their backs.
- Using their 'wobbly' hands the players play 'leap frog' by playing every other note starting with the longest (lowest) note. For example:

- When they have played the shortest (highest) note the players 'leap frog' down again.
- Ask the players to repeat the activity with their strong hands, putting their weak hands behind their backs.
- Swap players in each group and repeat the activity.

Focus 2: Pitch – scales   KS1–2

Play 'up and down the stairs' on tuned percussion:

- Using their 'wobbly' hand, the players 'go up the stairs' by playing every note starting from the longest (lowest) with a slow steady beat:

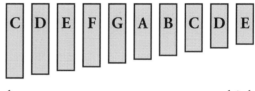

low   ⟶   high

- When the highest (shortest) note is reached they slide the beater down again 'falling down the stairs'.
- Ask the players to repeat the activity with their strong hands, putting their weak hands behind their backs.
- Swap players in each group and repeat the activity.

ORGANISATION
Circle

INSTRUMENTS
One tuned percussion between 2–4

Focus 3: Pitch – high and low   KS1–2

Play rainbow notes on tuned percussion:

- Using their 'wobbly' hand, the players find two notes with the same letter-name but different sizes. For example:

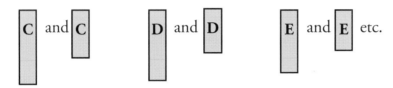

- The players play the low C and then the high C drawing a rainbow shape or semi-circle in the air (moving from left to right) and playing each note in turn going up. For example:

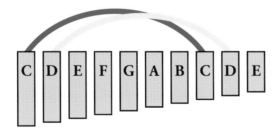

- Once they have played to the highest note (usually A), the players repeat the rainbow shapes in the opposite direction (moving from right to left).
- Ask the players to repeat the activity with their strong hands, putting their weak hands behind their backs.
- Swap players in each group and repeat the activity.

Focus 4: Pitch – scales   KS1–2

Play scales using left and right hands:

- Starting with the left hand on low C the players play 8 notes going up alternating left and right hands.
- Everyone chants 'Left right, left right', etc, as the scales are played.
- Repeat the activity going down starting with the right hand on the high C.
- Swap players in each group and repeat the activity.

NAME GAME

Focus 1: Pulse	KS1–2	Focus 2: Pitch and dynamics	KS1–2

ORGANISATION
Circle

INSTRUMENTS
None

Chant names over a steady beat:

- As a class, set up a steady beat by doing two claps and two *SHH*s. (When making the sound *SHH* open hands to feel the silent beats):

CLAP CLAP *SHH SHH* **CLAP CLAP** *SHH SHH*

- In turn round the circle everyone says their name in the *SHH SHH* space (don't make the *SHH* sound, but still feel the beats). For example:

    Wayne   **Jen-ni-fer**
CLAP CLAP (*SHH SHH*) **CLAP CLAP** (*SHH SHH*)

For children with little experience or with special needs the class repeats each name:

    Individual   Class copies
    Su-san   **Su-san**
CLAP CLAP (*SHH SHH*) **CLAP CLAP** (*SHH SHH*)

Repeat the game asking the children to find unusual ways of saying their names. For example: high and squeaky, low and gruff, going up or down in pitch, quiet or loud whispers, etc.

PLUG THE GAP

ORGANISATION
Circle

INSTRUMENTS
Focuses 1 & 2
None

Focus 1: Pulse and rhythm — KS1–2

Improvise rhythm patterns which fit within four beats:

- As a class, clap four times to a steady beat followed by four silent beats, saying *SHH* to feel the gaps:

CLAP CLAP CLAP CLAP *SHH SHH SHH SHH* CLAP CLAP etc.

- Ask the children how many *SHH* sounds there are in the gap between the groups of 4 claps. (Answer: 4 *SHH*s)
- The leader claps a solo rhythm in the gap between the groups of claps over the *SHH*s (i.e. plugging the gap).
- In turn each child round the circle plugs the gap by making up their own rhythm on the spot. The rhythm should last no more than the four *SHH* beats. (See diagram below).

Focus 2: Timbre – vocal and body sounds — KS1–2

Plug the gap with different body and vocal sounds. For example, patting knees or vocalising (e.g. *du-bi-du-bi*).

	Leader plugs the gap with a rhythm		Next child plugs the gap with a rhythm	
All: CLAP CLAP CLAP CLAP	*SHH SHH SHH SHH*	CLAP CLAP CLAP CLAP	*SHH SHH SHH SHH*	CLAP CLAP etc.

Focus 3: Timbre – instrumental sounds   KS2

Transfer the game onto untuned percussion
instruments:

- All the players play the four beats (claps) on untuned
  percussion instruments.
- Each player plugs the gap in turn by playing a solo
  rhythm on his/her instrument.

Focus 4: Pitch   KS2

Repeat focus 3 with the addition of several tuned
percussion instruments:

- Choose several children to play a steady beat pattern on
  xylophones etc. using any 4 notes from the
  pentatonic scale:

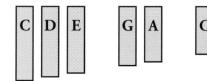

- The players decide an order in which to play the
  notes and repeat the pattern as an ostinato, even
  during the solos. For example: E G A C repeating.

ORGANISATION
Circle

INSTRUMENTS
Focus 3
One untuned
percussion
between two
Focus 4
One or more
tuned percussion

SHADOWING

Focus: Tempo and dynamics   KS1

Shadow the way instruments are played using movements:

- Play a drum in two different ways – first tapping and then stroking the skin (with finger nails).
- The children pretend to hold a drum and 'shadow' by copying the movements.
- Now introduce loud and quiet (dynamics) and fast and slow (tempo) for the class to follow. Make one type of sound then change to another. For example:

Tap it quickly and quietly

Slow circular movements with finger nails on skin

Tap it slowly and loudly

Start quietly with a steady beat and get gradually louder

Play three loud sounds followed by three quiet sounds

- Pass the drum to a new leader. Repeat the game.

STOP/START

Focus 1: Sound and silence	KS1–2

Respond to signals to stop and start playing:

- Number the children round the circle 'one' 'two' 'one' 'two' etc.
- All the number 'ones' choose an untuned instrument.
- The leader makes up a start/ stop signal on a cymbal or vibraslap.
- The leader plays the start signal. The children join in quietly, playing anything on their instruments.
- After a short time the leader plays the stop signal. (It may take a few goes for the children to respond quickly).
- Give the instruments to the number 'twos' and repeat the game with a new leader.

Focus 2: Structure	KS1–2

Repeat the game, but after the stop signal the leader points to an individual child (with an instrument). The child continues playing by improvising a solo:

Signals:

Start	Stop/ point	Start	Stop/ point
All play together	solo 1	All play together	solo 2

ORGANISATION
Circle

INSTRUMENTS
One untuned percussion between two (including a cymbal or vibraslap)

ACTION CONDUCTING

ORGANISATION
Circle

INSTRUMENTS
Focus 1
None
Focus 2
A selection of
tuned and
untuned

Focus 1: Texture – body sounds in layers   KS1–2

Build up layers of sounds and rhythms by showing others what to do through actions:

- The Action Conductor stands in the middle of the circle.
- Without speaking, the Action Conductor in turn shows each child which type of body sound to make. For example: gently pat knees with a steady beat, rub hands quickly or clap a rhythm.

(Simplify for younger children by deciding on two different types of sound or rhythm for the Action Conductor to use before starting the game).

- As soon as a child is shown what to do, s/he copies and keeps making the sound until the Action Conductor gives a stop signal.
- Several children in the circle may be shown the same sound or rhythm.
- To vary the music the Action Conductor can give individual or group signals to stop, start and get louder or quieter.

Focus 2: Texture – instrumental sounds in layers   KS 1–2

Repeat the game using instruments:

- Every other child in the circle chooses an instrument to play. (For younger and less experienced children have a smaller group of players using similar instruments. Children not playing copy the Action Conductor's movements).
- Again the Action Conductor shows players which types of sound to make through gestures. For example: a sideways arm movement shown to a xylophone player indicates a slide.
- After the players have performed they pass the instruments to the next child on the right and repeat the game.

ADD A BEAT

Focus 1: Metre   KS1–2

Add beats together to make different metres (beat groupings):

- Pass a clap round the circle facing the child to the right as you do so.
- Pass the clap round again but this time keep a steady beat. One child can tap out a steady beat on a woodblock to keep everyone 'in time'.
- When the clap has passed right round, pass two claps (each child claps twice) keeping the same steady beat. Slightly accent (clap louder) number 1.
- Next, pass three claps round.
- Repeat the game chanting the numbers out loud but clapping only on beat number 1:

Focus 2: Timbre – body sounds   KS2

Choose a different body sound (e.g. stamp) and make that sound on beat 1 only instead of saying the number.

Focus 3: Timbre – instrumental sounds   KS2

Play the game using tuned and untuned percussion. (Instruments such as cymbals and metallophones which make long ringing sounds are unsuitable for this game).

ORGANISATION
Circle

INSTRUMENTS
Focus 1 & 2
None
Focus 3
A selection of tuned and untuned

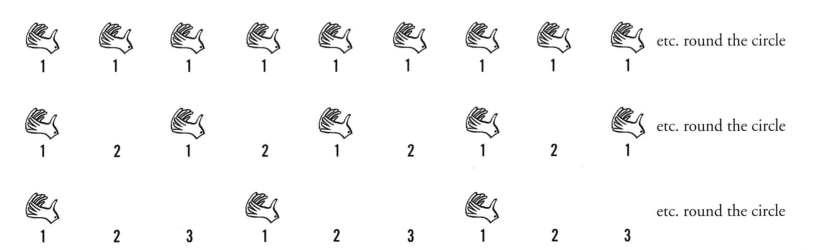

ADD A SOUND

ORGANISATION
Circle

INSTRUMENTS
None

Focus 1: Pitch and timbre   KS1–2

Imitate and add sounds together in a similar way to the cumulative game 'I went to the shops and I bought…':

- The leader makes an unusual vocal sound. For example:

  z z z z z z z z Z Z z z z

- The next child round the circle copies this sound and then adds a new sound. For example:

  z z z z z z z z z Z Z z z **Beep**

  Bop

- The next child adds another new sound and so on.
- The sequence of sounds gets longer and longer. Once it is is too long to be remembered, start again.

Focus 2: Melody   KS2

Repeat the game but make up short vocal 'tunes' using skat-singing sounds (e.g. *du-bi du-bi du* or *bop bop shu wah*).

CARD SIGNALS

Focus 1: Rhythm   KS1–2

Communicate and respond to the 3 card signals using a song. The pictures drawn on the cards are signals to:

CLAP SING HUM

- Ask the children what each card means.
- Sing a familiar song or action song showing the card **SING**. For example, *This Old Man*.
- At the end of line 1 quickly swap the card to **CLAP**. Everyone stops singing and claps the rhythm of the words only.
- At the end of line 2 quickly swap the card to **HUM**. Everyone stops clapping and hums the tune only.

Line 1	SING	This old man, he played one,
Line 2	CLAP	He played nick nack on my thumb.
Line 3	HUM	Nick nack paddy whack, give a dog a bone,
Line 4	SING	This old man came rolling home.

Focus 2: Texture – body sounds in layers   KS1–2

Respond to two visual symbols at the same time:

- Introduce two cards simultaneously. Be careful: you can't sing and hum at the same time.
- Divide the class into two groups. Group 1 follows the card in your left hand and group 2 follows the card in your right hand.

ORGANISATION
Group

RESOURCES
Photocopies of 3 cards (see page 18) or make your own cards with similar symbols

INSTRUMENTS
None

Card Signals

CHANGE A SOUND

Focus 1: Pitch and timbre   KS1–2

Improvise and make changes to vocal sounds:

- The leader makes a vocal sound. For example:

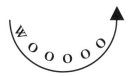

- The next child round the circle repeats the sound but changes it. For example:

1. Going up and then down (instead of down and then up):

2. Changing the type of sound:

- The next child changes it again and so on.

- When everyone has had a turn, compare the last sound with the first sound. (Tape record the game and play back to do this effectively).

Focus 2: Melody   KS2

Repeat the game making up short vocal 'tunes' using skat-singing sounds (e.g. *du-bi du-bi du* or *bop bop shu wah*).

ORGANISATION
Circle

INSTRUMENTS
None

CLOCK GONE WRONG !

Focus 1: Pulse and metre   KS1–2

Respond to signals and count groups of steady beats:

- As a class, count the numbers of the clock (1–12) steadily and evenly. (To simplify the game limit the count to six or eight).

- Choose a player to keep the beat on a two-toned woodblock (tick/tock).
- Count again, but this time add one number then go back to number 1 and count up to the next number, etc:

  1, 12, 123, 1234, 12345, 123456, 1234567, etc. to 12

- Choose a player to stand in the middle with a triangle ready to play on any number. This will be the signal to restart the counting from number 1.

- Everyone begins counting 1–12, but as soon as the triangle (the restart signal) is heard the counting goes back to number 1. For example:

Triangle:						△	△								△	
Count:	1	2	3	4	5	6	1	2	1	2	3	4	5	6	7	8	9	1 etc...
Woodblocks:	▬ ▬ ▬ ▬ ▬ ▬ ▬ ▬ ▬ ▬ ▬ ▬ ▬ ▬ ▬ ▬															

- Try the game at different speeds.

Focus 2: Texture - sounds in layers   KS2

Repeat the game with two groups together keeping to the same pulse (given on the woodblocks), but following their own restart signal:

	Triangle:						△	△								△	
Group 1	Count:	1	2	3	4	5	6	1	2	1	2	3	4	5	6	7	8	9	1 etc...
Group 2	Bell:	◎		◎						◎								
	Count:	1	2	1	2	3	1	2	3	4	5	6	7	8	9	10	11	1	2 etc...
	Woodblocks:	▬ ▬ ▬ ▬ ▬ ▬ ▬ ▬ ▬ ▬ ▬ ▬ ▬ ▬ ▬ ▬															

CONVERSATIONS

Focus 1: Mood and character   KS1–2

Improvise and communicate moods and feelings
through musical conversation:

- From two different starting points, pass two bean
  bags round the circle while chanting this rhyme (or
  make up your own):

  **Who shall we talk to? Wait and see;
  With any luck, it'll be me!**

(To simplify the game pass one bean bag round. At the
end of the chant, the teacher leads the musical
conversation allowing inexperienced children to express
themselves with greater confidence).

- Choose one child to accompany the rhyme on
  xylophone 3 (see diagram opposite) with a two
  note pattern. For example, play C and G as a
  repeating see-saw pattern.

        etc. repeating

- At the end of the rhyme the two children holding
  the bean bags leave them in their places and come
  into the circle and sit in front of xylophones 1 and 2,
  facing each other. (The see-saw pattern continues
  until the children start to play).
- The players have a musical conversation taking it in
  turns to play any rhythm or note pattern they feel
  in response to each other, varying pitch, dynamics
  and speed. (Encourage the children to use two
  beaters).
- At the end of the conversation, the see-saw pattern
  begins again, now played by the next child in the
  circle. The players return to their places and the
  chant is repeated.

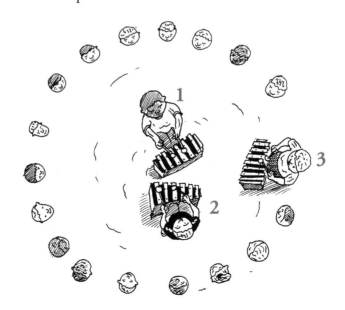

ORGANISATION
Circle

INSTRUMENTS
Three xylophones
placed as shown in
diagram

Focus 2: Melody and accompaniment   **KS2**

Play melodic conversations over the see-saw pattern
accompaniment:

- Take off the F and B bars of the xylophones to
  make a pentatonic scale:

C D E G A C

- Repeat the game but ask the see-saw pattern
  accompaniment player to continue playing
  with the conversations.
- Encourage the conversation players to
  keep in time with the accompaniment
  and avoid playing sliding sound effects.

EIGHTS

Focus: Pulse and metre   KS1–2

Measure groupings of eight beats using different body sounds:

- Click fingers eight times to a steady beat.
  The children should make the sound with their
  voices if they cannot do a finger click. (For younger
  children limit the count to four slow beats).
- Then straightaway the class clap eight times
  followed by eight lap pats and lastly eight stamps:

| click x 8 | clap x 8 | lap pat x 8 | stamp x 8 |

- Perform the whole sequence without gaps.
- Now try it as a round, in two groups first and then
  in four groups. Each group starts at the beginning
  of the sequence entering eight sounds apart:

Group 1 | click x 8 | clap x 8 | lap pat x 8 | stamp x 8 |

Group 2 | click x 8 | clap x 8 | lap pat x 8 | stamp x 8 |

ORGANISATION
Circle

INSTRUMENTS
None

FAVOURITES

ORGANISATION
Circle

INSTRUMENTS
Focus 1
None
Focus 2
One tuned
percussion or
several chime
bars

Focus 1: Structure – question and answer   KS1–2

Use word rhythms in a question and answer framework:

- Ask the children to discuss their favourite foods.
- As a class, set up a steady beat: lap clap lap clap, etc.
- Say this chant slowly to the steady beat. There are many ways to say the rhythm of the words. Find one that feels natural:

> **What do you like to eat?**
> **Say it to the beat.**

- Ask one child to answer, for example:

> **I like to eat fish and chips.**

- Repeat the chant until everyone has had a turn.
- Choose different favourites and make up new chants. For example:

Question: What do you watch on TV?
                   Say it after me.
Answer: I watch ....(Neighbours)...on TV.
Question: Colours of the rainbow –
                   Choose any one.
Answer: I choose ......(red).....

Focus 2: Melody   KS 1–2

Use note patterns in a question and answer framework:

- Sing the chant on two notes. A child answers using the same two notes. For example:

Question:
What do you like to eat?   Say it to the beat.

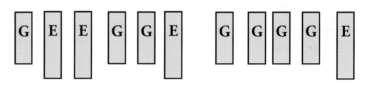

Answer:
I like to eat ice cream.

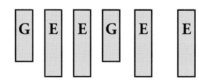

- Next, sing the question and answer using several notes.

MEXICAN WAVE

Focus 1: Timbre and links with movement   KS1–2

The Mexican wave was first seen at the World Cup in 1986 and is now seen at all major sporting events.

Send waves of sound and movement round the circle:

- Choose a leader to start the wave.
- Ask the children to do the Mexican wave by lifting their arms up and down once only round the circle in a domino effect.
- Using a vocal or body sound (e.g. rubbing hands) pass it round the circle in the same domino effect.

Focus 2: Texture and links with movement   KS1–2

Send several waves of movement round the circle at the same time:

- Starting with the leader, the right hand is placed in turn on the shoulder of the neighbour to the right in a domino effect. Hands should be kept on the shoulders.
- At any time (even before the hand-on-shoulder wave has gone completely round the circle) the leader may decide to start a second wave by placing his/her hand on the neighbour's head.
- The leader can start other waves by using other movements such as standing up or sitting down.

Repeat the game sending several waves of sound round the circle:

- This time the leader uses body sounds (e.g. gently patting knees) in free time or with a repeating rhythm.
- One by one, in a domino effect, the children join in and keep repeating the body sounds.
- The leader at any time may decide to start a second wave by changing the body sound from patting knees to clapping hands.
- Children must wait until the new wave has reached them before changing from patting to clapping.
- The leader can start other waves by using other body sounds such as clicking fingers or patting head.

ORGANISATION
Circle

INSTRUMENTS
None

ONE STEP BEHIND

ORGANISATION
Circle

INSTRUMENTS
None

Focus 1: Timbre   KS1–2

Imitate a series of sounds keeping one step behind the leader:

- As the leader, make up a sound and ask the class to join in. For example, rubbing your hands together.
- Make up a new sound with another part of the body, for example, patting your knees. The class does not change to your sound but continues to rub hands.
- Call out 'Change' and everyone changes to patting their knees. At the same time you make another new sound. For example, tapping your head. The class is always one step behind the leader.
- Call out 'Change' and everyone changes to tapping their heads. Again you make another new sound:

Leader:	rubbing	patting	tapping
	hands	knees	head, etc.
Class:		rubbing	patting
		hands	knees, etc.

- Choose other leaders.

Focus 2: Rhythm and timbre   KS1–2

Imitate a series of sounds using one rhythm and keep one step behind the leader:

- As the leader, clap a short rhythm and ask the class to repeat it.
- Make the same rhythm on your knees (the class continues to clap).
- Call out 'Change' and everyone changes to playing the rhythm on their knees. At the same time you play the rhythm with a new sound, for example, stamping. The class is always one step behind the leader.
- Call out 'Change' and everyone changes to stamping. Again you play the rhythm with another new sound.
- Choose other leaders.

Focus 3: Rhythm   KS2

Repeat focus 2 making up different rhythms for each body sound. It is a good idea to follow a difficult rhythm with an easy one and an easy one by a more difficult one.

ONE TO EIGHT

Focus 1: Pulse and timbre – vocal and body sounds KS2

Use numbers to co-ordinate sounds and create rhythmic patterns:

- As a class, chant a count of 8 with a slow steady beat several times:

  1   2   3   4   5   6   7   8   repeating

- Individually, each child chooses a number. Everyone claps on their chosen number while continuing to count. For example:

Child A: 1   2   3   4   5   6   7   8

Child B: 1   2   3   4   5   6   7   8

Child C: 1   2   3   4   5   6   7   8

etc.

- Repeat the activity asking the children to listen for other children clapping on their number.
- Repeat the activity but stop counting out loud (ask the children to count in their heads).

- Repeat the activity but, in addition to clapping, ask the children to say a word or make a vocal sound on another number.
- Finally, add a movement on a third number. For example:

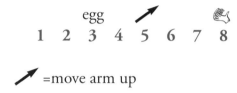

egg
1   2   3   4   5   6   7   8

↗ =move arm up

Focus 2: Pulse and timbre – instrumental sounds   KS2

Transfer the clapping part of the game onto untuned percussion instruments:

- Each child plays his/her instrument instead of clapping.
- Next, ask the children to choose two numbers next to each other and repeat the game.

ORGANISATION
Circle

INSTRUMENTS
Focus 1
None
Focus 2
One untuned percussion per child

PASS A SOUND

ORGANISATION
Circle

INSTRUMENTS
Focus 1
None
Focus 2
A drum

Focus 1: Timbre   KS1–2

Pass different sounds round the circle:

- Pass a clap round the circle facing the child on the right. Each child must make eye contact as they pass the clap.
- Using a stopwatch time how long it takes to pass the clap right round the circle and try to get it as fast as possible.
- Repeat the game passing different sounds. For example: *'sh'* or *'bzz'*.

Focus 2: Pulse   KS1–2

Repeat the game with a steady beat on a drum and pass the sound in time with the drum.

Focus 3: Texture – sounds in layers   KS2

Pass a clap one way round the circle, a *'sh'* the other way. At one point the clap and *'sh'* will coincide.

ROUND AND ROUND

Focus 1: Rhythm and timbre – body sounds   KS1–2

Perform a round using different sounds:

- Choose a round you know well; for example, *Frère Jacques.*
- Practise the rhythm of each phrase using different body percussion; making a different sort of sound for each line. For example:

Pat knees:

Frère Jacques, frère Jacques,

Tap shoulders:

Dormez vous, dormez vous,

Tap either side of head:

Sonnez les matines, sonnez les matines,

Stamp:

Ding dang dong, ding dang dong.

- Divide the children into four groups. Each group performs the sequence of body sounds whilst singing the song in their heads.

- Perform the body sounds again. This time each group starts one phrase apart making a rhythmic round. For example:

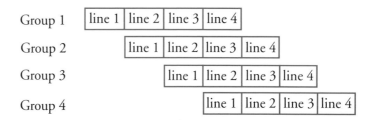

Focus 2: Rhythm and timbre – instrumental sounds   KS2

In 4 groups, transfer the rhythm of the complete round onto untuned percussion instruments:

- Decide the type of sound for each group (e.g. wood, metal, shakers, skin).
- Each group performs separately then together as a round.

ORGANISATION
Group

INSTRUMENTS
Focus 1
None
Focus 2
A selection of untuned percussion

STAND UP/SIT DOWN

ORGANISATION
Circle

INSTRUMENTS
One xylophone

Focus 1: Pitch   KS1–2

Use pitch shapes (notes moving from high to low, etc.) to signal different actions or movements:

- Play the following set of signals on a xylophone using hard beaters and ask the children to move accordingly:

Stand up: slide from low to high
Sit down: slide from high to low
Move a-long: tap out the rhythm of the words
(move round one place in the circle)   on one note

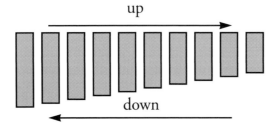

up

down

- Choose a leader by placing the xylophone in front of a child in the circle.
- The leader plays the stand up and sit down signals several times.

- When the signal to move along is played the children move round one place in the circle and a new leader will be in front of the xylophone. If the children are in the sitting position when the move along signal is given, the children slide along to their new place.

Focus 2: Dynamics   KS1–2

Divide the circle into two halves with one half only responding to stand up and sit down signals played loudly and the other half only responding to these signals played quietly.

Focus 3: Pulse and tempo   KS1–2

Repeat the game adding this signal to the set:

Clap hands   alternately play any two notes as a steady
to the beat: beat repeating pattern – fast or slow

When the leader plays this signal the children join in by clapping to the beat.

Focus 4: Pitch   KS2

Make up other pitch shapes to signal other types of movements or body sounds and add them to the set.

Basics

Sorting and Matching

Sorting and Matching considers the similarities and differences of sounds in a practical and creative way through imitation, movement and sets.
The activities mainly develop aural awareness and discrimination.

MATCHING SOUNDS

Focus 1: Timbre   KS1–2

👂 Listen to instruments and match them with the same sounds:

- With the children sitting in a circle, hide one instrument of each pair behind a screen placing the others in the centre of the circle.
- Choose a child to go behind the screen.
- Sing the song *Take the Parcel* which uses the same tune as *London Bridge is Falling Down*. At the same time pass a bean bag (the 'parcel') round the circle.

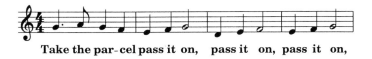

Take the par-cel pass it on,   pass it on, pass it on,

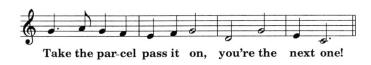

Take the par-cel pass it on, you're the   next one!

- When the song stops, the child holding the bean bag goes into the circle to play the game, leaving the bean bag in his/her space.
- The child behind the screen makes a short sound on one of the instruments. The child in the circle plays the matching instrument.

- Ask the class to name the instruments **after** the child in the circle has matched the sounds to those behind the screen.
- Sing the song again and repeat the game.

To extend the activity:

- Make sounds on two, three and then four instruments played one after another.
- Use similar sounding instruments from the same family (for example: from the shaker family select maracas and wicker shakers).

Focus 2: Dynamics   KS1–2

👂 Repeat the activity and ask the child behind the screen to play at different dynamic levels. The child in the circle matches the dynamic on the corresponding instrument.

Focus 3: Tempo   KS1–2

👂 Repeat the activity and ask the child behind the screen to play a steady beat at a slow or fast speed. After listening carefully the child in the circle matches the speed by playing the corresponding instrument at the same time.

EXAMPLE THEME
None

RESOURCES
None

INSTRUMENTS
Several pairs of instruments (e.g. two woodblocks two tambourines two pairs of Indian bells, etc.)

MIRRORING WITH MOVEMENT

EXAMPLE THEME
None

RESOURCES
None

INSTRUMENTS
Focus 1
2 drums, guiro
maracas, claves
woodblock
Focus 2
One tuned
percussion

Focus 1: Duration – long and short   KS1–2

👂 Listen and respond to long or short sounds with movement:

- Play continuous sounds on a drum by stroking the drum with fingers or fingernails. Ask the children to mirror the sound with movements. For example by making a long gesture with their hands.
- Now play short sounds on a drum by tapping with flat fingers. Vary the speed and ask the children to mirror the changes with movements. For example walking on the spot at different speeds.
- Divide into two groups: Group 1 mirrors the long sounds and Group 2 mirrors the short sounds.
- Choose 6 children to play the instruments below as indicated:

LONG	SHORT
1. Drum (fingernails)	4. Drum (fingers flat)
2. Guiro (up & down continuously)	5. Claves
3. Maracas (shake continuously)	6. Woodblock

- Signal one child to begin playing. The two groups listen to determine whether it is a long or short sound. The corresponding group then mirrors the sound (for example, if the claves play, the group playing short sounds will mirror).
- Direct the players, alternating long and short sounds. Later, try overlapping the sounds so that both groups mirror at the same time.
- Choose individual children to direct the sounds.

Focus 2: Pitch   KS1–2

👂 Listen and respond to high and low sounds with movement:

- Play from low to high moving up slowly one note at a time. Ask the children to mirror the sounds with movements, for example, by stretching arms and bodies upwards as the sounds get higher.
- Play any high note followed by any low note. Repeat the sounds. Ask the children to mirror the sounds with movements, for example, by moving arms up and then down.
- Choose individual children to play.
- Repeat the activity with the instrument unseen by the children.

SORTING SOUNDS 1

Focus: Timbre   KS1

👂 Listen to instruments and sort them into families:

- One by one each child chooses an instrument.
- Through demonstration and discussion the children sort their instruments into four groups or families:

    sounds made by hitting **wood**

    sounds made by hitting **metal**

    sounds made by **shaking or scraping**

    sounds made by hitting **skin**

- Describe the sounds of the instruments in each group. For example, metal instruments make tinging and clanking sounds.
- Number each group, for example:

No. 1	No. 2	No. 3	No. 4
Wood	**Metal**	**Shakers & Scrapers**	**Skin**
Woodblock	Indian bells	Maracas	Drums
Wooden agogo	Triangle	Tambourines	Bongos
Claves	Cymbal	Guiro	Tambour

🎵 Play the **Families of Sounds** game:

- On a blackboard draw a 1: all the wooden instruments play. Rub it out and the wooden instruments stop playing.
- Repeat this activity with each number group.
- Then combine groups by having more than one number on the board at the same time.
- Incorporate loud and quiet sounds: a large number 1 indicates loud sounds, a small number one indicates quiet sounds.

EXAMPLE THEME
None

RESOURCES
None

INSTRUMENTS
A selection of wood, metal, shakers & scrapers and skin

SORTING SOUNDS 2

EXAMPLE THEME
None

RESOURCES
None

INSTRUMENTS
One tuned or
untuned per child

Focus: Duration – long and short   KS2

👂 Listen to instrumental and vocal sounds and sort them by duration – sounding long or short:

- From a selection of instruments choose volunteers to demonstrate and sort them into two groups. (Encourage the children to use vocal and body sounds as well). For example:

Long and sustained sounds when played with one action or one long breath:

> Cymbal – metallophone – Indian bells – triangle – vibraslap (hit once)
> Hum (one complete breath)
> Recorder note (one complete breath)
> Bowed violin (one complete bow)

Short sounds when played with one action or short breath:

> Guiro (quick short scrape)
> Maracas – tambourine (one shake)
> Xylophone – woodblock (hit once)
> Hand clap
> Pizzicato (plucking) note on violin
> Recorder note (sound one short note)

Which materials vibrate the longest and which the shortest?
Can you describe the start and finish of a sound?
(e.g. a cymbal hit with a beater sounds loud at the beginning and then fades away).

🎵 Perform the sounds in a circle:

- Give each child an instrument (or a vocal or body sound).
- In turn each child makes one sound with their instruments, voice or body sound. Immediately the sound has finished the next child plays. With long sounding instruments (e.g. cymbal) the next child must wait until the sound has completely finished before playing his/her sound.
- Go round the circle again playing only the long sounds and then playing only the short sounds.

SORTING AND SETS

Focus: Timbre and pitch   KS2

👂 Listen to and sort the sounds of various instruments:

- Set up several groups of instruments around the room on tables.
- Label each instrument with its name.
- Ask the children to find out the type of material which makes the sound on each instrument (e.g. metallophone bars are made of metal).
- Sort instruments into sets according to certain characteristics or materials and draw Venn diagrams to represent the sets. For example, this diagram shows instruments that can be played with a beater, without a beater or both.

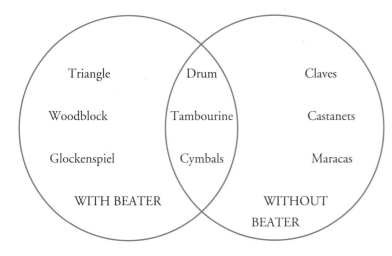

- Draw new diagrams considering the following characteristics or materials:

metal – not metal
blown – not blown
circular – not circular
pair – not pair (e.g. claves, Indian bells are pairs)
skin – not skin

Extend the activity using diagrams which sort in three ways. For example:

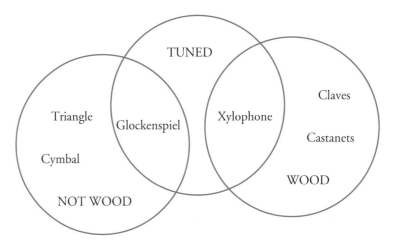

Draw new diagrams considering other characteristics or materials. For example:

sustained sounds – short sounds – tuned

EXAMPLE THEME
None

RESOURCES
1 sheet of plain paper per child

INSTRUMENTS
A selection of tuned and untuned percusssion

FRAMEWORKS

EXAMPLE THEME
Ghosts and Ghouls (Other suggestions: Types of Weather, Rivers and Waterfalls, Night and Day)

RESOURCES
Worksheet 👓

INSTRUMENTS
A selection of tuned and untuned

Focus: Contrast and form   KS2

The *Ghosts and Ghouls* framework is in ternary form (A B A) which means the first and third sections are the same. Sections A and B are contrasted by different instructions for sounds, dynamics (loud and quiet) and pauses. These instructions or rules are set up to guide the improvisers, but they still have freedom to decide when to play.

🎲 Improvise Ghost and Ghoul music using the framework on the worksheet:

- Choose a group of 4–10 children to explore ways of playing the instructions for each section on instruments. Choose another child to be the footstep player with the rest of the class forming the breeze group.
- Ask the group of 4–10 players to improvise together for about a minute following the instructions for section A. It is very important that they listen to the overall effect of the music and be aware of other members in the group.

👂 Listen to and discuss the improvisation:

Do you think the group followed the instructions and captured the atmosphere of the section? If not, how could the improvisation be improved?

Repeat the last composing and listening activities for section B using the same set of players.

🎵 Ask the group to perform the sections one after another without pause, accompanied by both the footstep player and ghost breeze group. Choose a conductor to give signals to begin the piece, to show when to move on to the next section and when to finish. Tape record the performance.

👂 Play back and discuss the performance:

Was it a good idea to have the footstep player and ghost breeze group playing all the time? If so, why? *(Answer: The sounds helped to link the sections and provide a background for the rest of the music).*
Is there any way the beginning or ending could be improved? For example would it sound better if players began or dropped out one at a time?

Choose new players and repeat the whole activity.

Frameworks – Ghosts and Ghouls

Section A	Section B	Section A
Short sounds	Long trembly sounds	Short sounds
Quiet	Get louder then quieter	Quiet
Long pauses	No pauses	Long pauses

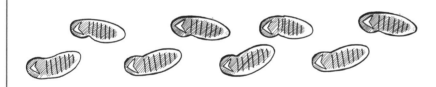

One player makes slow footstep type sounds all the time.

Ghost breeze ━━━━━━━━━━━━━━━

Make very quiet long **'shh'** and breath sounds throughout. Breath at different times.

As a class, compose a new Ghost and Ghouls piece:

● Make a list of instructions of other ways to play the instruments that capture the atmosphere. Besides length of sound, dynamics and general directions also think about using word rhythms. For example:

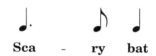

Sca - ry bat

● Sort the instructions into groups to make two or three contrasting sections.

Words

Words provides a direct stimulus for music making, both through their natural rhythm and expression. Spoken to a steady beat like a chant or rap, word rhythms reinforce rhythmic understanding and awareness.

WORDS

EXAMPLE THEME
Animals (Other suggestions: Machines, Transport, Toys, Water)

RESOURCES
Picture cards sheet ✂, p.46 (optional)

INSTRUMENTS
None

Focus: Pulse and rhythm   KS1

♫ As a class, chant the animal word rhythms to a steady beat:

● Feel a pulse with your feet and speak the bear word rhythm at the same time:

Rhythm (speak/clap):	Bear	Bear	Bear	Bear
Pulse (feet):	1	2	3	4

● Do the same using the rabbit word rhythm:

Rhythm (speak/clap):	Rabbit	Rabbit	Rabbit	Rabbit
Pulse (feet):	1	2	3	4

> Which animal word has the same rhythm as the pulse? *(Answer: 'Bear')*
> Which animal word has a different rhythm to the pulse? *(Answer: 'Rabbit')*
> How many sounds does 'Rabbit' have? *(Answer: 2)*

♫ Chant the *Hip Hop rhyme* feeling the beat (pulse) with your feet. An example is given on ⊚ A1:

	Hip	hop	rabbit	hop
Pulse:	1	2	3	4

	I saw a	rabbit	going to the shop	
Pulse:	1	2	3	4

▣ Ask each child to think of an animal name which has one or two sounds or syllables (it doesn't matter if some are the same).

♫ Chant the *Hip Hop rhyme* with new animal names:

● In turn individual children chant the rhyme with their own animal name (in the box). The class joins in with the *hip hop* shown in brackets and then repeats the rhyme. For example:

Child 1: (Hip   hop) | dog | (hop)
I   saw   a   dog   going to the   shop

All: Hip   hop   **dog**   hop
I   saw   a   dog   going to the   shop

Child 2: (Hip   hop) | monkey | (hop)
I   saw   a   monkey   going to the   shop

All: Hip   hop   **monkey**   hop
I   saw   a   monkey   going to the   shop

👂 After a number of chants ask the following questions:

> How many sounds (syllables) did Child 1's animal word have? *(Answer in the above example: 1).*
> How many sounds (syllables) did Child 2's animal word have? *(Answer in the above example: 2).*

To extend the activity talk about animal words with three syllables (porcupine, anteater, crocodile, etc.) and repeat the game.

WORDS IN SEQUENCE 1

EXAMPLE THEME
Animals (Other suggestions: Machines, Transport, Toys, Water)

RESOURCES
Enlarge and make several copies of the picture card sheet on page 46 and cut out the pictures (optional)

INSTRUMENTS
A selection of untuned percussion

Focus: Structure   KS1

♫ Explore word patterns:

- Ask the children to choose one- and two-syllable words associated with a topic. The example below uses animals.
- Sort the words into two columns (for pre-readers use the animal picture cards on page 46).

Column 1	Column 2
Dog	Rabbit
Cat	Chicken
Bear	Squirrel
Cow	Tiger
Pig, etc.	Monkey, etc.

🎲 Make a sequence using one- and two-syllable words:

- Ask the children to choose **2 words,** one from each column.
- Encourage them to put them in any order to create a sequence of 4 words (or set out the cards).

♫ As a class, perform the sequence:

- Clap a steady beat while the children say the words. Repeat the same pattern several times without a gap. For example:

	Bear	Rabbit	Rabbit	Bear (repeating)
Pulse :	1	2	3	4

	Tiger	Tiger	Cat	Tiger (repeating)
Pulse :	1	2	3	4

- Once this is secure ask the children to say the words **and** clap the rhythm of the words at the same time.
- Divide the class into two groups with one group clapping a steady beat and the other group clapping the word rhythms, then swap.

🎲 Working in pairs, ask the children to invent more sequences.

♫ Choose pairs to perform the sequences on percussion instruments while chanting the words. Repeat the sequences without chanting. More experienced children will be able to put together several versions.

Listening Game I:

- Draw several of the children's word sequences on the board (or show the sequences with sets of pictures).
- Choose one of the patterns to clap (without saying the words).

Whose sequence am I clapping?

Listening Game II:

- Ask a pair of children to perform their sequence on instruments with one child playing the beat (pulse) and the other the word rhythms.

Who is playing the steady beat?
Who is playing the word rhythms?

Picture Cards

LYRICS AND LOUDNESS

Focus: Dynamics   **KS1–2**

Listen to the song *Three Seeds* which uses the traditional tune *Three Crows* (A2, 3):

> Why did the first seed not grow at all?
> (*Answer: Because it was cold and frosty*).
> Why did the second seed grow a little bit?
> (*Answer: Because it rained and was wet*).
> Why did the third seed grow and grow?
> (*Answer: Because it was warm and sunny*).
> Was the music quiet all the way through ?
> (*Answer: No, it was quiet in verses 1 and 2, then got gradually louder in verses 3 and 4*).

As a class, sing the song *Three Seeds* (A2, 3). Then perform the song again with dynamics, actions and movements:

- Demonstrate the actions shown on the worksheet and ask the children to join in.
- Once the class is familiar with the actions, choose three children ('seeds') to do the following movements for each verse:

Verse	Movements
1:	The 'seeds' are standing up at the beginning of the song. One at a time they curl up when each successive 'planted' word is sung.
2:	The first seed remains curled up.
3:	The second seed opens out a little.
4:	The third seed stretches right up.

EXAMPLE THEME

Three seeds
(Other suggestions:
Ten Green Bottles
Three Blind Mice)

RESOURCES

Worksheet
(optional)

INSTRUMENTS

A selection of untuned percussion

1. Three seeds plant - ed in the ground, plant - ed in the ground, plant - ed in the ground, The

Three seeds plant - ed in the ground on a cold and fros - ty morn - ing. 2. The

© 1995 Middle Eight Music Ltd. Published by Cramer Music Ltd.

Lyrics and Loudness – Three Seeds (◎ A2, 3)

	Dynamics	Actions
1. **Three seeds planted in the ground, planted in the ground, planted in the ground, Three seeds planted in the ground on a cold and frosty morning.**	Sing quietly	Show three fingers; push seed into ground with thumb (x3) Hug shoulders
2. **The first seed didn't grow at all, didn't grow at all, didn't grow at all, The first seed didn't grow at all on a cold and frosty morning.**	Sing quietly	Show one finger; shake head (x3) Hug shoulders
3. **The second seed grew a little bit, grew a little bit, grew a little bit, The second seed grew a little bit on a wet and windy morning.**	Sing a little louder	Show two fingers; open arms a little Palms facing upwards feeling the rain
4. **The third seed grew and grew and grew, grew and grew and grew, grew and grew and grew, The third seed grew and grew and grew on a warm and sunny morning...**	Sing louder and louder	Show three fingers; open arms continuously Feel sun on outstretched arms and face

- Choose three players (seeds) to accompany the song and match the movements by playing untuned percussion instruments at the dynamic levels shown below:

  Verse   Instruments

  1:    All the players play a steady beat or copy the rhythm of the words.

  2:    The first seed (player 1) improvises freely playing very quietly.

  3:    The second seed (player 2) improvises freely beginning quietly and then getting a little louder.

  4:    The third seed (player 3) improvises freely playing gradually louder and louder.

- Repeat the activity choosing other groups of children to play and move.

Use dynamics to reflect the words of other traditional songs. For example:

- *Ten Green Bottles* – Divide the class into ten groups. In each successive verse one group drops out and the singing gets gradually quieter.
- *Three Blind Mice* – The children sing following the dynamics shown below:

Three blind mice	sing quietly
Three blind mice	
See how they run	getting louder
See how they run	
They all ran after the farmer's wife	sing louder and louder
Who cut off their tails with a carving knife	
Did ever you see such a thing in your life	getting quieter
As three blind mice?	quietly

WORDS IN SEQUENCE 2

Focus: Structure KS2

EXAMPLE THEME
Sea adventure
(Other
suggestions:
Sports, Funfairs,
Celebrations,
Exploration)

RESOURCES
Worksheet ✏
per group of 4–5

INSTRUMENTS
A selection of
tuned and
untuned

♫ Explore word rhythms and vocal sounds:

- As a class, chant and (clap to a steady beat) the words on the worksheet *Sea Adventure*. Each column of words uses a different number of syllables (claps).

- In groups of 4-5 ask the children to think of other words associated with an adventure at sea and sort them into the three columns by writing them down on the worksheet.

- Ask the children to suggest different ways in which the words can be spoken using even and uneven rhythm, long and short sounds and unusual vocal sounds. Here is an example of words spoken using different combinations of long and short sounds:

deep——sea——di–ver
long   long   short short

deep sea di – ver
short short short short

🎲© In the same groups of 4–5, make sequences using two-, three- and four-syllable words and write them down on the worksheet.

♫ Transfer the sequences onto instruments.

Words in Sequence 2 – Sea Adventure

Can you think of any other words to add to the adventure word table? Write words with two, three or four syllables in Columns 1, 2 or 3 as shown:

Column 1 **two syllables**	Column 2 **three syllables**	Column 3 **four syllables**
seaweed	octopus	deep sea diver
lighthouse	waterfall	sunken treasure
sailing	sandy shore	coral island

Compose a sequence of words:

- This example of a sequence uses words from one column only:

seaweed	seaweed	lighthouse	sailing

- Make up several sequences using words from one or more columns.

1				
2				
3				
4				
5				

WORDS IN LAYERS

Sea adventure
(Other
suggestions:
Sports, Funfairs,
Celebrations,
Exploration)

RESOURCES
Worksheet 👁
and the Calico
Jack rhythm card
sheet enlarged
and cut into 4
cards

INSTRUMENTS
A selection of
untuned
percussion

Focus: Texture   **KS2**

♫ Chant *Calico Jack* on the worksheet (👁 A4) (Calico Jack was an 18th century pirate):

- As a class, chant the words and keep a steady beat by tapping feet left and right.
- Then clap the rhythm of the words while chanting them.
- Clap the **rhythm** of the words **only** (don't say the words out loud, chant them in your head!).

🎲 Choose word rhythms from the chant to form an ostinato accompaniment (repeating pattern):

- Divide the class into two groups: Group 1 claps one of the four lines (phrases) as an ostinato, e.g. '**Spies the band**', while Group 2 claps and chants *Calico Jack* complete.
- Divide into three groups: Groups 1 and 2 clap different phrases as repeating patterns choosing different body sounds (e.g. Group 1 claps '**Calico Jack**'; Group 2 lap pats '**buried in the sand**'). Group 3 claps and chants *Calico Jack* complete.

♫ Clap and chant *Calico Jack* as a round in two groups:

- Group 1 begins. Group 2 enters after one line (when Group 1 chants the word 'spies').
- Now try the round in 3 or 4 groups beginning one line apart.
- From each group choose several children to play the rhythm patterns on untuned instruments.

🎧 Listen to and identify the notation on the *Calico Jack* rhythm cards:

- Write the words on the backs of the 4 word rhythm cards and place them in the order of the chant.
- The children chant the words again following the notation on the cards in sequence.
- Ask the children to clap the rhythm of the words without chanting (following the cards again).
- Hold up a card and ask a child to clap the rhythm.
- Ask the children to clap the cards in a new order.

🎧 Listening game – accompaniments:

- Ask one child to choose and play one of the *Calico Jack* rhythm cards as an ostinato accompaniment while the class chants *Calico Jack* complete.

Which card was played as the ostinato?

Words in Layers – Calico Jack (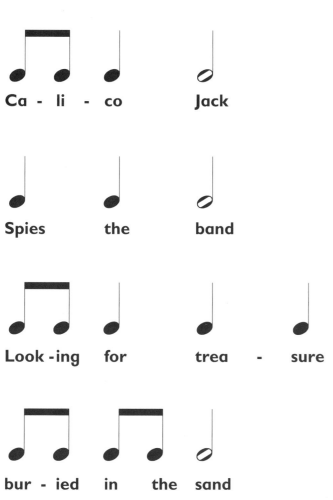 A4)

Ca - li - co   Jack

Spies   the   band

Look -ing for   trea - sure

bur - ied in   the sand

Accompany the chant by choosing one line and keep clapping the rhythm.

Words in Layers – Calico Jack

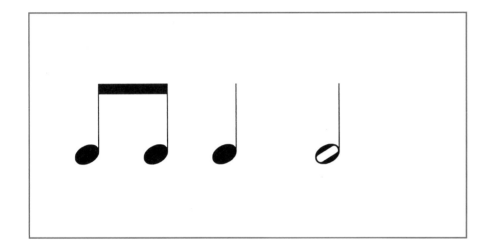

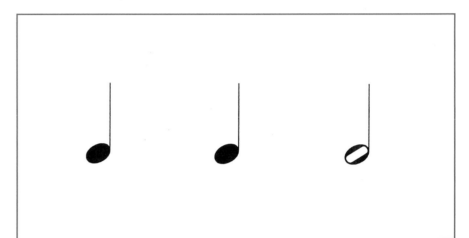

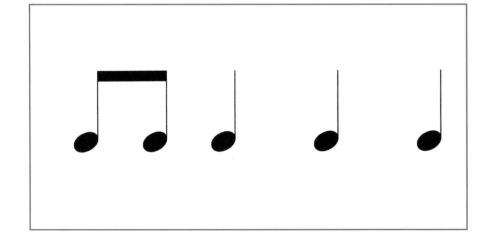

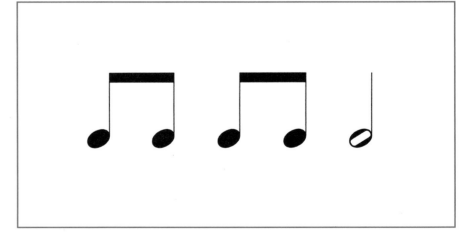

QUESTIONS AND ANSWERS

Focus: Structure   **KS2**

Make up answers for the questions in sections 1 and 2 on the worksheet. Let the children work in pairs or alternatively, choose volunteers to demonstrate and compose through class discussion.

Transfer the question and answer rhythms onto untuned instruments:

- Choose a pair to play to the class.
- Player 1 plays the rhythm of the question on one instrument and player 2 plays the answer on another instrument.

> Did the rhythm of the answer feel different to the rhythm of the question? If yes, perhaps it was because:
> a) the answer did not balance the question by lasting the same length of time.
> b) the character of the answer rhythm was completely different to the rhythm of the question. (An extreme example would be a question having 10 syllables followed by an answer of 1 syllable).

In two groups chant the question and answer phrases composed on the worksheet:

- Choose a pair to chant and play their phrases to the class.
- To help the two groups learn the rhythm, ask the players to play the question and answer phrases as a follow my leader:

Player 1 plays and chants the question:	Group 1 copies the question:
I am a mega bug, what do I do?	**I am a mega bug, what do I do?**

Do the same for the answer with player 2 and group 2.

- When secure, both groups chant and play their phrases one after another without copying.

On tuned instruments, players improvise tunes for each group to sing. Limit the range of notes to five at first to avoid wide leaps which can make the tune difficult to sing or remember. For example:

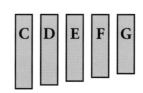

EXAMPLE THEME
Insects (Other suggestions: Jobs and Employment, Travel, TV Programmes)

RESOURCES
Worksheet, one between two

INSTRUMENTS
A selection of tuned and untuned

Questions and Answers

Follow these instructions to complete sections 1 and 2:

- Working in pairs ask your partner to pat a steady beat.
- Over this work out the rhythm of the **question** phrase by chanting the words to the beat. Then try to clap the rhythm of the words while chanting.
- Keeping in mind the rhythm of the question, make up **answers** to the question and work out how to chant and clap the rhythm of the words. The answers do not need to rhyme.
- Ask your partner to clap the question and you clap the answer.

1. Make up your own answers for the question:

Question phrase:

> **I am a mega bug, what do I do?**

Answer phrase:

> **You eat slimy worms the whole day through.**

Answer phrase:

> ....

Answer phrase:

> ....

2. The phrase below does not ask a question or give an answer, but being in two parts the musical effect is similar. Make up your own answer for the **Your dog** line:

My dog: **My dog itches 'cos he's teeming with fleas,**

Your dog: **Your dog twitches as he follows buzzing bees.**

Your dog:

> ....

Your dog:

> ....

Numbers

The main body of material in **Numbers** is centered around the element of pulse. This provides the basic foundation on which to build complex rhythmic ideas and to explore other musical elements (e.g. dynamics and pitch).

NUMBERS 1

EXAMPLE THEME
Animals
(Other
suggestions:
Post, Friends,
Streets)

RESOURCES
None

INSTRUMENTS
A selection of
untuned
percussion

Focus: Pulse and rhythm   KS1

♫ Chant the *lion rhyme* (🔊 A5) and clap on the four door numbers each time you say them:

Li-on's	knock-ing	on	a	door,
One	two		three	four.
Hur-ry	up	his	knu-ckle's	sore,
One	two		three	four.

🎲 Make a simple rhythm using the four numbers:

- Choose a door number (1, 2, 3 or 4) for the lion to knock on. As a class, chant the rhyme and clap on the door number. Do not clap on the other numbers. For example:

	clap		
One	two	three	four.

Clap on the same number for the second count of four.

- Chant the rhyme again but this time choose two door numbers to knock on. For example:

	clap	clap	
One	two	three	four.

👂 Listening game – Door knock numbers:

- Let the class help choose an instrument which makes a *door knock* sound.
- Choose one child to be the lion and play the instrument.
- The lion secretly decides which numbers to play on.
- Together chant the rhyme while the lion plays.

Which door did the lion knock on?

Follow the same steps for the *monkey rhyme* (🔊 A6), choosing an instrument suitable for a *tap on the window pane* sound.

Mon-key's	tap-ping	on	a	pane,
One	two		three	four.
Let	her	shel-ter	from the	rain,
One	two		three	four.

♫ Now chant the lion rhyme followed without pause by the monkey rhyme with the chosen players and instruments.

NUMBERS IN LAYERS 1

Focus: Texture   **KS1**

This activity follows on from Numbers 1.

Compose two rhythms to play at the same time:

- Divide the class into two groups.
- Before chanting the *lion rhyme* (page 58) ask each group to choose a number to clap on. For example:

Group 1:	clap			
Group 2:				clap
	One	**two**	**three**	**four**

- Repeat the activity but ask each group to choose two numbers to clap on. For example:

Group 1:	clap		clap	
Group 2:	clap			clap
	One	**two**	**three**	**four**

- Choose two players (one from each group) to play the rhythms on *door knock* sounding instruments while the class repeat the chant.

Follow the same procedure for the *monkey rhyme* choosing instruments suitable for *tap on the window pane* sounds.

EXAMPLE THEME
Animals
(Other suggestions: Post, Friends, Streets)

RESOURCES
None

INSTRUMENTS
A selection of untuned percussion

NUMBERS 2

EXAMPLE THEME
None

RESOURCES
Worksheet ✐
per pupil

INSTRUMENTS
A selection of
untuned
percussion

Focus: Pulse and rhythm   **KS2**

♫ As a class, practise chanting a count of 8:

- Keeping a steady beat repeat the count without
  pause:

1 2 3 4 5 6 7 8 1 2 3 4 5 6 7 8

- Do the same again but this time clap on every
  number. Everyone should try to clap exactly on
  each beat (number) so that it sounds like one big
  hand clap rather than lots of little hand claps
  around the beat.

🎲 Compose a number rhythm (Active-8 the
numbers!):

- Write a count of eight on the board.

- Ask the class to suggest several numbers to clap on
  and then circle these numbers. For example:

① 2 ③ ④ 5 ⑥ ⑦ 8

♫ As a class, practise clapping this number rhythm:

- Give a 7–8 count-in to start everyone together.
- Chant every number keeping a steady pulse and
  clap as indicated. Repeat the number rhythm
  several times without pausing.
- Clap the number rhythm at different speeds and
  dynamic levels, e.g. quietly, loudly or starting loud
  and getting quieter.

> At what speed did you think it would be best to
> practise?
> What happened to the speed when you clapped
> loudly, or softly, etc.? Did you keep a steady beat?

🎲 Individually compose a number rhythm by
completing the composing section on the worksheet.

Numbers 2 – Number Rhythms

Worksheet

Compose a number rhythm:

- Decide which numbers to clap on and then circle these numbers. For example:

  (1) 2 (3) (4) 5 (6) (7) 8

- Before circling the numbers try out your rhythm by quietly patting with two fingers on the palm of your hand.

  1 2 3 4 5 6 7 8

To practise your rhythm ask a partner to chant the count while you clap your rhythm (the circle numbers) several times without pause. Don't forget to ask for a 7 – 8 count in.

Listening Game

- Listen to a number rhythm and along one of the rows below circle the numbers on which a clap or instrumental sound is played.
- Follow the numbers with your pencil and try to keep up with the count.
- The rhythm may need to be played several times before you manage to write it all down.

  1 2 3 4 5 6 7 8

  1 2 3 4 5 6 7 8

  1 2 3 4 5 6 7 8

Did the rhythm have any pattern? For example:

  (1) (2) 3 4 (5) (6) 7 8

♫ After the children have practised their rhythms with a partner (as shown on the worksheet) go on to practise and perform their number rhythms in the following ways:

All practise at the same time:

- Everyone chants the count quietly while clapping their own rhythm.

Practise in chains:

- Number a group of children 1–10 in a chain.
- While everyone chants the count of eight quietly, each pupil in the chain claps their own number rhythm one after another without pause.
- Make another chain of 10 children and repeat the activity until everyone has had a go. (Practising in chains is particularly helpful in identifying children who are rhythmically weak and need extra help).

Three group chain:

- Divide the class into three groups.
- All the members of group one clap their own rhythm twice through at the same time, while chanting the numbers. Then as group one ends, without pause the second group begins chanting and clapping their number rhythms and so on. When group three has finished go round the chain once more.

- Repeat the exercise again but this time tell the children to count the numbers in their heads rather than out loud. (This will help the children feel the pulse or beat more naturally).
- Give each group a selection of untuned percussion instruments on which to play their rhythms. For example:

Group one	Group two	Group three
Wood	Shakers	Skins

(If you do not have enough instruments let one half of each group perform then swap).

- Go round the three group chain again, shortening the number rhythms each time round:

  1st time round each group chants and plays their number rhythms **twice.**
  2nd time round each group chants and plays their number rhythms **once.**
  3rd time round each group chants and plays their number rhythms **up to the first 4 counts only.**

Listening game – Number Rhythms (worksheet):

- Choose one child to clap his/her rhythm to the class and another child to chant the count of eight numbers including a 7–8 count-in. This is the easy version of the game (see chart right).
- The rest of the class writes the rhythm down by ear on one of the blank number rows on the worksheet.
- Choose another another child to clap his/her rhythm using the moderate or difficult version of the listening game in the chart below. (With both versions, because no one counts out loud, the class will need to keep track of the beat by counting the numbers in their heads).

VERSION	RHYTHM	COUNTING	PULSE
Easy	clap	someone chants the numbers	
Moderate	play on un-tuned percussion	no counting out loud, apart from the 7-8 count in	someone taps or claps the pulse
Difficult	play on tuned instrument	no counting out loud, apart from the 7-8 count in	no pulse is given

NUMBERS IN LAYERS 2

EXAMPLE THEME
Engine (Other
suggestions:
Clockwork
Body Beats)

RESOURCES
Worksheet ✐
per child

INSTRUMENTS
A selection of
untuned
percussion

Focus: Texture   KS2

👂 Listen to the example *3 in 1 Engine* piece on the worksheet (🔊 A7). The three number rhythms are played together on percussion instruments and repeated several times without pause. Player 1 starts and then player 2 joins in followed by player 3. The repeating patterns of rests and circles are called ostinati.

> What words can you think of to describe the sound of this engine?

♫ Divide the class into three groups and, following the worksheet, clap the rhythms of this example with group 1 following player 1's row and so on. Practise each group separately before putting all three groups together.

🎲 Working individually compose *3 in 1 Engine* pieces using the section on the worksheet.

♪ In groups of 4 perform the *3 in 1 Engine* pieces:

● Each child's piece in the group should be practised in turn.

● The composer conducts (co-ordinates) his/her own piece and the other three members of the group clap the rhythms.

● In rotation give each group a short time to practise one of their pieces using instruments before ending with a performance.

👂 Listen to and discuss each performance:

> What type of engine did you think the music represented? For example, did it sound like a slow, fast, lazy or busy engine?
> Did the group play together 'in time' or did the players' rhythms tend to drift apart?
> Was the piece well balanced, or should some players play louder or quieter?

Numbers in Layers 2 – 3 in 1 Engine (trio) Worksheet

This example of a *3 in 1 Engine* piece is a **trio** (a piece of music for three players) (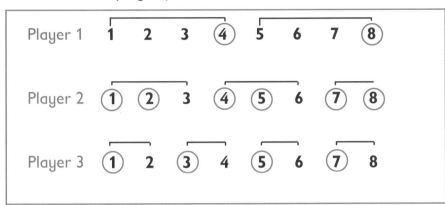 A7):

Player 1	1	2	3	④	5	6	7	⑧
Player 2	①	②	3	④	⑤	6	⑦	⑧
Player 3	①	2	③	4	⑤	6	⑦	8

- Each row of numbers has a repeating pattern of rests and circles called an ostinato. For example, player 1's ostinato is 'miss three' then 'play one'.
- An ostinato is similar in effect to an engine, repeating over and over and never pausing for rest.

Compose a 3 in 1 Engine (trio) piece:

- For each row of numbers compose a different ostinato (repeating pattern of circles and rests). Don't worry if the last repeating pattern of a row is incomplete (see player 2's rhythm opposite).
- Always keep in mind that the three number rhythms will eventually be played together.

Player 1	1	2	3	4	5	6	7	8
Player 2	1	2	3	4	5	6	7	8
Player 3	1	2	3	4	5	6	7	8

In a group of 4 practise your 3 in 1 Engine piece:

- You (the composer) become the conductor and chant and point to the numbers. The other three members of your group clap the rhythms.
- Rehearse each player separately before putting all three players together and repeating the whole piece several times without pause.

NUMBERS AND WORDS

EXAMPLE THEME
Planets (Other
suggestions:
Machines, Food,
Clothes, Capital
Cities)

RESOURCES
Worksheet 🖉
per child

INSTRUMENTS
A selection of
tuned and
untuned

Focus: Rhythm   KS2

👂 Listen to the three word rhythms being played one after another on the *Planet Rhythms* worksheet (🔊 A8). The musical notation is also given as an optional way of writing the rhythms down.

♪ Using 🔊 A8, practise the rhythms by clapping and chanting the *planet rhythms* in the gaps (echoing on beats 2 and 4).

🎲 Working individually, compose *planet rhythm* sequence 1 on the worksheet.

♫ Perform *planet rhythm* sequence 1:

- Working in pairs, the partner counts aloud the eight beats while the composer of the sequence claps and chants the name of the *planet rhythm*.
- Next, each pair claps both their *planet rhythm* sequences together and repeats them without pause.
- Choose one pair at a time to play their *planet rhythm* sequences together using untuned percussion instruments.

🎲 Working individually compose *planet rhythm* sequence 2 on the worksheet.

♫ Perform *planet rhythm* sequence 2:

- In pairs the children practise clapping *planet rhythm* sequence 2 as before with the help of a partner.
- Then, choose individual children to improvise note patterns using their *planet rhythm* sequence 2 on a tuned instrument. Ask the children to play in one of the ways shown on the worksheet, i.e. Space hopper, Lift off, Re-entry/touch down.

👂 Listening game – Identifying note patterns:

- Choose one child to play his/her sequence with one type of note pattern – Space hopper, Lift off or Re-entry/touch down.

Which type of note pattern was played?

Numbers and Words – Planet Rhythms
Worksheet

Three planet rhythms ( A8):

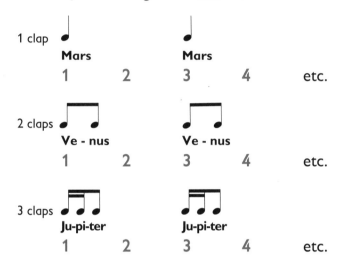

Compose planet rhythm sequence 1:

Choose **ONE** planet rhythm only and write the word above the numbers you want to clap it on. For example:

Your sequence:

1   2   3   4   5   6   7   8

Compose planet rhythm sequence 2:

Use more than one planet rhythm. For example:

Mars	Mars	Ve - nus	Mars		Ju-pi-ter	Mars	
1	2	3	4	5	6	7	8

Your sequence:

1   2   3   4   5   6   7   8

On a tuned instrument improvise a note pattern in one of the following ways using planet rhythm sequence 2:

- **Space hopper –** leaping about from low to high notes ( A9).
- **Lift off –** starting on low notes and getting higher ( A10).
- **Re-entry/touch down –** starting on high notes and getting lower ( A11).

LINKING NUMBERS

EXAMPLE THEME
Desert Winds and Sands (Other suggestions: Water, Snakes, Domestic Appliances)

RESOURCES
One copy of Worksheet ✎ per group of 4

INSTRUMENTS
A selection of tuned and untuned

Focus: Duration – long and short   **KS2**

♫ Perform the *Desert winds and sands* piece on the worksheet. An example is given on (💿 A12):

- Choose one child to chant the two counts of eight keeping a fairly slow steady beat.
- Over this ask the class to perform the first sequence of different length sounds by whistling quietly along each line. Repeat the same procedure for the second and third rows using the vocal sounds indicated.
- Divide the class into three groups and perform all three rows together.
- Ask several children to demonstrate ways of producing long and short sounds on various types of instruments. (This will give the children some idea of the sounds the instruments make and how to play them before beginning to compose their own desert music).

How can short sounding instruments sound for a long time? *(Answer: by fast tapping).*
How can long sounding instruments sound for a short time? *(Answer: by damping).*
Which instruments do you think are most suitable for desert music?

🎲 In groups of four compose desert music using the section on the worksheet.

♫ Allow the children time to practise their individual sequences using a vocal or body sound. Then in turn ask each group to perform their desert music by playing their sequences together on instruments of their choice.

👂 Listen to and discuss each performance:

- Did the group capture the atmosphere of a desert?
- If not, how could the piece be improved? Perhaps some players need to play more quietly or change their instruments for more suitable sounds.

Linking Numbers – Desert music

Long and short sounds:

The lines that link numbers together show how long the sounds last. For example, begin the whistling sound on 1 and keep going right up to (but not after) the count of 3. Whistling would restart at 5 and continue to the second count of 2, and so on.

An example of Desert Music called *Desert winds and sands*: (A12):

Desert wind
whistle **1 2 3 4 5 6 7 8 1 2 3 4 5 6 7 8**

Footsteps in the sand
shh **1 2 3 4 5 6 7 8 1 2 3 4 5 6 7 8**

Sand blown around
hiss **1 2 3 4 5 6 7 8 1 2 3 4 5 6 7 8**

In a group of 4 compose a piece of Desert music:

- Each member of the group composes one row each.
- Show where a sound begins, how long it lasts and where it ends by joining up the dots below the numbers. All sorts of patterns can be created, but keep in mind the effect you are trying to create: wind, sand, snake rattling its tail, etc.

1 2 3 4 5 6 7 8 1 2 3 4 5 6 7 8

1 2 3 4 5 6 7 8 1 2 3 4 5 6 7 8

1 2 3 4 5 6 7 8 1 2 3 4 5 6 7 8

1 2 3 4 5 6 7 8 1 2 3 4 5 6 7 8

Performing:

- Practise your sequence of long and short sounds by making a vocal or body sound while a partner chants the numbers. Then perform all four rows together using instruments as one member quietly chants the numbers.
- Think about how you might use dynamics (playing quietly or loudly) to make the music more interesting.

NUMBERS AND SYMBOLS

EXAMPLE THEME
None

RESOURCES
Worksheet ✎
per child

INSTRUMENTS
A selection of
tuned and
untuned

Focus: Dynamics   KS2

♪ As a class, clap a steady beat to a sequence of different dynamic (loud and quiet) levels following the number counts on the worksheet (💿 A13):

- Practise chanting and clapping a steady count of 8.
- Learn the meaning for each dynamic abbreviation and symbol on the worksheet. The abbreviations are of Italian words used in most music notation.
- Clap on the numbers and follow the first sequence (A), keeping the same dynamic level until the next dynamic is reached. The accent mark only effects the note it is placed above.
- If the children find any section difficult, practise the section separately at a slow tempo (speed).

> What happened to the 'steady' beat when you clapped loudly? Did it slow down, stay the same, or speed up? *(Most children tend to speed up)*.
> What happened to the 'steady' beat when you clapped quietly? Did it slow down, stay the same, or speed up? *(Most children tend to slow down)*.

- Repeat the activity for sequences B and C.
- Perform the sequences using other body sounds.

♪ Perform the sequences on instruments:

- Choose a child to play a tuned or untuned instrument.
- Ask the class to chant the count of eight quietly while the child performs the sequence. Then perform the sequence without chanting.
- Choose two or more children to perform two or more sequences at the same time. Each child should use a different instrument.

🎲 Individually, compose a sequence of dynamics by adding abbreviations and symbols to the 4 counts of eight on the worksheet (sequence D).

♪ After the children have practised clapping their own sequences choose several children to perform them to the class on instruments.

👂 Listen to and discuss each performance:

> Did the sequence begin or end loudly or quietly?
> Were any accents used?
> Could you hear a crescendo or diminuendo (getting louder or getting quieter)?

Numbers and Symbols – dynamics

Worksheet

Abbreviation	Italian	English meaning
p	piano	play quietly
mf	mezzo forte	play moderately loud
f	forte	play loudly

Symbol	Meaning
>	accent used to show when to play individual beats or notes louder
	gradually get louder
	gradually get quieter

Clap the number sequences to a steady beat and vary the dynamics (how loud to clap) as indicated (⊙ A13). Each sequence of dynamics gets more difficult. Try to keep the beat steady when changing dynamic (don't speed up or slow down). Compose your own sequence of dynamics on row D.

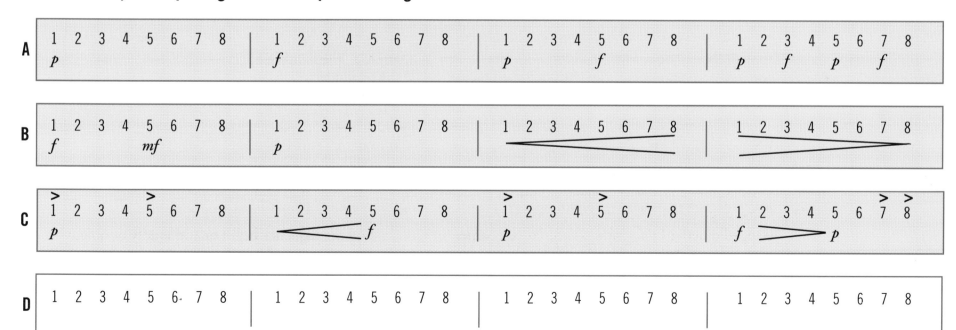

NUMBERS IN GROUPS

EXAMPLE THEME
None

RESOURCES
Worksheet 👓
and a sheet of
plain paper per
group of 4-5

INSTRUMENTS
A selection of
untuned
percussion

Focus: Metre   KS1–2

♫ As a class, perform groupings of steady beats using body sounds (examples given on 💿 A14):

- For a grouping of **two** beats the children pat their laps for beat 1 and clap for beat 2 (see worksheet).
- Repeat in the same way for groupings of **three** and **four** beats (see worksheet).

♫ Perform a sequence of number groupings:

- Call out one of the number groupings (i.e. either **two**, **three** or **four**). The class joins in with the corresponding grouping using lap and clap sounds.
- The class keeps playing this number grouping until you call out another number grouping. The class then changes to the new number grouping.
- Choose children to call out the number groupings.

♫ Introduce a **five** number grouping which may be grouped as three plus two. Clap to the right (for the group of three) and to the left (for the group of two):

five

1	2	3	1	2 etc.
lap	clap	clap	lap	clap
	R	R		L

♫ Divide the body sounds between two groups, starting with **threes** and **fours**. Group 1 makes the 'lap' sounds; group 2 the 'claps'. For example:

	three			**four**			
	1	2	3 etc.	1	2	3	4 etc.
Group 1	lap			lap			
Group 2		clap	clap		clap	clap	clap

🎲 In groups of 4–5 compose a sequence of number groupings on untuned percussion (see worksheet).

👂 Listen to recordings or performances of a variety of music and try to work out how the beats are grouped. For example:

- In *The Liberty Bell* by Sousa (theme to Monty Python's Flying Circus) the beats are grouped in twos.
- In the *Blue Danube* by J. Strauss (a fast waltz) the beats are grouped in threes.
- In *Ten Green Bottles* the beats are grouped in fours but could also be felt as a slower grouping of twos. (NB. It is often impossible to differentiate between **two** and **four**).
- In Mars from *The Planets Suite* by Holst and *Take Five* by Dave Bruebeck they are grouped in fives.

Numbers in Groups

Worksheet

Perform these number groupings to a steady beat using the body sounds shown (🔘 A14):

two

1	2		1	2		1	2		1	2 etc.
lap	clap		lap	clap		lap	clap		lap	clap

three

1	2	3		1	2	3		1	2 etc.
lap	clap	clap		lap	clap	clap		lap	clap

four

1	2	3	4		1	2	3	4 etc.
lap	clap	clap	clap		lap	clap	clap	clap

five

1	2	3	1	2		1	2	3 etc.
lap	clap	clap	lap	clap		lap	clap	clap
	R	R		L			R	R

In a group of 4–5 compose a sequence of number groupings on untuned percussion instruments:

- Decide on two number groupings to use.
- Choose pairs of instruments for each number grouping and decide who will play. For example:

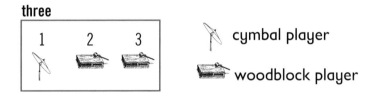

cymbal player

woodblock player

- Write the number sequence down and choose a leader to call out the number groupings (see example below).

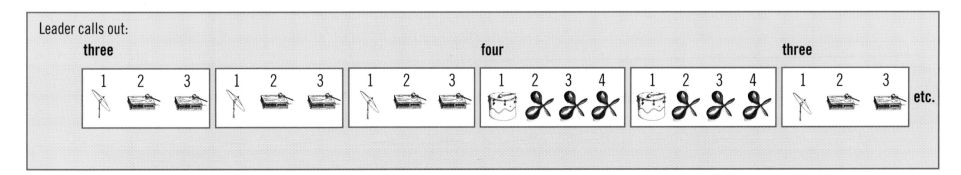

NOTES AND NUMBERS

EXAMPLE THEME
None

RESOURCES
Worksheet 🖉
per group of 4-5

INSTRUMENTS
1 set of chime
bars and 4-5
tuned percussion

Focus: Pitch   KS2

👂 Number the instruments as shown on the worksheet and perform the number sequences to the class:

> What happens to the sounds when the numbers get bigger? *(Answer: the sounds get higher).*

🎵 Divide the children into groups of 4-5 and ask them to take it in turns to play the example number sequences on the worksheet.

🎲 Compose several number sequences and a mirror sequence and then write them down on the worksheet.

🎵 Perform the new number sequences to the class.

👂 Listening game – Play the number sequences below and ask the children to fill in the missing numbers by ear on the worksheet. (The numbers in bold are the ones missing on the worksheet):

1   2   **1**   **1**   2   1

1   2   3   **3**   **2**   1   3   **1**

1 2 3 1 **1 2 3 1** 3 4 5 0 **3 4 5 0** *

*This is the beginning of *Frère Jacques*.

🎵 Perform number sequences using a set of chime bars (This technique is similar to bell ringing):

- Choose eight children and give each one a numbered chime bar as shown on the worksheet.
- Place the children in order one to eight according to their chime bar number.
- Point to and call out the numbers with a steady beat as the children play in sequence.

Notes and Numbers

Perform the number sequences below:

- Number the chime bars/xylophones as shown:

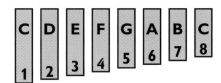

- Play the numbers to a steady beat. The number 0 means a silent beat:

1	2	3	0	4	5	0	6	7	0	8
1	2	3	2	3	4	3	4	5		
5	4	3	0	2	0	1				
3	3	4	4	5	5	6				
8	6	0	4	2	0					
1	3	5	7	0	5	0	7	0		
8	7	7	6	0	5	5	4	0	3	3	2

Compose your own number sequences:

Compose a mirror sequence :

Example:

1 1 2 2 3 0 4 5	5 4 0 3 2 2 1 1

Number Listening game:

As the sequences are played try to fill in the missing numbers:

1	2	_	_	2	1							
1	2	3	_	_	_	3	_					
1	2	3	1	_	_	_	_	3	4	5	0	_	_	_	_

This page is blank

Pictures and Symbols

Pictures and Symbols provide a stimulus for discussion about sound and enables children (especially early learners and pre–readers) to focus on creative work. Pictures and symbols can be used as cues, placed in sequence or organised to make a musical frieze. They are the first step in associating sounds with notation and develop a broad understanding of how sounds can be combined.

PICTURES AND CUES 1

EXAMPLE THEME
The Rappin'
Tappin' and
Clappin' Clown
(Other
suggestions:
Tiger, Builder,
Weather
Forecaster)

RESOURCES
Worksheet 🖎

INSTRUMENTS
None

Focus: Timbre   KS1

Ask the children to make up sounds for each part of the clown's body. For example:

Head	scratch
Mouth	laugh or hum a nursery rhyme
Hands	clap a rhythm
Knees	fast patting
Feet	stamp with right foot quietly, left foot loudly

Make up a piece of clown music using the worksheet:

- Point to parts of the clown's body at random to show which sounds the children should make. The children keep making the sound until another part of the body is pointed to.
- Sometimes change quickly, sometimes change slowly.
- Choose a child to point to the picture and repeat the activity.

After the performance ask the following questions:

What was the first and last sound played?
Which sound was used the most?

Pictures and Cues 1 – The Rappin', Tappin' and Clappin' Clown

Worksheet

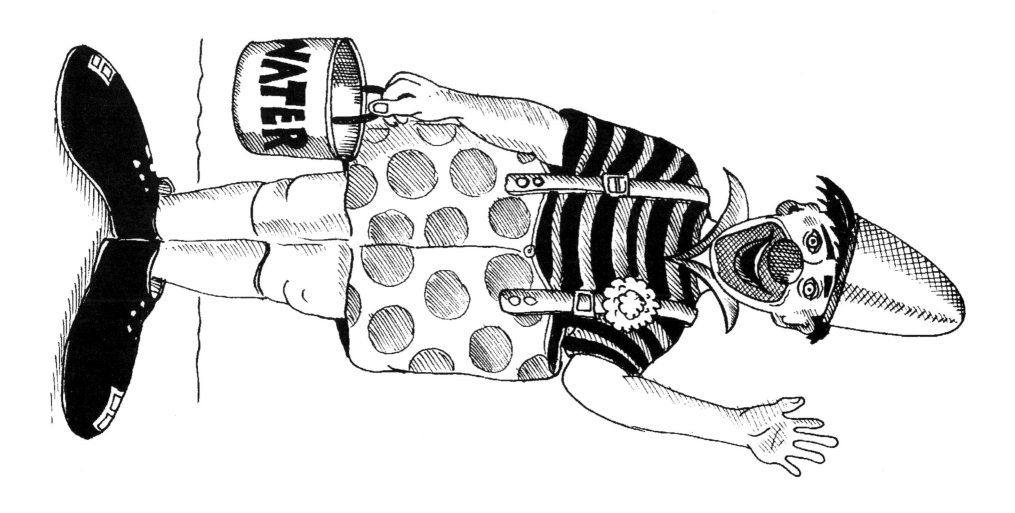

PICTURES AND CUES 2

EXAMPLE THEME
Magician (Other suggestion: Postman – big letter/small letter)

RESOURCES
A small and large picture of a rabbit plus a scarf placed inside a box or hat.
Alternatively enlarge the worksheet 🖼 and point to the pictures.
2 small pieces of card per child

INSTRUMENTS
A selection of tuned and untuned

♪ Follow the directions given by the magician to play loudly, quietly or be silent:

- Pull the big rabbit picture out of the hat and ask the children to clap loudly.
- Pull the small rabbit picture out of the hat and ask the children to clap very quietly.

> Is that the quietest you can clap or can you clap more quietly?

- Pull the scarf out of the hat and ask the children to be silent.
- Choose a child to be the magician. The magician pulls out a picture and puts it back in the hat. The children keep clapping quietly or loudly until the magician pulls out the other picture or scarf.
- Use other body sounds instead of clapping. For example, rabbit hopping sounds – pat the right and left knee quickly.

🎲 Draw pictures to represent loud and quiet sounds played on instruments:

- Demonstrate the sounds of four types of instruments. For example: skins, scrapers, shakers and tuned.

> What pictures could you draw to represent the sounds of each instrument? *(For example, a scrape on a guiro could sound like a lion roaring).*

- Ask each child to draw a large and small picture to match the loud and quiet sounds made on one instrument. Each picture should be on a separate piece of card.

♪ Perform quiet or loud sounds on instruments using the children's own pictures as directed by a magician:

- Choose one child to be the magician and place his/her pictures in the magician's hat along with the scarf.
- Choose 2–3 children and give each one an instrument that represents the magician's picture.
- The children play anything they wish as long as it is at the dynamic level given by the magician.

> Do you think the players could play even more quietly for the small picture?

- Repeat the activity choosing a different magician and players.

Pictures and Cues 2 – The Magician's Hat

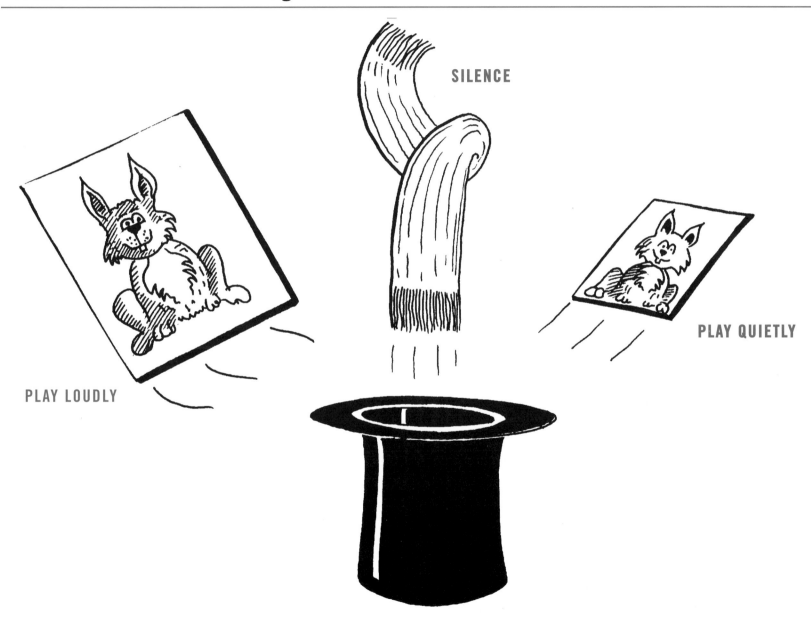

SILENCE

PLAY LOUDLY

PLAY QUIETLY

PICTURES IN SEQUENCE 1

EXAMPLE THEME
None

RESOURCES
One set of 4
picture
instrument cards
per group of
three children
(make the cards
by photocopying
the instrument
pictures on
pages 286-289)
Two of the cards
in each set
should have the
same picture

INSTRUMENTS
Several sets of
untuned
percussion
(matching the
chosen pictures)

Focus: Timbre and structure   KS1

👂 Recognise a sequence of sounds shown by pictures:

● Place one set of cards in sequence. For example:

● Play the sequence of sounds using the matching
  instruments. The sound you make on each
  instrument may have a regular pattern or be quite
  free; it doesn't have to be any particular length.
● Play the sequence twice through.

  Were all the sounds different? Were any the same?

● Change the order of the pictures and ask 3 children
  using one instrument each to play the new sequence.

👂 Identify one sequence from another:

● Select another set of cards and play the new
  sequence.
● With both sequences in view, play one of them.

  Which sequence was played?

🎲 Compose a sequence of sounds using picture cards:

● Divide the class into groups of three. Each group
  has a set of 4 cards (two of the pictures are the same)
● Ask them to find the instruments on the cards and
  create a sequence as above.
● Hand out four more cards with the same pictures
  and encourage the children to make longer
  sequences.

🎵 Perform the sequences.

PICTURES IN SEQUENCE 2

Focus: Tempo – fast and slow   KS1

♫ As a class, perform the tortoise and hare fast and slow picture score on the worksheet:

- Practise patting knees very slowly for the tortoise picture then quickly for the hare picture. Each child pats at their own speed for each picture as long as it is relatively fast or slow.
- Point to the chart and follow the path around.
- On reaching each picture the children pat at the speed indicated until the next picture is reached.

Individually compose new fast and slow picture scores:

- Ask the class to think of two pictures to represent fast and slow. Both pictures should belong to the same 'family' (e.g. cycle and train - transport).
- Each child draws a path on the paper.
- The children then draw their fast and slow pictures at various intervals along the path. Pictures of the same type should not follow each other in the sequence.

♫ Perform the picture scores using instruments:

- Choose 4–6 children and individually ask them to select an instrument and explore playing fast and slow.

> Could the slow playing be even slower? What types of movement would help the group play more slowly? *(Answer: Slow motion and broad, long or wide movements).*

- Choose a child to conduct their own picture score by pointing and following the path around. The group plays fast or slow accordingly.
- Perform the picture score again, but ask the group to play very quietly.

> Did the group manage to play quietly all the time or did they get louder? *(Children will naturally tend to play louder when playing faster).*

- Choose another group of players and perform another fast and slow picture score.

EXAMPLE THEME
Tortoise and Hare (Other suggestions: Aeroplane and Car, Walking and Running, Rain and Snowfall)

RESOURCES
Worksheet 📠
One sheet of plain paper per child

INSTRUMENTS
A selection of tuned and untuned

Pictures in Sequence 2 – Fast and Slow Picture Score

Tortoise = slow Hare = fast

PICTURES IN SEQUENCE 3

Focus: Timbre, rhythm and pitch KS1

♪ Perform the sequence of snake and ladder pictures on the chart in three different ways:

- Make a hissing sound for the snake and climbing ladder sound for the ladder.
- Use a word rhythm for each of the pictures. For example:

Naugh-ty snake Climb-ing the lad-der

- On a tuned instrument slide the beater down for the snake and play notes going up for the ladder. Ask the class to sing the slide and notes to 'la' as you or a child plays the sequence.

Ask the children to make up and draw their own snake and ladder sequences. The same pictures may follow each other in the sequence.

♪ Perform the new sequences as suggested above, but also ask the children to think about playing quickly or slowly, quietly or loudly.

Identify snake and ladder sounds in sequence:

- Play a sequence on a tuned instrument using the word rhythms and/or an up and down pattern:

Which sound started the sequence, snake or ladder? How many snake sounds did you hear in the music?

EXAMPLE THEME
Snakes and Ladders (Other suggestions: Stairs and Lifts, Firefighters' Ladder and Pole, Climbing and Skiing)

RESOURCES
Worksheet
One sheet of plain paper per child

INSTRUMENTS
One tuned percussion

Pictures in Sequence 3 – Snakes and Ladders

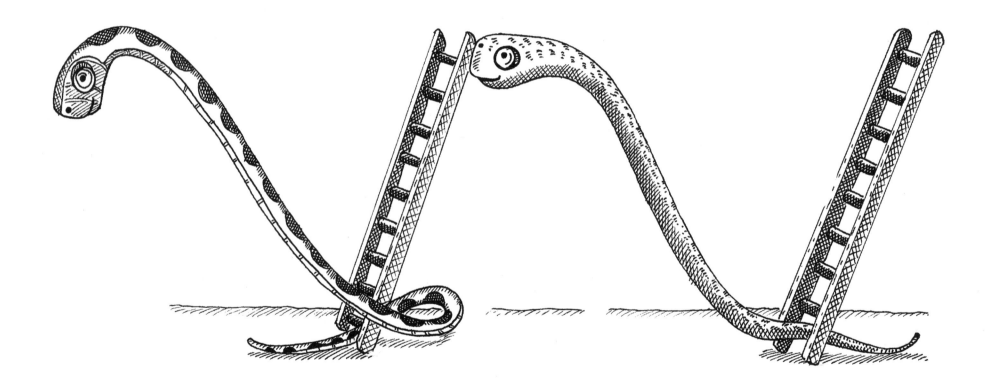

SHAPES IN SEQUENCE

Focus: Rhythm   **KS1**

♫ Perform a sequence of sounds represented by shapes. For example:

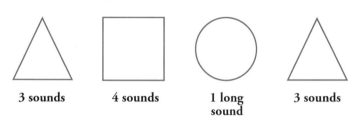

3 sounds   4 sounds   1 long sound   3 sounds

- Demonstrate vocal and/or body sounds for each of the above shapes. (With younger children, incorporate gestures or movements). For example:

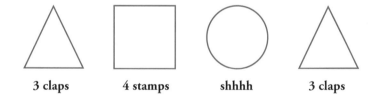

3 claps   4 stamps   shhhh   3 claps

- As a class, perform the sequence.
- Place the shapes in a new order and ask individual children to perform the sequence using the same sounds.

▦ In groups of 4–5 invent new sounds for each shape (e.g. using animal sounds) and compose new sequences:

> Which animals make long sounds? *(For example: snake – hisssss, cow – moooo, cat – purrrrr).* Which animals make short sounds? *(For example: dog – woof woof, monkey – eek eek eek).*

- The children choose one animal sound for each shape then imitate it with their voices. For example:

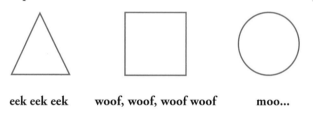

eek eek eek   woof, woof, woof woof   moo...

- Ask the groups to compose sequences using sets of cards or 3D shapes. For example:

♫ Perform the sequences using the new sounds.

EXAMPLE THEME
None

RESOURCES
Sets of cards or 3D objects illustrating triangles, squares and circles

INSTRUMENTS
A selection of untuned percussion

♫ Transfer the vocal sounds onto percussion
instruments:

> What instruments can make long sounds?
> *(For example: cymbal, maracas or cabassa played*
> *continuously, vibraslap).*
> What instruments can make short sounds?
> *(For example: woodblock, agogo, castanets).*

- Each group chooses one instrument for each shape
  and performs the sequence.

👂 Listening game – Stop on the Shape:

- Choose one group to play their sequence of shapes
  on instruments.
- Stop the group at any time during their sequence.

> Which shape did the group stop on - triangle,
> square, or circle?

SYMBOLS IN SEQUENCE

Focus: Pulse and timbre   **KS2**

♫ As a class perform the sequences of body sounds on the worksheet, following the symbols according to the key:

Which sequences have a pattern ?
(Answer: B and C).
Which sequences were easier to perform – those with or without a pattern?

📷 Working in pairs write down new body beat sequences on squared paper (between 8 and 12 boxes) or on the worksheet.

♫ Practise the sequences in pairs then perform them to the class.

👂 Listening Game:

● Perform one of the sequences to the class.

Which sequence was it?

● Choose individuals to perform other sequences for the class to identify.

EXAMPLE THEME
None

RESOURCES:
Worksheet ✏
one between two

INSTRUMENTS
None

Symbols in Sequence – Body Beats

Perform the body beat sequences:

Practise each line of body beats one at a time following the key on the right
and saying the words out loud.
Each box represents one steady beat.
For example: A = lap clap click click lap clap lap clap lap click click

KEY

✖ = click once

● = clap once

▬ = place two hands on lap once

Compose new body beat sequences:

DIAGRAMS

Focus: Pulse and Dynamics KS2

♫ As a class, clap at different dynamic (loud and quiet) levels following the worksheet:

- Practise clapping a steady beat at three different dynamic levels as shown by the LED meter readings on the worksheet (dB = decibel):

Quiet	**(-15 dB)**
Moderately loud	**(0 dB)**
Loud	**(10+ dB)**

Notice that a moderately loud reading is shown by 0 dB.

- For the meter reading with no LED boxes highlighted (i.e. silence) practise making a 'rest sign' for every beat.
- Choose a conductor to point to the four LED meters on the worksheet.
- While the class continually claps a steady beat, the conductor directs them to clap quietly, moderately loudly or make 'rest signs' by pointing to the four meter readings in any order.

> What happened to the 'steady' beat when you clapped loudly? Did it slow down, stay the same, or speed up? *(Most children tend to speed up).* What happened to the 'steady' beat when you clapped quietly? Did it slow down, stay the same, or speed up? *(Most children tend to slow down).*

- Repeat the activity, but ask the conductor to point to a different meter reading every four beats.
- To produce more subtle changes of dynamic levels ask a conductor to slide a pointer up and down the LED meter with 'empty' boxes. The higher the number the louder the clapping.

♫ Choose a group of 5 to 7 players and transfer the activity onto untuned instruments. Repeat the activity with another group of players until everyone has had a go.

Ask the children to draw other types of diagram and symbols to indicate changing dynamics levels. For example, block diagrams, graphs, etc.

EXAMPLE THEME
None

RESOURCES
Worksheet
Graph and plain paper

INSTRUMENTS
A selection of tuned and untuned

Diagrams – L.E.D. Meters

Recording level meters found on some tape recorders are used to indicate the volume of the sounds being recorded or played back. The meters measure the sound level in decibels (dB) and are made from LEDs (Light Emitting Diodes) that look like little square boxes. The louder the sound, the higher the numbers lighting up.

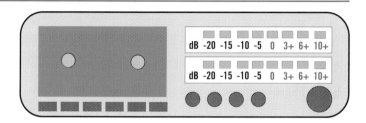

| dB | -20 | -15 | -10 | -5 | 0 | 3+ | 6+ | 10+ | = silence |

| dB | -20 | -15 | -10 | -5 | 0 | 3+ | 6+ | 10+ | = quiet |

| dB | -20 | -15 | -10 | -5 | 0 | 3+ | 6+ | 10+ | = moderately loud |

| dB | -20 | -15 | -10 | -5 | 0 | 3+ | 6+ | 10+ | = loud |

Point to the four LED meters in sequence to show others when to be silent, play quietly, play moderately loudly or loudly.

| dB | -20 | -15 | -10 | -5 | 0 | 3+ | 6+ | 10+ |

quiet ——————————————————— loud

Point to the four LED boxes above the numbers to show others to gradually play more loudly or more quietly.

MUSICAL FRIEZE

Focus: Structure and texture   KS1–2

👂 Listen to and follow the *Wake Up!* musical frieze chart (💿 A15). The score uses sounds that could wake someone in the morning and shows how the sounds are played together to make the piece of music:

- A cymbal crash is given as a cue to begin each of the three sections and end the piece. Point to the various pictures to help the class follow the score.
- **SECTION A:** The alarm clock sound begins and keeps going right up to section B (arrow lines = keep going). Then, over the alarm clock sound, the door knock and car sounds take it in turns to play (alternate) until section B.
- **SECTION B:** The radio plays its song up to section C, while at the same time the bird calls three times.
- **SECTION C:** The sounds enter one by one, beginning with the alarm clock, and keep going until the final cymbal crash.

> Which pictures have high or low sounds?
> Which pictures have fast or slow sounds?

🎵 Rehearse and perform the score:

- For picture groups 1-4 below, choose two or three children to play the instruments shown. Choose another child to play the cymbal with the rest of the class forming picture group 5 (radio):

Picture group	Sounds	Instrument / voice
1. Alarm clock	'tick tock' and 'alarm' sounds	woodblocks claves and bells
2. Door knock	door knock sounds	tambours or large woodblock
3. Car	car horn sounds	horns, kazoos or cowbells
4. Bird	bird calls	recorder or bird whistles
5. Radio	repeat the first line of this song: *Early one morning just as the sun was rising….*	voice

- Discuss and help each group work out how to perform their sounds. Remember that the arrows indicate to keep making or repeating the sound until the next cue.

EXAMPLE THEME
Wake up! (Other suggestions: Sounds of the City or Forest, At the Airport, Launderette)

RESOURCES
Worksheet 📋
1 small sheet of card per child

INSTRUMENTS
See table oppposite plus a selection of others

- Rehearse each section separately before trying to perform the score from beginning to end.
- The cymbal player determines the length of each section by giving the cue to move on.

🎲 Compose a new *Wake Up!* musical frieze:

> **What other things could wake you up in the morning?**

- Decide on four new pictures and ask the children to draw each one on a small piece of card, so that you end up with four or more separate cards of each picture.

> **What type of sounds could you make for each picture?**

- With suggestions from the class compose a section of *Wake up!* music by sticking some of the pictures on to the board to show when each sound is made. Draw lines to show continuous sounds.

♫ Perform this section of *Wake Up!* music.

Go on to compose and perform one or two more sections then perform the whole piece.

Musical Frieze – Wake Up (💿 A15)

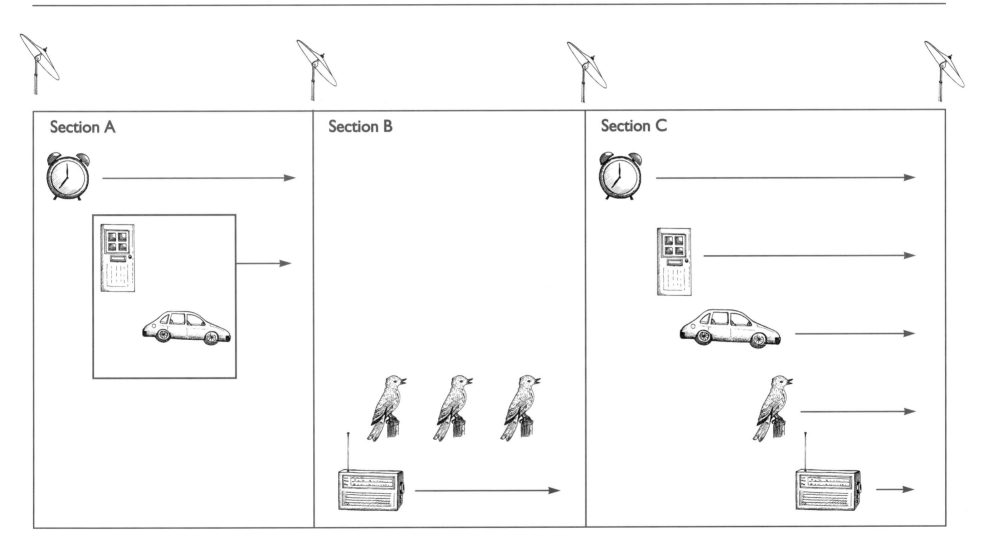

SCENES IN SOUND

EXAMPLE THEME
Sea Life (Other suggestions: Forest, Farms, Factories)

RESOURCES
Worksheet 👓
1 sheet of plain paper per child

INSTRUMENTS
A selection of tuned and untuned percussion

Focus: Texture   KS2

The *Seaweed City Scene* on the worksheet consists of four types of picture: 1. Fish, 2. Sea snake, 3. Seaweed and bubbles, 4. Sea bed:

👂 Listen to the *Seaweed City Scene* sounds made for each type of picture:

● First they are played separately (💿 A16).

> How are the sounds for each picture contrasted? Think about the instruments' timbre (sound quality), rhythms and dynamics (loud and quiet).
> *(Answers: The fish picture is played on a glockenspiel – metal – using the word rhythm 'mackerel and kippers'.*
> *The seaweed and bubbles are played on a xylophone – wood – with sounds moving from low to high.*
> *The sea snake is represented by the shaker, scraper and rattle sounds played one after another.*
> *The effect for the sea bed uses gentle 'shh' vocal sounds and rubbing sounds).*

● Now listen to the four types of sound played together to make a *Seaweed City Scene* in sound (💿 A17). The sea bed sound plays all the time, but the other sounds have gaps between their repetitions.

🎲 Compose music for the *Seaweed City Scene*:

● Divide the class into four groups and use the instruments and sounds indicated on the worksheet (group 1 – Fish, group 2 – Seaweed and bubbles, group 3 – Sea snake, group 4 – Sea bed).
● Each group follows the suggested composing ideas given on the worksheet or works out their own ideas.

♪ Perform the *Seaweed City Scene* :

- Practise the sounds for each group separately.

> Could the sounds for each picture be improved?
> For example, by playing more slowly or more
> quietly?

- Choose a conductor from group 4.
- To start the piece the conductor points to the sea
  bed group to begin making their sounds
  continuously.
- Using stop and start signals the conductor indicates
  individually to the other three groups when to start
  and stop playing. Over a period of one or two
  minutes the conductor varies the combination of
  the groups, sometimes having all three playing at
  the same time, at other times only one.

> Did the sounds contrast each other?
> Did the music balance or were some groups
> playing too loud?

⊞ Ask the children to draw their own scenes featuring
other kinds of aquatic life. Choose several pictures and
turn them into scenes in sound.

Scenes in Sound – Seaweed City Scene (🔊 A16, 17)

Worksheet

Group 1 – **Fish:** 3–4 players using glockenspiels, metallophones. Make up repeating patterns using fish word rhythms and notes CDEGA.

Group 2 – **Sea snake:** 7 players using percussion instruments which make menacing sea snake sounds. Play them quickly one after another, like a pass-the-sound game. Think about loud and quiet, long and short.

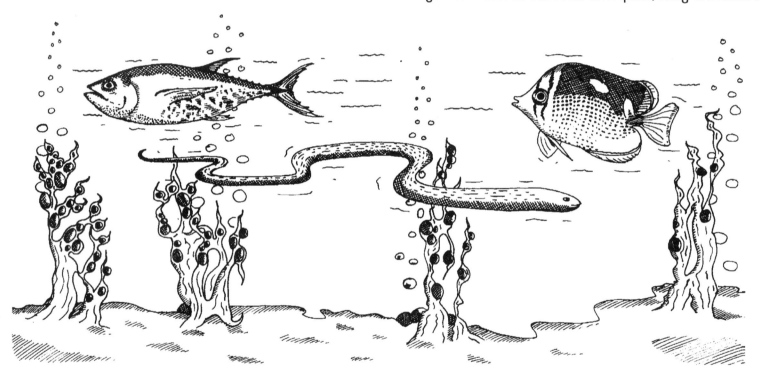

Group 3 – **Seaweed and bubbles:** 3–4 players using xylophones. Starting from low notes gradually rise to high notes.

Group 4 – **Sea bed:** rest of class using vocal and body sounds. Make quiet and gentle swelling continuous sounds.

GRIDS AND BOXES 1

Focus: Timbre and structure   KS1–2

Listen to and follow the example *Water Works* grid score on worksheet 1 (A18), performed with *real* water sounds. All the rows are played together.

Compose the first row (Part 1) of the blank grid score (worksheet 2) on the board:

- Ask the class to think up a body or vocal sound related to the water theme. For example 'rain' – patting on palms.
- With suggestions from the class place a symbol for the sound in several boxes along the row (see example score on worksheet 1).

Perform the first row (Part 1):

- Count and point to the boxes in order. The class pats when boxes contain the rain symbol and is silent on empty boxes.
- Each box does not have to be exactly the same length. Just point to the next box when you feel ready.

Follow the same procedure for each of the other rows.

Perform two or more rows at the same time (for early years limit the grid to one or two rows):

- Divide the class into two groups with group 1 following Part 1 and group 2 following Part 2. Ask the following questions before performing:

> In which columns do groups 1 and 2 make their sounds together? *(The answer for the example score on worksheet 1 is columns 5 and 7).*
> In which column do both parts have empty boxes? *(The answer for the example score on worksheet 1 is column 4).*

- Divide the class into four groups and put four parts together with each group following one of the four parts.

EXAMPLE THEME
Water Works (Other suggestions: Circus, Sports, Jungles, Traffic)

RESOURCES
Worksheet 1
Worksheet 2

INSTRUMENTS
A selection of tuned and untuned

Grids and Boxes – Water Works grid score (⊛ A18, 20)

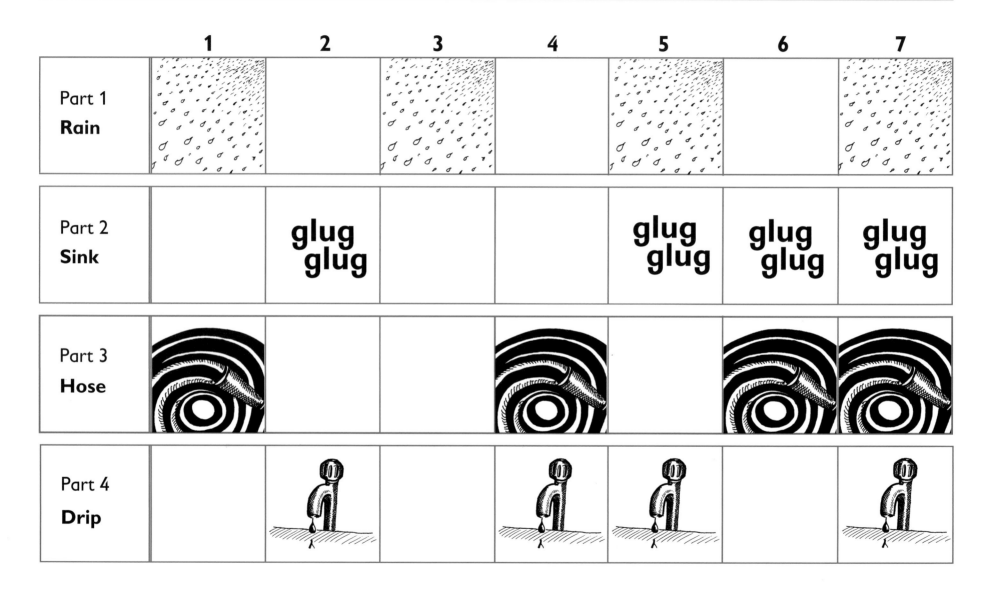

Grids and Boxes – blank grid score

	1	2	3	4	5	6	7
Part 1							
Part 2							
Part 3							
Part 4							

🎲 Choose instruments for each symbol:

> Which instruments do you think are the most suitable to play each part? *(For example: Rain – drumming fingers on a drum, Sink – scraping a guiro, Hose – shaking maracas, Drip – tapping claves).*

● Choose volunteers from each group to work out and demonstrate ways of playing the instruments for each part.

🎵 Give several of the chosen instruments to 3–4 players in the corresponding groups and perform the score. Repeat the performance with a different set of players from each group.

👂 Listen to and discuss each performance:

> Did you like the way the sounds of each row were combined (played together)?
> Did any one part stand out from the others or did the instruments blend and balance?

🎲 Make up a water chant and use it to introduce the grid score. For example:

> **Water, water, cool and wet,**
> **Wash away my soil and sweat.**
> **In a glass you're good to sip,**
> **Water, water, gurgle, drip.**

🎵 Perform the grid score with a steady beat accompaniment (measuring an equal amount of time for each column):

● Choose one child to play the beat on a drum or xylophone using the repeating note pattern C and G. (This is called an ostinato.)
● Move from column to column every four steady beats:

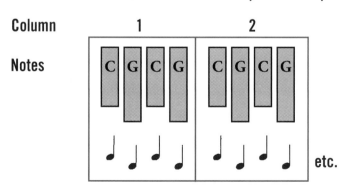

● Use the steady beat to accompany the water chant as well as the grid score and the whole piece of music will feel unified.

GRIDS AND BOXES 2

Focus: Rhythm and structure   KS2

 Ask the class to think of a word rhythm to clap over a steady beat (see the steady beat repeating pattern in Grids and Boxes 1 on page 102). For example:

Wa- ter, wa- ter, cool and wet.

♪ Perform the first row (Part 1) of the completed *Water Works* grid score (worksheet 2):

- Ask the class to chant the rhythm once for each number, but only clap the rhythm on boxes containing a symbol.
- Point to the numbers to help the class follow the boxes.

♫ Using the same rhythm follow the same procedure for each part.

♫ Perform two or more rows together:

- Divide the class into two groups both clapping the *Water, water, cool and wet* rhythm, but following different parts.

- Divide the class into four and perform all four parts together.
- Repeat the activity with each group using a different body or vocal sound. For example:

Rain – pat the rhythm on your hand.
Sink – say the rhythm using the vocal sound 'glug'.
Hose – do the rhythm using the vocal sound 'hiss'.
Drip – do the rhythm using a vocal clicking sound.

- Chant the word rhythm and ask the class to think or say the word rhythm in their heads. This will help them keep in time and feel or measure the length of empty boxes.

♫ Transfer the word rhythms onto instruments:

> Which instruments match the sound of each symbol? *(For example, shakers could sound like the hiss of a hose pipe).*

- From each group choose several children to play the *Water, water, cool and wet* rhythm on instruments (tuned instruments use notes C D E G A – a pentatonic scale).

EXAMPLE THEME
Water Works
(Other suggestions: Circus, Sports, Jungles, Traffic)

RESOURCES
As for Grids and Boxes 1 (i. e. Worksheet 1 Worksheet 2)
If this activity is not being used as a follow on from Grids and Boxes 1, just use worksheet 1

INSTRUMENTS
A selection of tuned and untuned

Ask the class to make up different word rhythms for each part over a steady beat. Each rhythm should last the same amount of time and fit over the same number of beats. For example (A19):

Part 1	Rain,	rain,	go a - way
Part 2	Glug	goes the	sink
Part 3	Spray me	with cold	wa - ter
Part 4	Drip	drop	drip
beats	**1**	**2**	**3**	**4**

Perform the grid score over a steady beat using the four different rhythms:

- Divide the class into four groups and tell each group which rhythm to clap.
- At first ignore the grid score and ask each group to simply practise chanting and clapping the rhythms together. Start one group at a time and gradually build up till all four are clapping.
- Now follow the grid score a part at a time, with each group clapping and chanting on boxes that contain their symbol. Then try two, three and finally four groups together, each following their own part.
- Choose several children from each group to perform the grid score by playing the rhythms on instruments.

Listen to and follow the *Water Works* grid score on worksheet 1 (p.100) performed with rhythms (A20). This version of the grid score is introduced by the water chant (p. 102).

MAPPING

Focus: Form   KS1–2

Look at the worksheet and answer the following questions:

> How many obstacles are there? *(Answer: 6).*
> Can you describe each obstacle? *(For example: The mountain has steps going up and a slide going down).*
> How would you tackle each obstacle? *(For example: You would climb up the mountain getting gradually slower through exhaustion. Then at the top slide down getting faster and faster).*
> What part of the obstacle course keeps coming back again and again? *(Answer: The path).*

🎲 As a class, improvise vocal and body sounds for the obstacle course on the worksheet:

- Follow the path from start to finish by pointing to the picture.
- In between each obstacle, ask the children to pat knees left and right to suggest running along the path.
- As each obstacle is encountered, the children improvise vocal and/or body sounds. Here are some suggestions:

Obstacle	Vocal sounds
Mountain:	Begin making low sounds and go up step by step, gradually getting slower and then slide the voice down.
Tunnel:	Make long quiet spooky sounds going up and down with occasional fluttery sounds.
Mud:	Make low slurping, squelching noises.
Hurdles:	Jump from low to high using *beep*s and *boing*s.
Water:	Make swishing and splashing noises.
Balancing beam:	Make a *boing* sound then make long, wobbly sounds, ending with another *boing*.

- Encourage the children to find other sounds with their voices. Younger children may want to show the movements as they make the sounds. For example, miming arms and legs in mud.

By following this path a piece of music is created which has many contrasting sections but one of them (the path) keeps recurring. This is called a **rondo** form.

EXAMPLE THEME
Obstacle Course (Other suggestions: Local Street Plan, School Plan)

RESOURCES
Worksheet 👓

INSTRUMENTS
A selection of untuned percussion

Mapping – Obstacle Course

Compose music on instruments for the obstacle course:

- Divide the class into 7 groups (one for each obstacle and a smaller group to make the running sounds between each obstacle).

> What sort of instruments are suitable for making the running sounds along the path? *(For example, a two-tone woodblock, gato drum).*
> What sort of instruments are suitable for each obstacle? *(For example, for the mountain – a xylophone can make up and down shapes).*

- Give each group their chosen instruments.

Perform the musical obstacle course:

- The 'runners' group play their music for the path between each obstacle. The music should lead straight into the mountain obstacle music without a gap.
- As soon as the mountain obstacle music has finished the 'runners' group plays again until the tunnel music begins, etc.

After the performance discuss the following questions:

> Did the music give the 'feel' of each obstacle? *(For example, could you imagine yourself going up the mountain, wading through the mud etc.?)*
> Did the sounds used help to show the kind of obstacle being described? *(For example, did they use low and high sounds to show jumping the hurdles?)*

This page is blank

Dots, Lines and Spaces

Dots, Lines and Spaces is a simple form of graphic notation which helps to develop an understanding of fundamental musical concepts. Used as the basis for composing activities and listening games, this section provides an *approximate* but immediate way for children to interpret and notate shapes and patterns.

DOTS AND SPACES 1

EXAMPLE THEME
Focus 1
Clocks (Other suggestions: Heart Beats)

RESOURCES
Focus 1
Worksheet 🖺

INSTRUMENTS
Focus 1
A selection of untuned percussion

Focus 1: Pulse and tempo - fast and slow   KS1

👂 Compare fast and slow dot rhythms:

- Listen to and follow dot rhythm A on the worksheet (💿 A21):

> Did the rhythm remind you of anything?
> *(For example: a pulse or heart beat, a ticking clock, the radio time signal or just something steady and even).*

- Listen to and follow dot rhythm B on the worksheet (💿 A22):

> Did dot rhythm B go faster or slower than A?
> *(Answer: Faster, because the dots are closer together).*

🎵 As a class, clap dot rhythm A then dot rhythm B. Try to keep the beat or pulse steady whether clapping fast or slow.

🎲 Pretend to be ticking clocks in a clock maker's shop:

- Choose several children to be 'clocks' and give each an instrument on which to play ticking sounds (e.g. claves, woodblocks, a cymbal hit softly on the dome with a hard beater).
- One at a time, ask each 'clock' to play a steady ticking sound at a slow speed (rhythm A) and at a fast speed (rhythm B).
- Perform the ticking sounds together with some 'clocks' ticking fast and others ticking slow. A clock winder (conductor) could 'wind-up the clocks' and start them ticking one by one.

Focus 2: Rhythm   KS1

👂 Listen to and follow dot rhythms C and D on the chart (🔊 A23). These rhythms mix slow and fast (dots wide and close apart).

♪ As a class, clap dot rhythms C and D. To help feel the spaces between the dots say 'space' or 'gap' or make a rest sign with your hands.

🎲 Compose a dot rhythm - *Walking the Dog*:

- Ask a child to place several balls along a straight line at various intervals on the floor.
- Attach a piece of string (the lead) to a bean bag (the dog).
- Take the dog for a steady even walk along the line. When the bean bag passes a ball everyone claps (or barks) once.
- Use different size balls to show loud and quiet.

> The child walked steadily, but the rhythm of the sounds may have seemed jerky or uneven. Why was this? *(Answer: Because the spaces in between the balls were different lengths).*

👂 Notate dot rhythms by ear:

- On the spot, ask a child to clap a short rhythm. The class listens and then helps write the dot rhythm on the board.

> How many claps did you hear (how many dots are needed)?
> Where do the spaces or gaps come?

EXAMPLE THEME
Focus 2
Walking the Dog
(Other suggestion: Driving down the Street)

RESOURCES
Focus 2
Worksheet 🖼
Bean bag and piece of string, plus several balls of various sizes

INSTRUMENTS
Focus 2
None

Dots and Spaces 1 – Dot Rhythms (🔊 A21, 22, 23)

Walking the dog

DOTS AND SPACES 2

Focus: Rhythm   **KS2**

Listen to the eight rhythms on the worksheet several times (⊚ A24):

> Can you guess the order in which they are played? Listen out for the number of dots (sounds) each rhythm uses and the space (rest) between them. *(Answer: 7, 4, 8, 3, 5, 6, 1, 2).*
> How would you describe rhythms 1 and 2 and what is the difference between them? *(Answer: Steady beat or pulse. Rhythm 2 is faster than 1 because the dots are closer together).*

As a class, practise clapping dot rhythms 1-8. The rhythms don't have to sound exactly like the versions given on the tape. This type of notation is only an approximate guide and different people will interpret the dots and spaces in slightly different ways.

Listening game:

● Choose a child to improvise a note pattern (using any notes) to one of the rhythms on a tuned instrument.

> Which rhythm was used?

Ask the children to compose their own rhythms by clapping. Then ask them to write them down on the worksheet.

Choose several children to play their rhythms to the class on instruments.

Copy a child's rhythm onto the board so that the class can follow the rhythm as it is played:

> Was the rhythm notated correctly?
> Were the notes grouped in a special way?
> Did the rhythm feel energetic, relaxed, steady or uneven?

EXAMPLE THEME
None

RESOURCES
Worksheet ✎
per child

INSTRUMENTS
A selection of tuned and untuned percussion

Dots and Spaces 2 – Dot Rhythms (🔊 A24)

1 ●   ●   ●   ●   ●

2 ● ● ● ● ●

3 ●   ●   ● ● ● ●

4 ● ●   ●

5 ●   ● ●   ● ●

6 ● ● ●   ● ● ●   ● ● ●   ● ●

7 ●   ● ●

8 ●   ●   ●   ● ● ● ●

Write down your own rhythms, using dots and spaces:

Notate dot rhythms by ear:

1

2

3

4

Notate dot rhythms by ear:

- Clap or play the four rhythms below one by one
  (🔊 A25) and ask the class to write them down in
  the space provided on the worksheet. Give help by
  stating how many dots are being used so that the
  children only have to work out where the spaces go.
- Each rhythm may need to be played several times:

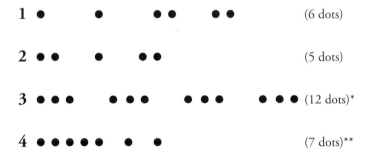

1 ●   ●   ●●   ●●   (6 dots)

2 ●●   ●   ●●   (5 dots)

3 ●●●   ●●●   ●●●   ●●● (12 dots)*

4 ●●●●● ● ●   (7 dots)**

* This rhythm uses 12 dots but ask the children to listen out for a
magic number (3).
** This is the rhythm from a well-known TV programme,
EastEnders.

- Choose several children to clap the beginnings of
  other well known tunes and ask the class to notate
  the rhythm using dots and spaces.

DOTS AND LINES 1

EXAMPLE THEME
None

RESOURCES
Worksheets
1 & 2

INSTRUMENTS
A xylophone
(or similar
instrument) and
hard beaters

Focus: Pitch   KS1

🎧 As a class, listen to and follow the **up** line played three times on worksheet 1 (💿 A26):

- First playing – listen only.
- Second playing – follow the sound up with your hand.
- Third playing – sing the line to *'la'* as it rises.

> How did the sound move from low to high?
> Did it leap, step, or slide? *(Answer: Slide).*

🎵 As a class, sing the **up** line without the tape. Raise a hand higher as the sound gets higher.

Repeat the same steps for the **down** line (💿 A27).

👂 Listening game – *Rocket*:

- Choose a child to play the **up** or **down** line on a tuned instrument by sliding a hard beater from low to high or high to low. (The xylophone rocket next to the up and down lines on worksheet 1 helps to show where to start on the instrument).

> Which line was played (did the rocket go up or down)?

👂 Playing by step (playing each note separately) is another way to go up or down. As a class, listen to and follow the **up and down** dot shape played three times on worksheet 1 (💿 A28):

- First playing – listen.
- Second playing – follow the 5 steps up and then down with your hand.
- Third playing – sing, counting up 5, then 5 down backwards.

🎵 As a class, perform the **up and down** dot shape on worksheet 1 using the actions shown – touch toes for the lowest dot and head for the highest dot.

🎵 Choose volunteers to play the **up and down** dot shape on a tuned instrument. Any notes can be used as long as they get shorter (going up) and longer (going down).

Dots and Lines 1 – Up and Down (💿 A26, 27, 28)

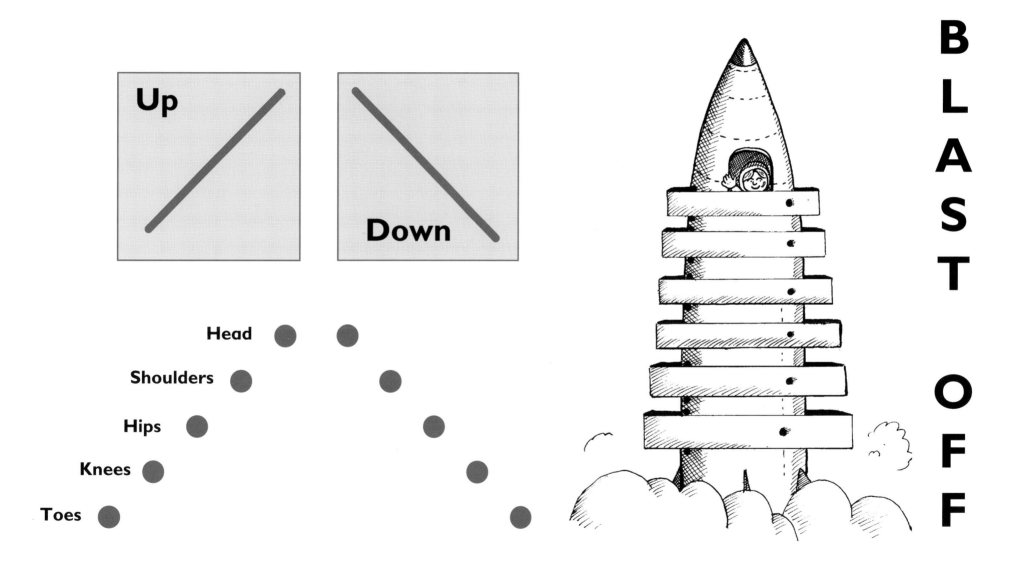

🎲 Choose volunteers to play up or down on a tuned instrument. Whether sliding (glissando) or playing by step (playing each note separately), there are lots of different ways to go up or down:

- Slowly or quickly, getting faster or getting slower.
- Loudly or quietly, getting louder or getting quieter.
- Evenly or jerkily.
- Using a rhythm e.g. *Three blind mice*.

♫ Perform the six **up and down** shapes on worksheet 2 on a tuned instrument:

- Depending on age and experience of the class choose one of the methods below:

1. One at time, ask volunteers to choose and work out how to play one of the shapes on an instrument. (Limit the number of shapes for the very young).
2. Divide the class into several groups and give each group a tuned instrument. Ask each group to choose collectively one shape and work it out, taking turns to play the shape.

- Although lines are used to show the shapes ask the children to slide or step from low to high.

🎲 Choose a child to play one of the shapes again, but this time ask him/her to think about:

- The different ways of going up and down discussed above (fast, slow, loud, quiet, evenly, jerkily, etc.).
- Using a mixture of stepping and sliding (e.g. for shape 1 – slide up and step down).

👂 Listen to the performance of each shape:

Which shape was played?
How was the shape played?
(For example, fast or slow, quietly or loudly, etc.).

Dots and Lines 1 – Up and down shapes

1

2

3

4

5

6

DOTS AND LINES 2

EXAMPLE THEME
Robot Music
(Other suggestions: Bird Calls, Sirens, Speech Patterns)

RESOURCES
Worksheets
1 & 2
1 sheet of plain paper per child

INSTRUMENTS
Ideally one tuned instrument per group of 4

Focus: Pitch   KS2

Listen to the first five dot and line shapes (note patterns) on worksheet 1 (A29). Each shape is played twice:

These are the answers to the questions in each box on worksheet 1:
No. 1 – *two peaks and one trough and two half-troughs.*
No. 2 – *two different notes.* **No. 3** – *three different notes; a hill shape.* **No. 4** – *the notes in the second group are closer together.* **No. 5** – *the line shows how long the sound lasts.*

- Listen to the A29 again. On the first playing of each shape follow the sound up and down with a hand movement. On the second playing sing the shape to *'la'*.

Explore ways of playing long and short sounds:

- Choose several children to demonstrate on xylophones, glockenspiels or metallophones.

How can a long sound (shape 5) be played on a xylophone? *(Answer: By fast tapping on the same note – tremolo).*

How can a short note (in shape 5) be played on a glockenspiel which usually 'rings' and fades away? *(Answer: By stopping the note vibrating with your hand – damping).*

Perform the shapes on worksheet 1 on instruments:

- Divide the class into groups of four with one tuned instrument per group.
- One person from each group chooses a shape to play from worksheet 1, but keeps their choice a secret from the rest of the class.
- Allow about 2–3 minutes for the players to work out the shape and practise. Encourage other members of the group to help the player.

Listening game:

- One at a time, choose one player from each group to play.

Can you guess which shape was played?
Was the shape played correctly? If not, what is it that needs to be corrected or improved?

Change players in each group and repeat the above performing and listening activities.

Dots and Lines 2 (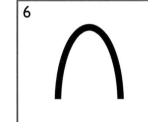 A29)

1 How many peaks (high points) and troughs (low points) does this shape have?

2 How many different notes are there?

3 How many different notes are there? What shape do the dots make?

4 What is the difference between the first and second group of three notes?

5 Each line is on the same level so you only need one note or sound, but what does the length of the line mean?

6

7

8

9

10

11

12

13 high   middle   low

14

♫ Practise the shapes in other ways:

- Ask the player from each group to play the same shape at the same time. Give a count-in to start the players together and point to the lines and dots as they are played. (This allows many children to perform the shape at the same time).
- Choose a player to play shape 2, 3, 4, 11, 12 or 13 and ask the class to echo the shape by singing the notes to 'la'.
- Enlarge and draw the three lines of shape 5 on the board. As you steadily move a pointer along the lines the class hums on one note. They should stop humming when the pointer comes to the end of a line, etc.

🎲 Individually compose robot music shapes by following the instructions on worksheet 2.

♫ Choose several children to perform their robot shapes to the rest of the class.

👂 Listen to and discuss each performance:

Can you guess what type of work the robot is doing?
Did the music feel robotic?

👂 Notate shapes by ear.

- Choose one child to play his/her robot shape.
- Ask the class to write down the shape. They will need to hear the shape several times.

Dots and Lines 2 – Robot Music

Imagine a robot doing work in a factory. The tasks given are very short and repetitive. It could be hammering rivets, putting tops on milk bottles or taking things from one shelf and putting them on a lower shelf.

Compose two robot music shapes for your instrument:

- Think about what type of work your robot will do.
- Your robot shapes should be short, so that you can repeat them over and over again.
- Think about the movement of the robot and how you might imitate this on your instrument.
- Always work out your shape by first playing and only then writing it down using dots and/or lines.
- Here are two examples:

Hammering nails

Filling a milk bottle and putting on the top

DOTS AND LINES IN SEQUENCE 1

EXAMPLE THEME
The Iron Foundry
(Other
suggestions:
Firework Display,
Traffic Jam,
Seaside)

RESOURCES
Worksheet 🖾

INSTRUMENTS
5 pairs of tuned
and untuned
percussion

Focus: Structure   KS1

♪ Discuss with the children how to play the three shapes on the worksheet, trying to capture the atmosphere of an iron foundry. Then, choose 10 players and give each player one of the instruments. Ask each player to find out which shape is linked to his/her instrument.

🎲 Sequence the *Iron Foundry* shapes:

● Ask the class to suggest an order for the players to play in.
● Stand them in a straight line to form a sequence and number them 1 to 10 (see example 1).

♪ Perform the sequence of shapes one after another without pause.

🎲 Ask the children to suggest ways of rearranging the players to make up a different sequence (The players keep the same instruments and play the same shape). For example:

● Pattern of pairs (see example 2).
● Start with the loudest and end with the quietest instruments, or the other way around.
● Start with the lowest and end with the highest sounding instrument, or the other way around.

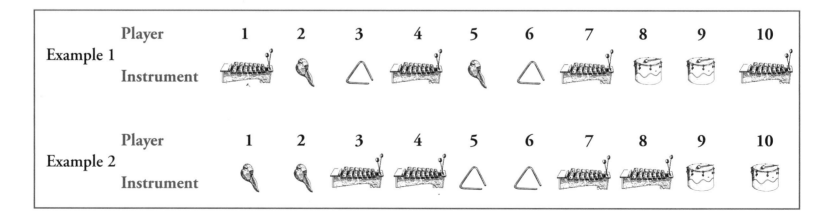

Dots and Lines in Sequence 1 – Iron Foundry Shapes

Xylophone or Glockenspiel

Shaker or Maracas   **Drum**

Triangle

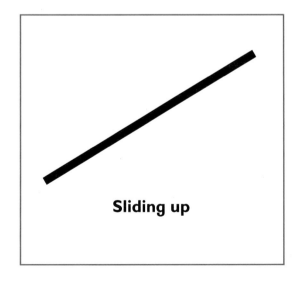

Sliding up

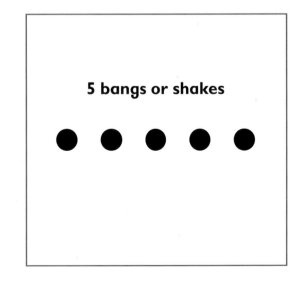

5 bangs or shakes

Long sound

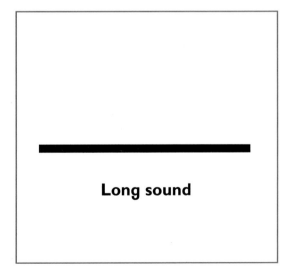

DOTS AND LINES IN SEQUENCE 2

EXAMPLE THEME
C3PO Star Wars
Robot Speech
(Other
suggestions:
Bird Calls,
Timber Yard,
Transport)

RESOURCES
Worksheet ✎
per child

INSTRUMENTS
A tuned
instrument and
two beaters per
group of 4-5
children

Focus: Structure   KS2

♪ Discuss how to play the three shapes on the worksheet:

- Choose volunteers to demonstrate on a tuned instrument.
- Choose volunteers to perform the shapes using vocal robot sounds.

👂 Listen to the example sequence using the three shapes which make up the *C3PO Star Wars Robot Speech* on the worksheet (🔊A30).

🎲 Ask each child to compose a robot speech sequence by following the instructions on the worksheet. (Give one tuned instrument per group of 4-5 children. Ask them to take turns trying out ideas before notating the tunes on the worksheet).

♪ Choose several children to perform their sequences to the class on an instrument or using robotic vocal sounds.

👂 Listen to each performance and answer one or more of the questions:

Which was the first and last shape played?
How many times was shape number 1 played?
Which were the first five shapes played? Write the order down like this:

/ / ⋰ / ∿

or as numbers: 1   1   2   1   3

(It may take two or three playings before everyone has the answer).

Dots and Lines in Sequence 2 – C3PO Star Wars Robot Speech

The C3PO robot from the Star Wars films does not talk with speech but uses sounds that are more like singing with whistling slides, bleeps and trills.

Compose a robot speech sequence by ordering and repeating the three shapes below:

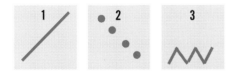

- Work out your sequence by playing before writing it down in the box below. This is an example of a sequence (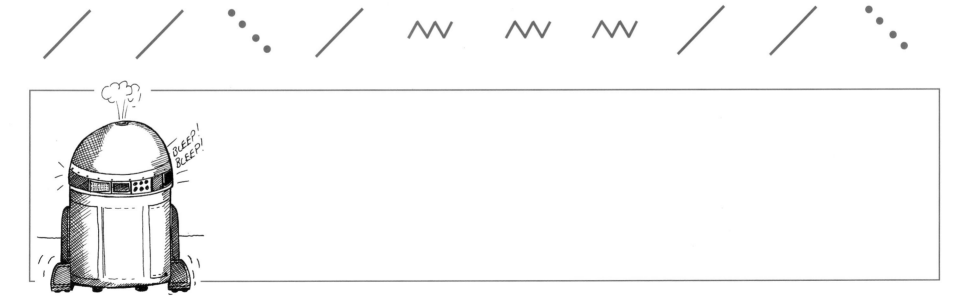 A30):

- You can vary where and how you play each shape on the instrument. For example, the three squiggly lines could be played at different places on the instrument. The notation gives only an approximate guide to the notes used in your sequence.

- Try to sing the tune using robotic vocal sounds.

- Think about tempo (speed) and use of dynamics (quiet and loud) to give the sequence character. For example, if your robot feels frustrated the tune may be played fast and loud.

- Think up ways of making a good beginning or ending. For example, by getting quieter or slower.

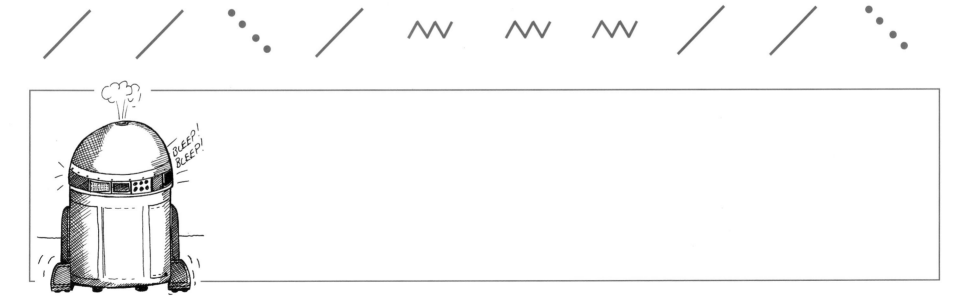

DOTS AND LINES IN LAYERS 1

EXAMPLE THEME
Big Ben's Clock
(Other
suggestions:
Forest Sounds,
Clockwork Toys)

RESOURCES
Worksheet 📖
(optional)

INSTRUMENTS
A selection of
tuned and
untuned
percussion
including a
glockenspiel, two
tone woodblock,
xylophone,
claves and drum,
cymbal or bell

Focus: Texture   KS1

👂 Listen to *Big Ben's Clock* , 💿 A31 (the worksheet is given to help you see how the music fits together. It may be useful to show this to the children depending on age and experience):

🎵 As a class perform *Big Ben's Clock* :

- Chant the rhyme:

	(Echo whisper)
Big Ben's clock,	*Big Ben's clock,*
Tick and tock.	*Tick and tock.*
Big Ben's clock,	*Big Ben's clock,*
Whir and knock	*Whir and knock.*

All the thingies, cogs and springs,
Work together till Ben rings.

- Practise patting the word rhythm 'Big Ben's Clock' on knees. Make a *'shh'* sound or use open hands to indicate and 'feel' the silent 4th beat:

	1	**2**	**3**	**(4)**
clap	●	●	●	*(shhh)*
	Big	*Ben's*	*Clock*		etc.

- Chant *Big Ben's Clock* again and accompany it by patting the word rhythm on knees.
- Choose four players to play the sounds in the boxes using the instruments indicated on the worksheet. (If you are not using the worksheet draw the four shapes on the board). Choose a fifth player to be **Big Ben** using a drum, cymbal or bell.
- Discuss how to play the four shapes on each instrument which are played in the echo parts of the chant as indicated.
- At the end of the chant all four players play together and keep repeating their shapes. Alternatively, players could enter one after another and gradually build up, beginning quietly and getting louder.
- The fifth player – **Big Ben** – stops the four players after a short period by 'ringing' (playing his or her instrument) several times.

🎵 Perform the chant again with a different group of players.

🎲 Make up new shapes to play in the echo whisper sections. Remember, a shape or sound must be quite short and fit in the time it takes to say **Big Ben's Clock**

Dots and Line in Layers 1 – Big Ben's Clock (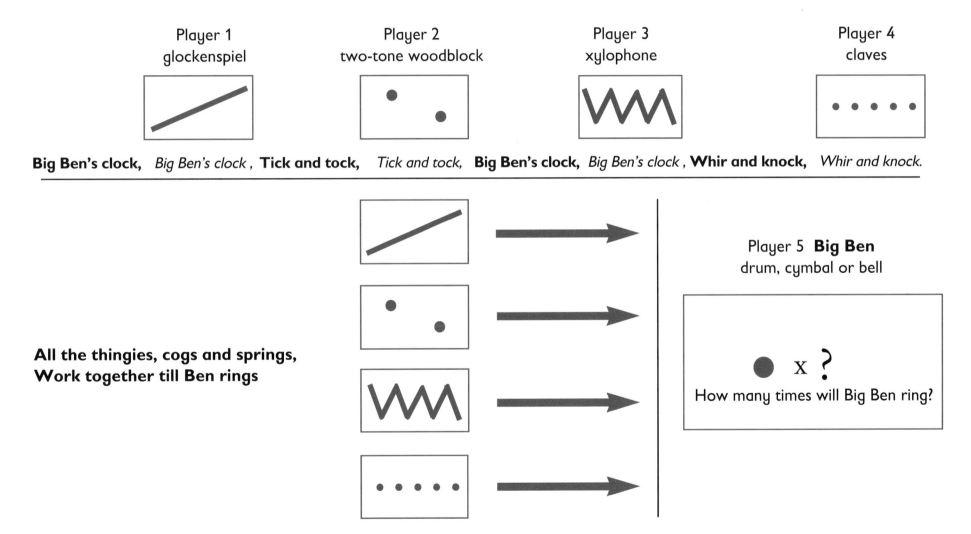 A31)

Player 1
glockenspiel

Player 2
two-tone woodblock

Player 3
xylophone

Player 4
claves

Big Ben's clock, *Big Ben's clock ,* **Tick and tock,** *Tick and tock,* **Big Ben's clock,** *Big Ben's clock ,* **Whir and knock,** *Whir and knock.*

All the thingies, cogs and springs,
Work together till Ben rings

Player 5 **Big Ben**
drum, cymbal or bell

● x **?**

How many times will Big Ben ring?

Play the sounds together and repeat them until Big Ben rings.

DOTS AND LINES IN LAYERS 2

EXAMPLE THEME
Machines (Other suggestions: Timber Yard, Building Site, Garage)

RESOURCES
Worksheet 👓

INSTRUMENTS
Two tuned and a selection of untuned percussion (see worksheet)

Focus: Texture   KS2

👂 Listen to the sound of a printing machine (🔊 A32). The machine is made up of several repeating sounds.

> What sort of words could you use to describe the sounds that the machine makes?

🎵 Choose several players to work out and play the machine shapes on the worksheet for each instrument. Then choose another pupil to be the conductor.

🎲 Improvise machine music with a conductor:

- The conductor directs the group of players by giving start and stop signals to individual players. By using these signals to vary the combination of players playing at any one time the conductor becomes the composer.
- When given the signal to start a player continually repeats the shape with or without a short pause in-between until given the signal to stop.
- Add other signals, such as raising and lowering an arm to indicate when to play loudly or quietly.

👂 Listen to and discuss each performance:

> Was the music varied enough?
> Did the music sound too cluttered because all the instruments were playing nearly all the time?
> Were the sounds balanced in volume?
> Which sounds and shapes went well together?

🎲 Compose new machine music shapes:

- Choose a new group of players to quickly compose machine shapes for their instruments.
- Draw a diagram on the board like the one on the worksheet and notate the shapes for each instrument in the circles.

Choose another conductor and repeat the activity.

Dots and Lines in Layers 2 – Machine Music

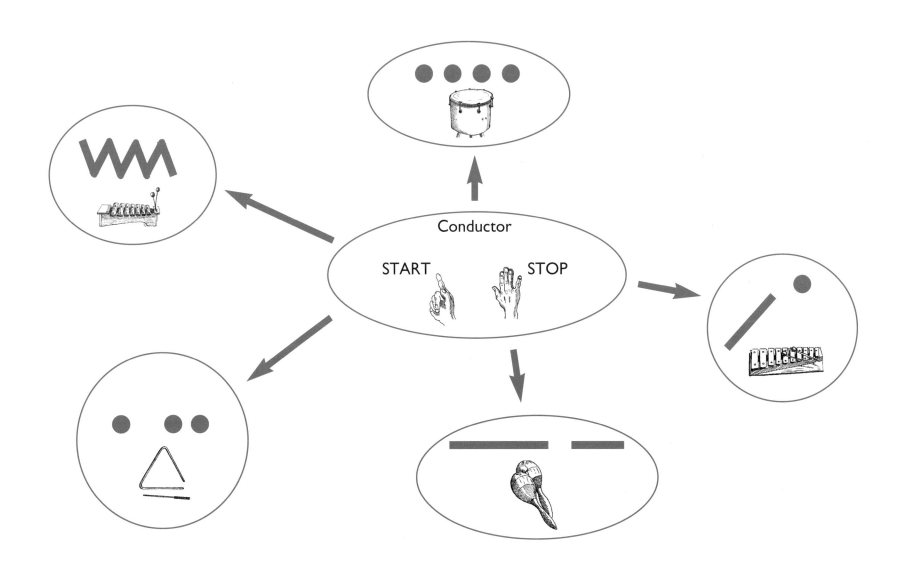

DOTS AND LINES IN SECTIONS

EXAMPLE THEME
Opposites –
Rat Race and
Moonwalk (Other
suggestions:
Desert and
Rainforest,
Waterfall and
Ponds)

RESOURCES
Worksheet 👓
and a sheet of
plain paper per
group of 4-5

INSTRUMENTS
A selection of
tuned and
untuned

Focus: Contrast and form   **KS2**

👂 Listen to and follow the Rat Race and Moon Walk graphic score on the worksheet (🔊 A33):

- The music is in two sections: section A captures the mood of busy non-stop city life, i.e. a rat race; section B captures the mood of someone walking on the moon. Each section is repeated several times.
- Each section uses the same instruments but they are contrasted by:

1. **Rhythm and pitch shape**.
2. **Structure and texture** (the way the shapes are played together). In section A there are always at least three parts playing together - player 1 alternates with players 2 and 3 while players 4 and 5 play continuously. In section B there are never more than two players playing at the same time - player 5 plays continuously while the others play one after another.
3. **Dynamics** (loud and quiet).
4. **Tempo** (fast and slow).

- Two contrasting sections played one after another make a **binary** form.

🎵 In groups of 5 perform section A using vocal and body sounds:

- The children decide who plays each part and what type of vocal or body sounds to use for each shape. (The same vocal sounds will be used for each section).
- Ask each group to practise the parts separately, then practise the pattern of player 1 alternating with players 2 and 3.
- Finally the children put all five parts together and repeat the section several times without pause.

The children should follow a similar procedure for section B making sure that there is a real contrast in the use of dynamics and tempo.

👂 Listen to and discuss each group's performance of both sections:

> Did section A capture the atmosphere of a 'Rat Race'? If not, would playing at a faster tempo help?
>
> Did section B capture the atmosphere of a 'Moon Walk'? If not, would playing at a slower tempo 'in slow motion' help?

♫ Perform the Rat Race and Moon Walk score using instruments:

- Ask volunteers to demonstrate how to play the shapes for each part on a variety of instruments.

Which instruments could be used for each part? *(For example, to play the up and down shapes of players 4 and 5 tuned instruments will be required).* Which instruments can make sounds suitable for the mood of both sections? *(For example, a cymbal can produce both harsh and gentle sounds).*

- In turn, ask each group to select their own choice of instruments for the performance. Allow a short period of rehearsal before the groups perform to the class. If enough instruments are available the groups can rehearse for a short period at the same time. If not, each group should have a very short rehearsal using the instruments prior to their performance.

👂 Listen to and discuss each performance:

Was there enough contrast of tempo and dynamics between the two sections? If not, how could they be improved?
Did the instruments balance or were some too loud?

In groups of 5 ask the children to compose two contrasting sections of music using vocal and body sounds. Each group should make a graphic score to show how their music fits together and how each section is contrasted.

♫ Perform the new scores to the class using vocal and body sounds or instruments as shown above.

Dots and Lines in Sections – Rat Race and Moon Walk (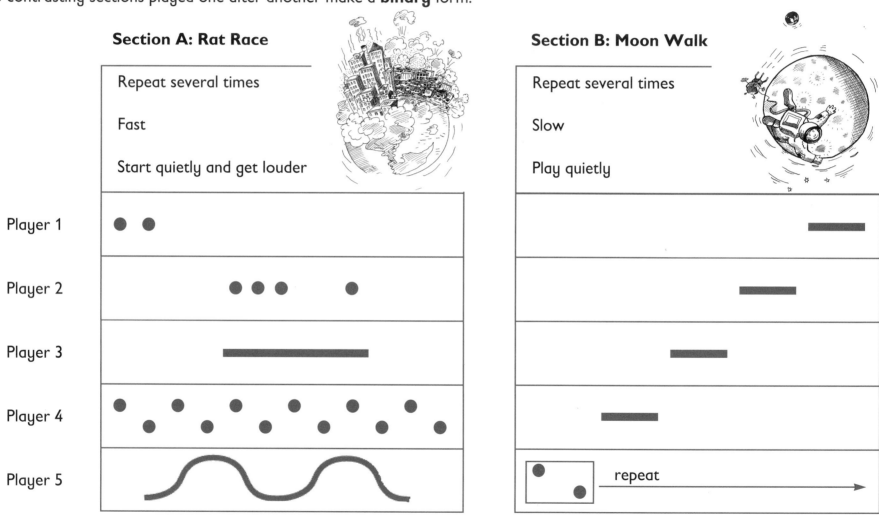 A33) Worksheet

For each section perform the sounds together. Think carefully about mood, dynamics (loud/quiet) and speed (tempo).
Two contrasting sections played one after another make a **binary** form.

Section A: Rat Race

> Repeat several times
>
> Fast
>
> Start quietly and get louder

Player 1	● ●
Player 2	● ● ● ●
Player 3	▬▬▬▬▬
Player 4	● ● ● ● ● ● ● ● ● ● ● ● ●
Player 5	〰〰〰

Section B: Moon Walk

> Repeat several times
>
> Slow
>
> Play quietly

	▬▬
	▬▬
	▬▬
	▬▬
	● ● → repeat

Projects

HIDDEN IN THE JUNGLE

GAMES
Copy Me
Plug the Gap

RESOURCES
Focus 1
Worksheet 1 👀
(optional)
Worksheet 2 👀

INSTRUMENTS
Focus 1
None

Year group R–2

In between the densely packed trees, shrubs and undergrowth of the jungle it is very difficult to see any of the creatures that live there. But, if the children use their ears they will soon know what type of creatures are there.

Focus 1: Timbre – vocal and body sounds

🎵 Sing the song *Hidden in the Jungle* on worksheet 1 (💿 A34). An instrumental section follows the song which relates to the **grid score** on worksheet 2. As the **five numbers** and the **GET READY BAR** are called out on 💿 A34, point to the numbers on the grid score and ask the children to count them out loud.

👂 Listen to the whole song (five verses with creature sounds) on 💿 A35 and ask the children to follow the sounds made by the animals on the grid score (worksheet 2), one row at a time.

🎲 As a class, make up a short vocal or body sound and action for the **snake** picture on the grid score (e.g. a hissing sound with wriggly arm movement). The sound should last no longer than the time it takes to count one box on the grid (four beats).

🎵 Perform the **snake** row on the grid score:

- When a box has a picture placed in it everyone makes the sound. When a box is empty everyone is silent!
- Without the recording, practise the **snake** row by pointing to each box in turn.
- Then using 💿 A34 sing verse 1 and go on to perform the row on the grid score as the numbers are called out.

(Alternatively, if you do not want to use the recording and cannot provide a piano accompaniment, chant the words of the song and keep a steady beat during the verse and grid score. Call out each number on the grid score every four beats).

🎲 Following the same procedure make up vocal and/or body sounds for the remaining rows of the grid (i.e. verse 2 – **monkey**, 3 – **elephant** and 4 – **lion**).

🎵 Sing the whole song and perform the corresponding row of the grid score after each verse using 💿 A36.

🎵 Repeat the performance but this time, choose a conductor to point to the boxes of each row in turn.

Hidden in the Jungle (💿 A34, 35, 36)

Hidden in the jungle there's a creature,

Can you hear the sound that it makes? (repeat)

Counting Section:
(One, Two, Three, Four, Five, GET READY)

Change the word **creature** for each verse:

Verse 1   **snake**

Verse 2   **monkey**

Verse 3   (an) **elephant**

Verse 4   **lion**

Verse 5   **creature**

Hidden in the Jungle – grid score (⊚ A34, 35, 36)

	1	2	3	4	5	
Snake Verse 1						**Get Ready**
Monkey Verse 2						**Get Ready**
Elephant Verse 3						**Get Ready**
Lion Verse 4						**Get Ready**

Focus 2: Texture - sounds in layers

♫ Perform two rows from the grid score (worksheet 2) at the same time:

- Divide the class into two groups with one group ready to follow the **snake** row and the other group ready to follow the **monkey** row.

> On which numbers (in which columns) do the snake and monkey make their sounds at the same time? *(Answer: Column 5)*

- Practise both rows together 'out of time' then go on to perform with 💿 A34 or a steady beat accompaniment.

If the children find this easy, divide into four groups and put four rows together.

Focus 3: Timbre – instrumental sounds

🎲 Find instrumental sounds to represent each creature:

- Choose volunteers to select and then explore different ways of making sounds on various instruments for each creature. For example, the elephant could be represented by a low sounding drum or a trumpeting sound on a kazoo.

> Which instruments do you think best represent each creature sound?
> Did you like the sound of the instrument, or the way it was played, or both?

♫ Perform the grid score (worksheet 2) using instruments:

- Choose several children to perform the sounds for each row (separately in order) after each verse of the song using 💿 A36 or a steady beat accompaniment.
- Perform two or more rows together without the recording.

RESOURCES
Focuses 2 & 3
Worksheet 1 👀
(optional)
Worksheet 2 👀

INSTRUMENTS
Focus 2
None
Focus 3
A selection of tuned and untuned
Tuned instruments use this pentatonic scale:
C D E G A

WHAT TIME IS IT ON THE CLOCK?

GAMES
Keep Fit
Plug the Gap

RESOURCES
A clock

INSTRUMENTS
Two sets of
chime bars

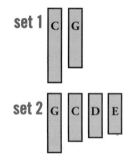

(Alternatively
use glockenspiels
or
metallophones)
plus a selection
of tick tock
sounding
percussion

Year group: R–2

Besides developing many musical skills, this project is a useful aid in teaching very young children to tell the time.

Focus 1: Pulse and accompaniment

♫ Sing and accompany the two note song *What time is it on the clock?* (◎ A37):

- Use a clock to show what time it is (which number to sing) each time through.
- Keep a steady beat by patting knees – right then left.
- Without the recording, play the steady beat C and G *tick tock* accompaniment (chime bar set 1) while the children sing and pat their knees. For an introduction play the accompaniment pattern twice.
- Choose a child to play the C and G *tick tock* accompaniment and sing the song again.

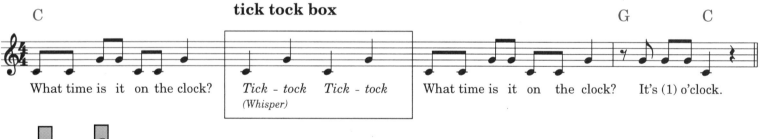

Repeat this *tick tock* accompaniment pattern throughout the song. It uses the same notes as the tune.

© 1995 Middle Eight Music Ltd. Published by Cramer Music Ltd.

Focus 2: Pitch – high and low

👂 Compare high and low sounds:

- Play the C and G *tick tock* notes (set 1).

> Which note is a high sound and which note is a low sound? *(Answer: The C note is low and the G note is high).*
>
> Just by looking, how could you tell the difference? *(Answer: By length or size. The C note is longer and bigger than the G note).*
>
> What other instruments are good at making *tick tock* sounds? Think about instruments that can make high and low sounds. *(For example: A two tone woodblock, metal agogos, two different sized triangles).*

♫ Invite volunteers to choose an instrument and explore making high and low *tick tock* sounds. Then choose several of the volunteers to accompany the song on their instruments.

Focus 3: Pitch and rhythm

🎲 Sing the song and improvise a clock chime over the words *tick tock tick tock* i.e. in the **tick tock box.** (Demonstrate using the following ideas then choose individual children to improvise their own clock chimes):

- Play one or more of the notes in chime bar set 2 (you don't have to use all four):

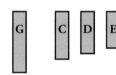

(This set of notes is the same set used by Big Ben's clock to chime the quarters of the hour. On the hour they are played in this order: CEDG CDEC ECDG GDEC).

- Use one of these ideas for the rhythm:

1. Play the notes to a steady beat, i.e. *tick tock tick tock*
2. Copy the rhythm of the phrase *What time is it on the clock?*
3. Use the rhythm of your name or other word rhythms.
4. Simply improvise the rhythm you 'feel'.

- Remember to only play during the **tick tock box.** Stop playing when the phrase *What time is it on the clock?* is sung for the second time.

Focus 4: Pulse

🎧 Listening games – Tell the time by listening to the beats in the **tick tock box.** For each **Tell the time** game below:

- Choose a child to be the time chimer who plays the 'C' note chime bar from chime bar set 2.
- Choose one child to provide a steady *tick tock* accompaniment on chime bar set 1 or other instrument.

Tell the time 1– 4 o'clock:

- Sing the song, but instead of whispering the *tick tock tick tock* words, ask the children to whisper the number count 1 2 3 4 .
- **Version 1:** The time chimer indicates the time and the number for everyone to sing (1– 4) by playing the chime bar on **one** of the *tick tock* beats. For example:

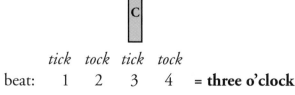

tick   tock   tick   tock
beat: 1   2   3   4   **= three o'clock**

- **Version 2**: The time chimer indicates the time by playing the chime bar once on each beat up to the chosen time. For example:

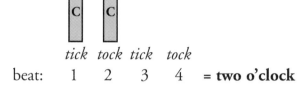

tick   tock   tick   tock
beat: 1   2   3   4   **= two o'clock**

- Make both versions slightly more difficult by whispering the original *tick tock tick tock* words of the song (asking the children to relate the words to the number count).

Tell the time 5–12 o'clock:

- Sing the song, but ask the children to extend the **tick tock box** by counting up to 12 *tick tock* beats.
- The time chimer indicates the time and number for everyone to sing (5–12) by playing the chime bar once on each beat up to the chosen time. For example, seven o'clock is played:

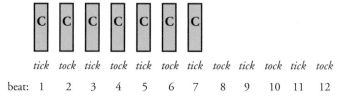

tick tock tick tock tick tock tick tock tick tock tick tock
beat: 1   2   3   4   5   6   7   8   9   10   11   12

ROCKET

Year group: R–3

Rockets that carry human beings into space make all kinds of sounds. Besides rocket engines or motors they are packed with computers and gadgets which tick, bleep, hum or whir around.

Focus 1: Timbre and dynamics

Select instruments and make up sounds for the rocket motors and computers, etc:

- Choose a player for each of the 10 sounds on the Rocket Count-down and Blast-off worksheet. Sit the players in a line and number them 1–10.
- One at a time, each player demonstrates the count-down sound for their number on an instrument of their choice. For example, player 7 could play the fuel pump sound by patting a tambour or drum.

Listen to and discuss each count-down sound:

> Could the sound be improved by playing slower, faster, louder, quieter, higher or lower?
> Would another instrument be a better choice for the count-down sound?

Perform the count-down sounds in sequence:

- Over a count-down of 10 –1 quietly spoken by the class the players enter one by one and keep playing as directed on the worksheet. The music gradually builds up until the words *blast off* are spoken which signals everyone to stop playing.
- Repeat the activity but ask the children to play very quietly throughout the count-down. Stop the count-down if the children play too loudly.

GAMES
Action

Conducting, Left and Right

RESOURCES
Worksheet

INSTRUMENTS
A selection of tuned and untuned (including one large tuned percussion instrument)

Rocket – Count-down and Blast-off

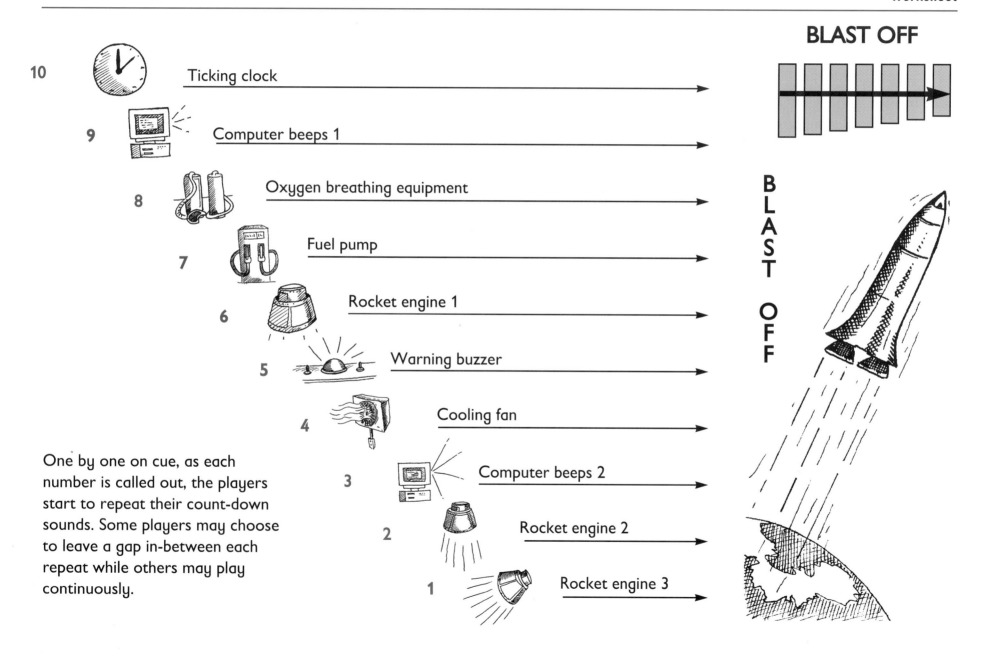

BLAST OFF

BLAST OFF

10 Ticking clock

9 Computer beeps 1

8 Oxygen breathing equipment

7 Fuel pump

6 Rocket engine 1

5 Warning buzzer

4 Cooling fan

3 Computer beeps 2

2 Rocket engine 2

1 Rocket engine 3

One by one on cue, as each number is called out, the players start to repeat their count-down sounds. Some players may choose to leave a gap in-between each repeat while others may play continuously.

Focus 2: Pitch – high and low

Choose one child to improvise rocket blast-off music by playing the notes from low to high in any way on the large tuned instrument. For example by:

- using a rhythm,
- repeating or fast tapping on each note,
- playing every note one after another or skipping over notes,
- moving quickly or slowly up to the high notes,
- playing loudly or quietly.

Perform the count-down sequence again with the player of the large tuned instrument starting the rocket blast-off music on the words *blast-off*.

Choose other players and repeat the activity, but reverse the entry of players and replace the words *blast-off* with *touch-down*. The player of the large tuned instrument must now improvise rocket touch-down music by playing notes from high to low.

Listening game:

- Choose a player to improvise rocket blast-off or touch-down music.

Did the rocket blast off or touch down?

ROOF TOP CAT

GAME
High and Low

RESOURCES
Worksheet 1
plus building
blocks
Worksheet 2
or squared paper
(depending on
age and ability)

INSTRUMENTS
One or more sets
of chime bars or
tuned
instruments with
the notes:

Year group R–3

The various heights of roof tops are used as a stimulus to explore pitch (high and low). In the related song *Roof Top Cat* the cat leaps from roof to roof and helps to show the note patterns of simple melodies.

> What are the roof tops like in your street or town centre? Are they all on one level or do they go up and down like the ones the Roof Top Cat jumps about on? (See picture on worksheet 1).

Focus : Melody

♪ Sing the song *Roof Top Cat* on worksheet 1 (🔊 A38):

𝄞 Listen to and follow the melody of *Roof Top Cat* on worksheet 1 (🔊 A38):

• Point to the roof tops (shaded squares) for each line of the song. The higher the roof top the higher the note.

> Which lines have the same pattern of roof tops (i.e. the same melody)? *(Answer: lines 1 and 3).*

♪ Sing the song again, but this time ask the children to do hand movements related to the height of the roof tops. For example, touch head for high roof tops, shoulders for the middle roof tops and knees for the low roof tops.

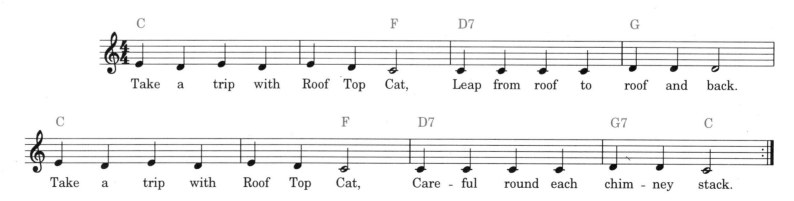

Take a trip with Roof Top Cat, Leap from roof to roof and back.

Take a trip with Roof Top Cat, Care - ful round each chim - ney stack.

Roof Top Cat – melody (⊚ A38) Worksheet 1

Take a trip with Roof Top Cat,

Leap from roof to roof and back.

Take a trip with Roof Top Cat,

Careful round each chimney stack.

E	Take		trip		Roof		
D		a		with		Top	
C							Cat,

E							
D					roof	and	back.
C	Leap	from	roof	to			

E	Take		trip		Roof		
D		a		with		Top	
C							Cat,

E							
D					chim -	ney	
C	Care -	ful	round	each			stack.

Ask the children to notate the melody using **Building Blocks, Squared Paper** or one of the **Alternatives** shown below to suit the age and ability of the class. The class can either observe and comment on volunteers or work in small groups.

Building Blocks:

- Looking at worksheet 1, build the melody for one line using large building blocks. Use one colour of block to represent the shaded roof tops (e.g. red) and another colour to support the middle and high roof top blocks:

> How many high roof tops (high notes) are there?
> How many middle roof tops (middle notes) are there?
> How many low roof tops (low notes) are there?

Take   a   trip   with   Roof   Top   Cat

Squared Paper:

- Draw the roof top patterns of each line on large squared paper. The pattern can be 'decorated' with windows, door and slate patterns, etc.

Take   a   trip   with   Roof   Top   Cat

- Ask the same questions given in the talking point box under **Building Blocks.**

Alternatives:

- Shade in the empty squares on worksheet 2.
- Place blocks on to squared paper.

♪ Play the melody on instruments:

- Sing the song again, but instead of singing the words, sing the corresponding roof top letter names, i.e.

  E D E D E D C, etc.

- On a barred tuned instrument ask the children to compare the C D and E notes with the three bars at the left hand side of each roof top line on worksheet 1.

Which note is the highest of the three notes? *(Answer: E, because it is the shortest).*
Which note is the lowest of the three notes? *(Answer: C, because it is the longest).*

- Ask the children to work out the melody of each line in turn and then try to sing and play the notes in time. (The class can either observe volunteers or work in small groups).

🎲 Compose new melodies (note patterns) to go with the words of the first line:

- Whether observing volunteers or working in small groups, ask the children to chant the words *Take a trip with Roof Top Cat* as they play the three notes in any order.
- When the children have found a melody they like, ask them to notate it using 1) building blocks, 2) squared paper, 3) squared paper and building blocks or 4) by simply shading in the squares on worksheet 2.

♪ Choose children to perform their new melodies for the first line and ask the class to sing them.

Roof Top Cat – notation

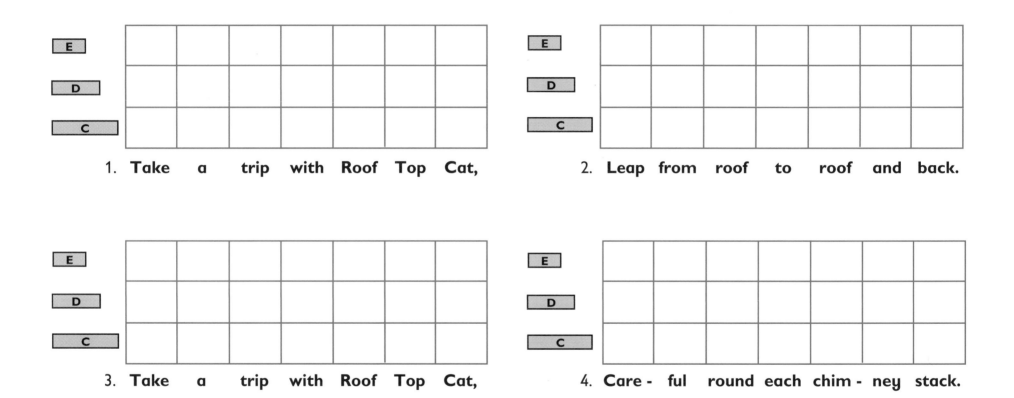

E D C

1. Take a trip with Roof Top Cat,

E D C

2. Leap from roof to roof and back.

E D C

3. Take a trip with Roof Top Cat,

E D C

4. Care - ful round each chim - ney stack.

WASH DAY

Year group: R–3

In past times wash day used to be a once or twice weekly event that would take up a whole day, but nowadays machines have taken a lot of the hard work out of washing our clothes. This project looks at all the different mechanical and manual sounds that we could hear on wash day.

Focus 1: Pulse and accompaniment

♪ Sing the song *Wash Day* on worksheet 1 (⊚ A39). The song uses the traditional tune of *The Wheels on the Bus*:

♫ Accompany the song:

- Ask the children to clap hands and knees alternately to a steady beat.
- Choose one child to play a steady beat on a drum or tambour while the class sings.

Make up more verses for other things that happen on wash day. For example: The tumble dryer goes round and stops, etc. The hands in the sink go rub, rub, rub, etc.

GAMES
Join In,
Card Signals

RESOURCES
Focus 1
Worksheet 1

INSTRUMENTS
Focus 1
A selection of tuned and untuned

Wash day – words ( A39)

Verse 1

The washing machine goes
round and round,
round and round,
round and round.

The washing machine goes
round and round,
All day long.

Verse 2

The water down the pipe goes
glug glug glug

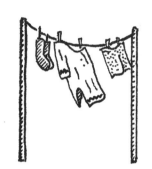

Verse 3

The clothes on the line go
flap flap flap

Verse 4

The iron on the board goes
left and right

Focus 2: Timbre – vocal and body sounds

Listen to the four wash day sounds on A40:

> Can you guess what is making each wash day sound?
> (Answer: Clothes flapping in the wind, water going down the sink, washing machine, clothes being ironed).
> Which words can you think of to describe the sounds?

As a class, think up a vocal or body sound for the things mentioned in each verse. For example:

Verse 1: **Washing machine** – 'swish' or 'zzzzz'.

Verse 2: **Water down the pipe** – 'glug'.

Verse 3: **Flapping of washing** – pat shoulders.

Verse 4: **Ironing** – rub up and down legs from hip to knee and back again.

Perform the song using the wash day vocal and body sounds:

- Instead of singing the words, make the vocal or body sounds for each verse to the rhythm of the words. For example:

Rhythm: **The wash- ing ma- chine goes,** etc.
Vocal sound: **Swish swish swish swish swish swish**

- If the class finds it difficult to remember the rhythm of the words choose a small group to sing the song while the rest make the sounds.

Perform the sequence of pictures on worksheet 2 using the vocal and body sounds (without singing the song):

- Point to each picture in turn.
- The class makes the sound for a picture until you point to the next one. The mug of tea indicates a tea break meaning rest or silence.

RESOURCES

Focus 2

Worksheet 1
Worksheet 2

INSTRUMENTS

Focus 2

A selection of tuned and untuned

Wash Day Sounds

Wash day sequence:

Wash day sounds on instruments:

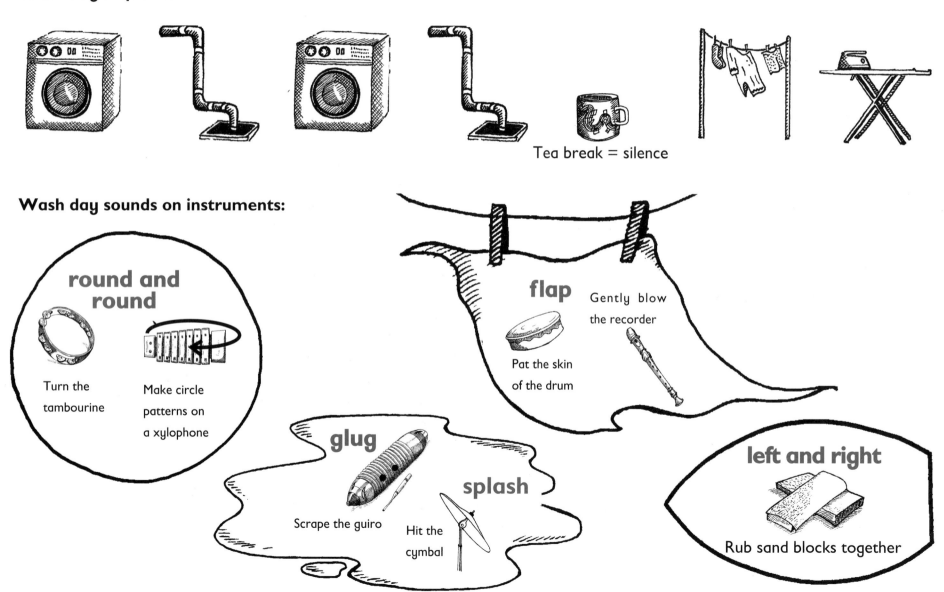

Tea break = silence

round and round

Turn the tambourine

Make circle patterns on a xylophone

flap

Gently blow the recorder

Pat the skin of the drum

glug

Scrape the guiro

splash

Hit the cymbal

left and right

Rub sand blocks together

Focus 3: Timbre – instrumental sounds

🎲 Explore ways of playing instruments to produce the wash day sounds for each verse:

- Choose several children to select instruments and demonstrate to the class.

> Which instruments do you think suit each wash day sound? *(See worksheet 2 for examples).*

🎵 Perform the instrumental sounds in between each verse of the song:

- Choose 4 groups of children to play the instruments chosen for each wash day sound.
- At the end of the first verse keep the steady beat accompaniment going (see page 151).
- Over this, the corresponding group of children plays their instruments. Then, after a short time go on to sing the next verse, etc.

Focus 4: Structure – sounds in sequence

🎲 With suggestions from the class, compose a wash day sequence by drawing pictures of the four wash day sounds on the board. To indicate rest or silence draw a mug of tea. Alternatively make cards from the pictures on worksheet 2.

🎵 Perform the sequence using instruments:

- Choose 2 or 3 players for each type of wash day picture.
- Choose a conductor to show when to move on to the next sound by pointing to each picture in turn.
- The players only play when their picture is being pointed to.

🎲 Individually compose a sequence of wash day sounds:

- The children may use the four wash day pictures and sounds or think up their own.
- Ask the children to draw a sequence of not more than ten pictures in a row. Remind the children that not all the pictures should be different and also that spaces or 'tea break symbols' can be used to indicate silence.

🎵 Ask each child to perform their own sequence using vocal and body sounds. Then, choose several sequences to perform using instruments.

RESOURCES

Focus 3

Worksheet 1 👓

Worksheet 2 🖼

Focus 4

As above plus one sheet of plain paper per child

INSTRUMENTS

Focuses 3 & 4

A selection of tuned and untuned

FIREWORKS

GAME
Shadowing

RESOURCES
Focus 1
Worksheet 1 👀
(optional)

INSTRUMENTS
Focus 1
A selection of
tuned and
untuned

Year group 1–4

A poem about fireworks is the stimulus for the activities which incorporate movement, word rhythms and percussion instruments.

Focus 1: Timbre

👂 Read the poem: *November the Fifth* on the worksheet 1:

> Do you think the words of the poem capture the atmosphere of bonfire night?
> What is your favourite type of firework? Can you describe what it does?

🎲 Improvise firework movements and vocal sounds:

- Read out the first verse and ask individual children to demonstrate movements and vocal sounds for the rocket. For example, move both arms upwards in a fast motion saying *whoosh*.
- Repeat the same procedure for the second and third verses (Catherine wheel and Roman candle).

🎲 In pairs make up a short piece based on one of the three fireworks using vocal sounds and movements.

♪ Perform the firework pieces.

🎲 Transfer the firework pieces onto instruments:

- Choose volunteers to explore ways of making firework sounds by thinking about the way the firework moves. For example, the rise and fall of a Roman candle can be imitated by 1) a shaker getting louder and quieter or 2) up and down patterns played on a xylophone.
- Ask each pair to choose an instrument and work out a sound for their firework.

♪ Perform the pieces as a firework display:

- Choose a conductor to direct the display of fireworks using stop and start signals.

> Will the firework display begin loudly or quietly? Are the fireworks going off at the same time or one after each other?

November the Fifth – words

And you, big rocket,
I watch how madly you fly
Into the smoky sky
With flaming tail

Catherine wheel,
I see how fiercely you spin
Round and round on your pin
How I admire
Your circle of fire

Roman candle,
I watch how prettily you spark
Stars in the autumn dark
Falling like rain
To shoot up again

And you, old guy,
I see how sadly you blaze on
Till every scrap is gone
Burnt into ashes
Your skeleton crashes

And so,
The happy ending of the fun,
Fireworks over bonfire done
Must waits a year now to remember
Another fifth of November

Leonard Clark

RESOURCES
Focus 2

Worksheet 1
(optional)
Worksheet 2

INSTRUMENTS
Focus 2

A selection of
tuned and
untuned

Focus 2 : Rhythm and texture

In groups of 4 –5 compose firework pieces using word rhythms:

- Each group chooses one verse, i.e. either the rocket or Catherine wheel or Roman candle, and selects suitable percussion instruments.
- The children in each group choose words or short phrases from their chosen verse and play them as word rhythms on the instruments.
- Ask the children to work out an order for the word rhythms choosing one or more phrases to play as repeating patterns (ostinati). Two players may play the same rhythm.
- Encourage each group to think about dynamics (loud and quiet). In the example on worksheet 2, the word rhythms get gradually louder.

Perform the firework pieces.

Listen to and discuss each performance:

Did the instruments chosen sound suitable for each firework rhythm? (For example, a busy rhythm played loudly on a cymbal may be too overpowering).
How did the groups use dynamics (loud and quiet) to portray the different fireworks?

Rocket verse word rhythms

**Players 1 and 2 begin
followed by 3 and 4.
They repeat their rhythms
(gradually getting louder)
until player 5 plays the
'big rocket' rhythm once.**

Player 5

big   roc-ket

Player 4

repeating

flam-ing tail

Player 3

repeating

mad-ly you fly

Players 1 and 2

repeating

smo-ky   sky

quiet   getting louder   loud

RESOURCES
Focus 3

Worksheet 1 👀
(optional)
Worksheet 2 👀

INSTRUMENTS
Focus 3

A selection of
tuned and
untuned

Focus 3: Links with movement

Add movements to the firework pieces composed in focus 2:

- In the same groups as focus 2, combine the groups into pairs of groups. One group performs their firework piece while the other group listens and creates a sequence of movements to fit with the music.
- The children in the movement group work individually, in pairs or as a whole group.
- If certain sections of the music are too short, the movement group may like to suggest that parts are extended.

What types of movement mirror the sounds in the firework piece? *(For example, the movement group could mirror a piece that begins with a big bang by leaping in the air).*

♫ Perform the combined music and movement firework pieces.

👂 Listen to and discuss each performance:

Did the movements match the sounds of the firework music?
Do the movements need to be larger or smaller to capture the mood?

Repeat the activity with the groups swapping their roles.

NOISY TRAFFIC

Year group 1–4

The sounds of traffic are used to create graphic scores using grids. The song warns of the harmful effects of noise and traffic pollution.

Focus 1: Pulse and metre

♪ Sing the song *Noisy Traffic* on worksheet 1 (🔊 A41).

🎲 Ask the children to make up actions to go with the words of the song.

🎧 The instrumental section that follows each verse of the song on 🔊 A41 relates to the grid score on worksheet 2. As the seven numbers are called out point to the numbered boxes on the grid score and ask the children to listen to the traffic sounds.

♪ As a class sing the song again using 🔊 A41. During the counting section repeat the pattern of body sounds calling out the numbers on each lap sound as shown:

1	2	3

lap clap clap clap lap clap clap clap lap, etc.

GAMES
Plug the Gap,
Stop/Start

RESOURCES
Focus 1
Worksheet 1 👓
(optional)
Worksheet 2 🖼️

INSTRUMENTS
Focus 1
None

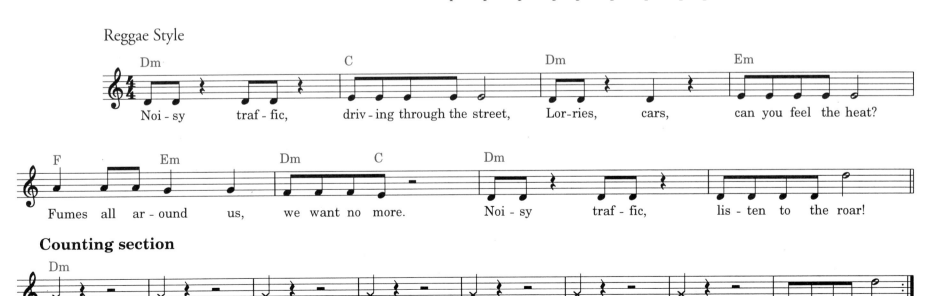

Reggae Style

Noi-sy traf-fic, driv-ing through the street, Lor-ries, cars, can you feel the heat?

Fumes all ar-ound us, we want no more. Noi-sy traf-fic, lis-ten to the roar!

Counting section

(One two three four five six seven) Lis-ten to the roar!

Noisy Traffic – words ( A41, A42)

1. **Noisy traffic, driving through the street,**
   Lorries, cars, can you feel the heat?
   Fumes all around us, we want no more.
   Noisy traffic, listen to the roar!

Counting section:
   (One two three four five six seven)
   Listen to the roar!

2. **Noisy traffic, clogging up our town,**
   Buses, vans, don't they make you frown?
   Fumes all around us, we want no more.
   Noisy traffic, listen to the roar!

Counting section:

3. **Noisy traffic, what a dreadful din!**
   Motorbikes, throw them in the bin.
   Fumes all around us, we want no more.
   Noisy traffic, listen to the roar!

Counting section:

Repeat verse 1:

Counting section:

Noisy Traffic—completed grid score (⊚ A41)

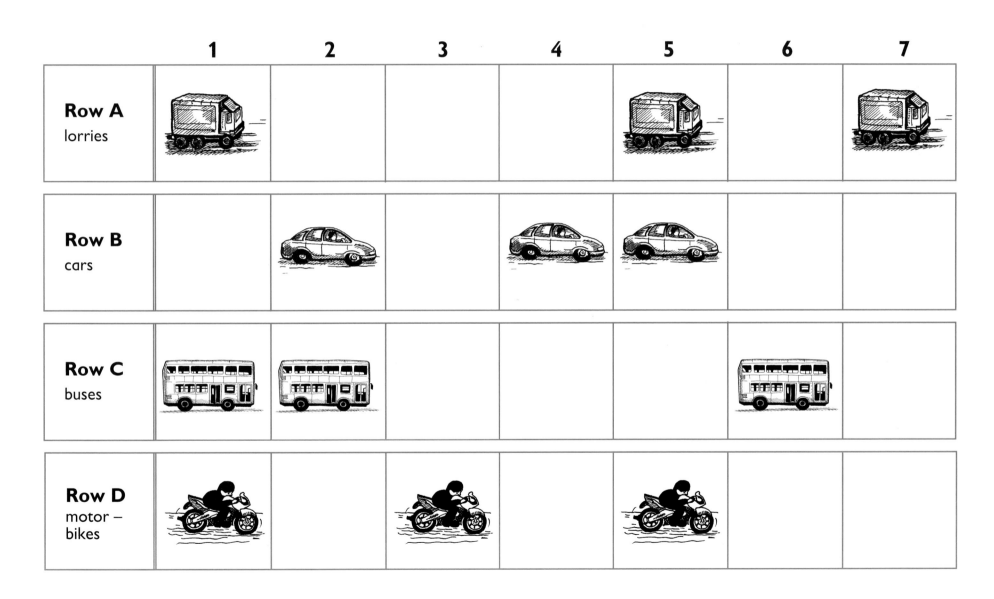

Noisy Traffic– blank grid score

	1	2	3	4	5	6	7
Row A							
Row B							
Row C							
Row D							

Focus 2: Timbre and structure

Discuss and describe different types of traffic and the sounds they make:

> What traffic sounds go high and low/ stay the same /get louder or quieter/ go fast or slow?
> What are the differences between traffic in the town, in the country and in different parts of the world?

As a class, complete an enlarged copy of the blank grid score (worksheet 3):

- The children choose one type of traffic sound and imitate it using their voices.
- Ask the children to choose three of the boxes along row A. Draw a symbol to represent the sound in the three boxes.

Perform row A without the recording:

- Point to the seven boxes in turn.
- The children make the traffic sound for every box with the symbol. An empty box indicates silence.

Choose traffic sounds for the remaining three rows and repeat the process for rows B, C and D.

Sing the song and perform each row of the grid score using A42:

- Divide the children into 4 groups, one for each row of the grid.
- Each group performs their row separately using the vocal sounds after singing a verse of the song.
- Then try combining two rows at the same time. (For example in the completed version on worksheet 2 the lorries' group makes their sounds in boxes 1, 5 and 7 and the cars in boxes 2, 4 and 5). Later combine three and then all four rows.

In groups of 4–5 compose new versions of the noisy traffic piece on the blank grid score (worksheet 3):

- Each group chooses other types of traffic and makes up vocal sounds for them.
- The groups devise new pictures for their traffic sounds and place them in three or four of the boxes along each row.

RESOURCES
Focus 2
Worksheet 1
(optional)
Worksheet 3
Worksheet 3
per group of 4–5

INSTRUMENTS
Focus 2
None

RESOURCES
Focus 3
Worksheet 1
(optional)
Worksheet 3
per group of 4–5

INSTRUMENTS
Focus 3
A selection of
tuned and
untuned

♫ Practise performing the grid scores:

- In each group one child acts as a conductor by pointing to the numbered boxes on the grid.
- In turn, each member of the group follows their corresponding row making the appropriate sounds.
- Then, the children try to perform three or more rows at the same time.

♫ As a class, sing the song with each group performing their grid score in turn between each verse.

👂 Listen to and discuss each performance:

> What did you like about the sounds?
> How did you recognise the different types of traffic?

Focus 3: Timbre – instrumental sounds

🎲 Transfer the grid scores composed in focus 2 onto instruments:

- Each group chooses instruments to represent their traffic sounds.
- The children explore ways of playing the instruments to create traffic sound effects.

♫ Perform the pieces using the instruments.

👂 Listen to and discuss each performance:

> Can you identify the types of traffic played on the instruments?
> Which was the loudest/quietest traffic?

TOP ATHLETE

Year group 1–4

Training to be a top athlete takes a lot of time and dedication. The song gives everyone the opportunity to become musically fit as well as physically fit.

Focus 1: Timbre and structure

♪ Sing the song *Top Athlete* (worksheets 1 or 2) which uses the traditional tune *Little Bird* (💿 A43).

🎲 Ask the children to think up actions to fit the words and play the rhythmic patterns shown on lines 5 and 6 of worksheet 2.

♪ An instrumental section follows the song which relates to the **grid score** on worksheet 3. As the **seven numbers** and the **GET READY** bar are called out point to the numbers on the grid score and ask the class to count them out loud. Each numbered box lasts for four beats.

👂 Listen to the whole song (5 verses with example grid score sounds) on 💿 A44 and ask the children to follow the example grid score (worksheet 4) one row at a time:

Verse 1 – running sounds (strings)
Verse 2 – javelin sounds (synthesizer)
Verse 3 – diving sounds (metal percussion)
Verse 4 – walking sounds (guitar and bongos)

♪ On a second playing of 💿 A44 ask the children to join in by making the suggested vocal and body sounds given on worksheet 4.

🎲 Make up a short movement or action for each of the sports on the grid score (worksheet 4). For example, pretend to throw a javelin.

♪ Sing the song and do the movements or actions for each row of the grid score using 💿 A45. Do the movement for boxes containing pictures and keep still on boxes that are empty.

GAME
Mexican Wave

RESOURCES
Focus 1
Worksheet 1 👓
(optional)
Worksheet 2 👓
Worksheets
3 & 4 ✏️

INSTRUMENTS
Focus 1
Drum, vibraslap
claves

Top Athlete – words and music (A43, 44, 45)

C · Dm · Cmaj7 · Dm7sus4 · C · B♭ · Am · G7 · C

On your marks, get set go,   See what's mov-ing high and low.   Leg or arm, head or toe,   Is it fast or slow?

B♭ · C · C · B♭ · Am · G7 · C

Heart beat pound-ing like a drum,   Mu-scle pops up like a plum   Top ath-lete, fit-ness freak, TRAIN-ING at your peak.

Counting or Grid Score section

C · G

(One   Two   Three   Four   Five   Six   Seven   GET READY)

Top Athlete – words (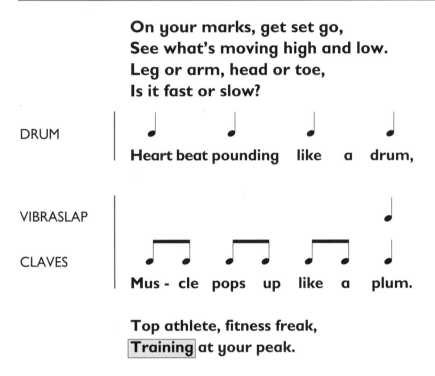 A43, 44, 45)

**On your marks, get set go,
See what's moving high and low.
Leg or arm, head or toe,
Is it fast or slow?**

DRUM

Heart beat pounding   like   a   drum,

VIBRASLAP

CLAVES

Mus - cle pops up   like   a   plum.

**Top athlete, fitness freak,
Training at your peak.**

Counting section:

one two three four five six seven (get ready)

SPORT WORDS

sprinting   running

walking

throwing   shooting

jumping   vaulting

swimming   diving

sailing   rowing

RESOURCES
Focus 2
Worksheet 1 ✂
(optional),
Worksheet 2 ✂
The class-
completed
grid score
(Worksheet 3 📝)

INSTRUMENTS
Focus 2
Drum, vibraslap
claves

🎲 As a class, compose the first row (A) of the blank grid score on worksheet 3:

● Choose a sport from the list on the worksheet (or think up another) and decide on a short vocal or body sound to represent it. The sound must not be too long as it will need to fit into the time it takes to count one box on the grid score.
● Place a symbol for the sound in three or more of the seven boxes.

🎵 Perform row A:

● Point to each box in turn 'out of time' (i.e. don't worry about making each box last exactly the same amount of time). When a box has a symbol placed in it everyone makes the sound for the sport. When a box is empty everyone is silent!
● Using 💿 A43 sing the song but, instead of singing the word **training**, sing the sport word you have chosen from the list (e.g. **running**). Go on to perform row A from the grid score as the seven numbers are called out.

(Alternatively, if you do not want to use the recording and cannot provide a piano accompaniment, chant the words of the song and keep a steady beat during the verse and grid score. Call out a number on the grid score every four beats).

Choose other sports for the remaining three rows and compose and perform as shown above. This class-completed grid score will form the basis of all the activities.

🎵 Perform all the rows of the grid score one at a time in order, using 💿 A45 (the version with 5 verses). Sing the song before each row and once again after row D.

Focus 2: Texture – sounds in layers

🎵 Perform several rows at the same time (many events at the Olympics occur at the same time):

● First, divide the class into two groups with one group following row A and the other following row B. Run through the grid score 'out of time' before trying it with 💿 A45 or a steady beat accompaniment.
● Next, divide into four groups and perform four rows together.

Top Athlete – blank grid score

	1	2	3	4	5	6	7	
A Verse 1								**Get Ready**
B Verse 2								**Get Ready**
C Verse 3								**Get Ready**
D Verse 4								**Get Ready**

RESOURCES
Focus 3

Worksheet 1 ☺
(optional)
Worksheet 2 ☺
The class-
completed
grid score
(worksheet 3 ▱)

INSTRUMENTS
Focus 3

A selection of
tuned and
untuned

Focus 3: Timbre – instrumental sounds

▱ Make sounds on instruments for each type of sport:

- Divide the class into four groups, one for each type of sport on the class-completed grid score (worksheet 3).
- Ask several children from each group to select instruments and explore different ways of playing and making the corresponding sports sounds. For example, a running sound could be played using hard or soft beaters, patting or tapping, etc. The sounds do not need to be rhythmical, but they should last no longer than a box on the grid.

> Which instruments do you think work best for each sport sound?
> Did you like the sound of the instrument, or the way it was played, or both?

♪ Sing the song again using 🔘 A45 and ask the children with instruments to perform the rows of the grid score during the counting sections.

👂 Listening game – sport sounds:

- Choose four players to play instruments which represent the four sports. For example:

Player 1 – xylophone = throwing
Player 2 – shakers = swimming
Player 3 – drum = jumping
Player 4 – claves = running

- Listen to each instrument then send the players behind a screen or ask the class to close their eyes.

> One instrument plays – which was it?
> Two instruments play – which were they?
> All four instruments play one after another – in which order did they play?

Top Athlete – example of completed grid score (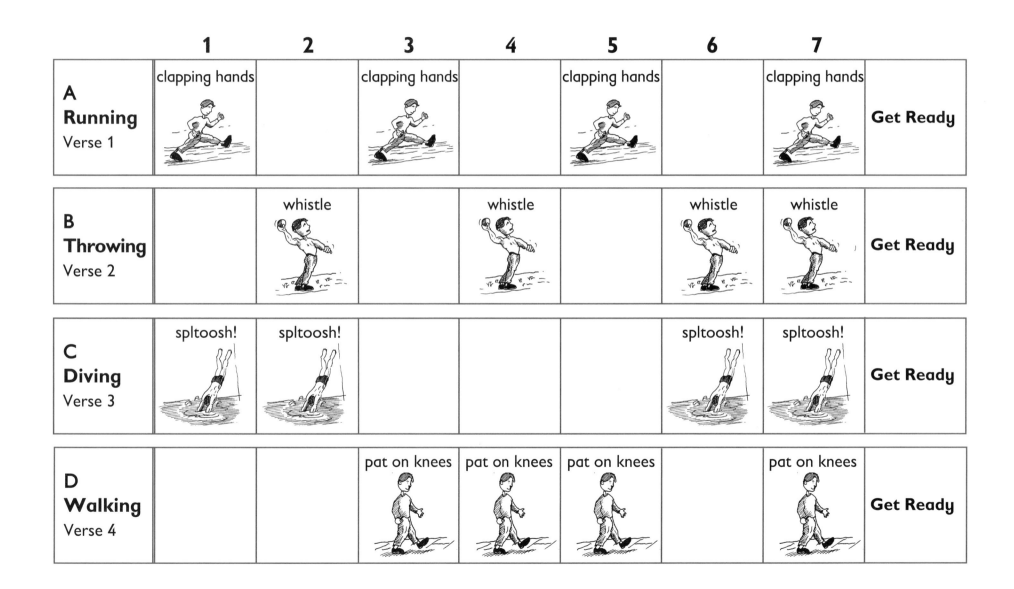 A44)

	1	**2**	**3**	**4**	**5**	**6**	**7**	
A **Running** Verse 1	clapping hands		clapping hands		clapping hands		clapping hands	**Get Ready**
B **Throwing** Verse 2		whistle		whistle		whistle	whistle	**Get Ready**
C **Diving** Verse 3	spltoosh!	spltoosh!				spltoosh!	spltoosh!	**Get Ready**
D **Walking** Verse 4			pat on knees	pat on knees	pat on knees		pat on knees	**Get Ready**

RESOURCES
Focus 4
Worksheet 1 👀
(optional)
Worksheet 2 👀
The class-
completed
grid score
(Worksheet 3 📖)
Worksheet 5 👀

INSTRUMENTS
Focus 4
A selection of
tuned and
untuned

Focus 4: Rhythm

👂 Listen to the four examples of sport word rhythms A, B, C and D on worksheet 5 (💿 A46).

📻 Make up word rhythms to replace the vocal or body sounds for each sport in the grid score composed by the class (worksheet 3). As in the examples on worksheet 5, the word rhythms need to fit into the time of four beats (a box of the grid).

🎵 As a class, perform the grid score using the sport rhythms:

- Practise chanting and clapping the sport rhythms to a steady beat.
- Sing the song again using 💿 A45 but, **don't** follow the rows of the grid score during the counting sections. Instead just clap and chant the corresponding rhythm 7 times.
- If the children find this easy, perform each row of the grid score. The children chant the word rhythm for every box, but only clap on boxes that contain a symbol.
- Next, divide the class into groups and try to put two or more rows together.

👂 Listen to sport word rhythms A and B played on tuned instruments (💿 A47). The note patterns are shown as graphic notation in examples AA and BB on worksheet 5:

Why do you think rhythm AA's note pattern uses just two sounds – high and low?
(Answer: To represent the running idea, i.e. two legs moving up and down).
Why do you think rhythm BB's note pattern uses notes going up and then down?
(Answer: To represent the up and down flight of the javelin).

Sport rhythms and note patterns ( A46, 47)

A   Run-ning fast-er, Run-ning fast-er

B   Ja - ve - lin   soar - ing

C   Dive   in   deep

D   Wib-ble wob-ble walk - ing

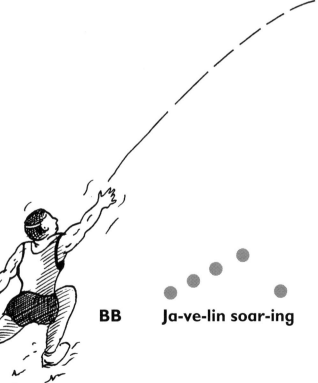

AA   Run-ning fast-er, Run-ning fast-er

BB   Ja-ve-lin soar-ing

Transfer the sport rhythms onto instruments:

- Divide the class into four groups and give each group a selection of instruments and one of the sport rhythms.
- Ask any group with a tuned instrument to take off the F and B notes. The remaining notes will make a pentatonic scale (a group of notes with five different letter names):

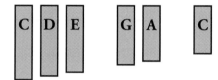

- Each group explores ways of playing their rhythm by thinking about the movement of the sport and deciding the type of instrument to use, which notes to play and whether to play quietly or loudly.

Sing the song using A45 and perform the rhythms during the counting sections:

- Choose several players from each group.
- During the counting sections, the corresponding group of players repeats their rhythm 7 times. (**Don't** ask them to follow the grid score because on top of everything else it would over-load the players with things to think about). The rest of the class can quietly chant the word rhythms to help keep the players in time.

Listening game – sport rhythms:

- Ask a child to play one of the four sport rhythms on an instrument.

Can you guess which rhythm was played?

WEATHER WITCH

Year group: 1–4

The weather and associated graphic symbols provide an excellent stimulus for exploring sound and creating music. A touch of magic is added by the related song which conjures up the vision of a Weather Witch casting spells to change the weather.

Focus 1: Accompaniment

♫ Sing the song *Weather Witch* on worksheets 1 or 2 (🔊A48, 49). (The song can also be performed as a chant without the recording or piano accompaniment).

♫ For an ostinato (repeating pattern) accompaniment choose one child to play the word rhythm *Weather Witch* on a tambour or deep drum:

Wea-ther   Witch

♫ Sing the song again with a group of 8 children chanting the echo words of the song.

Focus 2: Timbre – instrumental sounds

♫ Transfer the echo group's word rhythms onto percussion instruments:

> Which instruments do you think work best for each group of echo words?

● The players play separately at first then play together for the last two echo lines of the song. For example:

Player 1 – shaker:	*witch, witch, witch*
Player 2 – scraper:	*twitch, twitch, twitch*
Player 3 – shaker:	*glitch, glitch, glitch*
Player 4 – scraper:	*switch, switch, switch*
Player 5 – bells:	*high, high, high*
Player 6 – claves:	*dry, dry, dry*
Player 7 – tom tom:	*low, low, low*
Player 8 – cymbal:	*show, show, show*
All together:	*witch, witch, witch*
All together:	*switch, switch, switch*

GAMES
Shadowing
Stop/Start

RESOURCES
Focuses 1 & 2
Worksheet 1 👓
(optional)
Worksheet 2 👓

INSTRUMENTS
Focus 1
A large drum or tambour
Focus 2
As above plus a selection of untuned

Weather Witch – words and music (A48, 49, 50)

Weather Witch – words and weather symbols ( A48, 49, 50) Worksheet 2

Singing group:	Echo group:
Oh Weather Witch,	*witch, witch, witch,*
Give your wand a twitch,	*twitch, twitch, twitch,*
Cause a sudden glitch,	*glitch, glitch, glitch,*
Make the weather switch.	*switch, switch, switch.*
Now pressure high,	*high, high, high,*
Could mean warm and dry,	*dry, dry, dry,*
But with pressure low,	*low, low, low*
Many clouds could show,	*show, show, show.*
I wonder, I wonder, I wonder	
Which weather Weather Witch,	*witch, witch, witch,*
I wonder, I wonder, I wonder	
Which weather you will switch.	*switch, switch, switch.*

RESOURCES
Focuses 3 & 4
None

INSTRUMENTS
Focus 3
A tuned
instrument with
the notes
D E F G A and a
large drum or
tambour
Focus 4
A large drum or
tambour

Focus 3: Pitch

Echo (copy) note patterns in the Echo Spell game:

- Choose one child to be the Weather Witch and another child to keep a steady beat on the tambour or drum.
- The Weather Witch improvises note patterns on a tuned instrument using the *Weather Witch* word rhythm. Everyone echoes the note pattern, by singing the words *Weather Witch*. For example:

D D A

The player improvises
'Weather Witch' note
patterns on the spot.

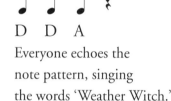

D D A

Everyone echoes the
note pattern, singing
the words 'Weather Witch.'

- The Weather Witch has several goes, varying the choice of notes each time.
- Choose other players and repeat the activity.

Focus 4: Timbre – vocal and body sounds

In a circle make up weather sounds:

What kinds of weather can you think of?
What type of sounds could you make for them
using your voice or body?

- In turn round the circle, each child makes up a weather sound effect using body and/or vocal sounds. After each turn everyone copies and then tries to guess the type of weather the sound represents.

Perform the weather sounds over a steady beat in the Ring of Weather game:

- Choose one player to beat out the *Weather Witch* rhythm on a drum in the middle of the circle.
- In turn round the circle without pause, the children perform their weather sounds in the time it takes to beat out **one** *Weather Witch* rhythm (3 beats and a rest).
- Next time round the circle everyone copies (echoes) the weather sound in between turns:

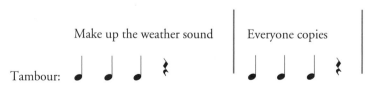

Make up the weather sound | Everyone copies

Tambour:

- Try the same game with movements or actions.

Focus 5: Texture – sounds in layers

👂 Listen to 💿 A50 and after the song you will hear the Weather Wand Section in which the Weather Witch makes the weather change from one type of weather to another. The weather sounds are made on instruments and there are eight different types as shown on worksheet 2. Listen to the Weather Wand section several times:

Can you match the weather sounds to the weather symbols on worksheet 2 and guess the order in which they are played?

(*Answer:*   **A = light rain (3)**   **E = wind (7)**
  B = sun (1)   **F = heavy rain (4)**
  C = cloud (2)   **G = snow (6)**
  D = frost/ice (5)   **H = storm (8)**

You may find there is disagreement, but this is natural – one sound can have different 'meanings' for different people).

🎲 In groups of 4 –5 compose or improvise (make up on the spot) weather music. (For younger and less experienced children choose volunteers to demonstrate to the class):

- Give each group a selection of instruments and one type of weather from worksheet 2.
- Each group makes their weather music using vocal and body sounds, instruments or a mixture. This is an example of a group's wind music:

3 players make long
vocal wind sounds:

2 players play short 'gusts'
on shakers – starting quietly,
getting louder
then fading away:

🎵 Perform the weather music compositions.

👂 Listen to and discuss each performance:

Can you guess which type of weather music is being played?

Is there any way the weather music could be improved? Should it be quieter or louder, higher or lower, faster or slower? Would it sound better on different instruments?

RESOURCES

Focus 5

Worksheet 2

INSTRUMENTS

Focus 5

A selection of tuned and untuned. Tuned instruments need the notes D E F G A B C

RESOURCES
Focus 6
Worksheet 2

INSTRUMENTS
Focus 6
A selection of tuned and untuned (including a tambour or drum). Tuned instruments need the notes D E F G A B C

Focus 6: Structure – sounds in sequence

Make a sequence using the weather music of each group from focus 5 in the Weather Wand section of the song:

- Choose one child to be the Weather Witch (conductor). Choose another child to play the *Weather Witch* accompaniment rhythm on the tambour or drum.
- The weather groups need to be ready to play. (Alternatively for younger and less experienced children instead of having groups choose individual players for each type of weather).
- Sing or chant the words of the *Weather Witch* song. At the end of the song ask the tambour player to keep playing the accompaniment rhythm throughout the Weather Wand section.
- In the Weather Wand section, the Weather Witch points to a group to begin playing. The Weather Witch can switch the weather at any time to one of the other weather groups.
- When another group begins to play the previous group is silent.
- When the Weather Witch has finished, sing or chant the words of the song again.

Can you remember the first and last type of weather group the Weather Witch pointed to? Can you remember the order of the weathers in the sequence? (If not, next time make a tape recording and during play-back ask the children to point to the weather symbols as the sounds change).

- Later, the Weather Witch could have several weather groups playing at the same time by using signals to start and stop individual groups at will.

Alternatively, make a set of cards using symbols on the worksheet. Then, with the help of the class arrange the weather symbols in sequence. The groups play their weather sounds in the order shown in the sequence. For example:

Although the order of the group is fixed, the Weather Witch can decide when to move from one group to the next by pointing to the symbols.

Focus 7: Rhythm

Listen to the two rhythms made from weather words and sayings on A51 (each rhythm is played several times on different instruments):

Rain, rain, go away,
Come again another day.

Every cloud has a silver lining.

Clap the rhythm of other weather words or sayings, see worksheet 3.

Perform the weather word rhythms during the Weather Wand section of the song:

● Choose several Weather Witches to clap or play the rhythms on instruments one after another over the *Weather Witch* accompaniment rhythm. The rest of the class chants the words. For example:

	Weather Witch 1 claps	Weather Witch 2 claps	etc.
All chant	*I'm on cloud nine.*	*It's raining cats and dogs.*	etc.

● Ask two or more children to play their weather sayings at the same time. One player should start with other players joining in one at a time. For example:

Weather Witch 1	*I'm on cloud nine*	*I'm on cloud nine.*	etc.
Weather Witch 2		*It's raining cats and dogs.*	etc.

RESOURCES
Focus 7
Worksheet 3
(optional)

INSTRUMENTS
Focus 7
A selection of tuned and untuned (including a tambour or drum). Tuned instruments need the notes
D E F G A B C

Weather Sayings

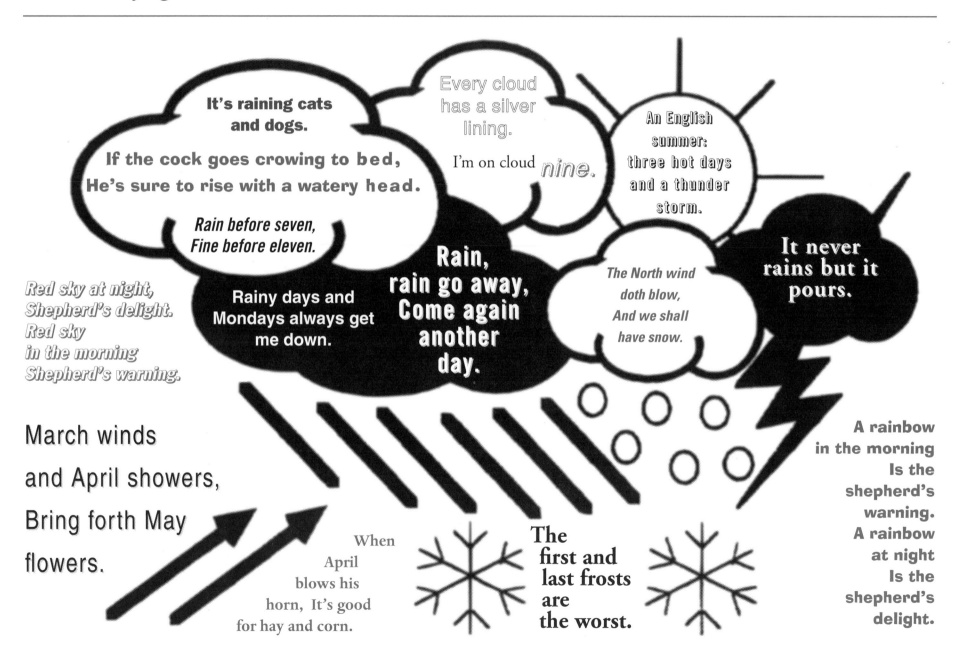

RESOURCES
Focus 8
None

INSTRUMENTS
Focus 8
Recorder,
whistle, shaker
or sand blocks
and kazoo or
harmonica

Focus 8: Timbre

👂 Listening game – Weather vane sounds:

● Choose four instruments and players to represent
each type of wind sound from the four points of
the compass. For example:

Blow North	Recorder: place hand over hole in the top joint
Whistle East	Whistle
South Says *Shhhh*	Shaker or sand blocks
West Wind Humming	Kazoo or harmonica

● Unseen by the rest of the class, ask one player to
play one of the instruments.

Which wind blew?

● Ask the players to play their instruments one after
another in any order.

In which order did the winds blow?

RESOURCES
Focuses 9 & 10
Worksheet 4 👀

INSTRUMENTS
Focus 9
Several tuned
and untuned
Focus 10
One xylophone or
glockenspiel

Focus 9: Rhythm

👂 Listening game – Weather vane word rhythms:

- Learn the rhythms of each compass point wind phrase shown on worksheet 4A (💿 A52).
- Choose a child to clap or play one of the rhythms repeatedly.

> Which compass wind rhythm is blowing? As soon as you know make the sound for that direction of wind, i.e. blow, whistle, *'sh'* or hum.

Focus 10: Pitch – high and low

👂 Listening game – Weather vane notes:

- All the wind phrases on worksheet 4B use the same three rhythms, but have different note patterns (look at the notes in the diagram).
- Point to and then play each of the note patterns to the children, so that they make the link between the compass wind point and note pattern. Then, play one of the note patterns at random.

> Which wind is blowing?

- Choose a child to play and repeat the activity.

Weather Vane Listening Games

A. Weather Vane Word Rhythms (A52)

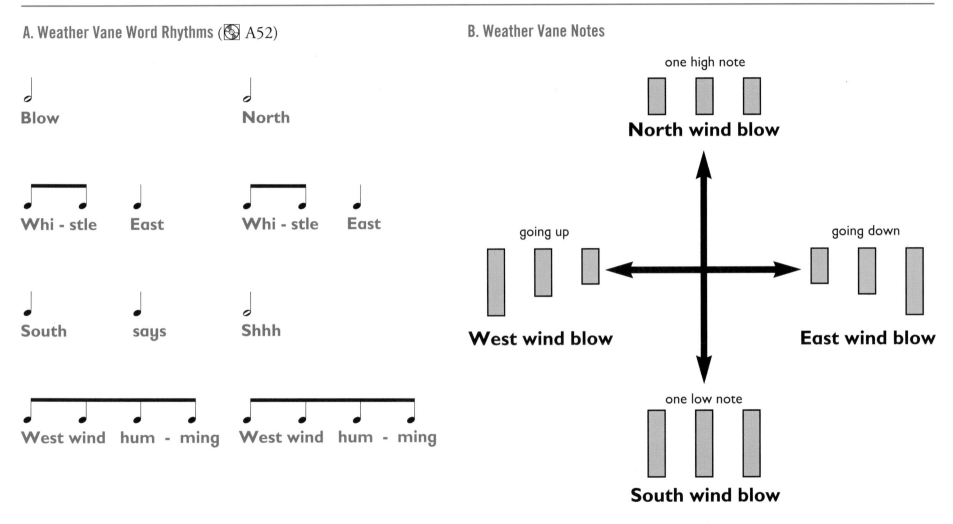

Blow

North

Whi - stle   East

Whi - stle   East

South   says

Shhh

West wind   hum - ming

West wind   hum - ming

B. Weather Vane Notes

one high note

North wind blow

going up

going down

West wind blow

East wind blow

one low note

South wind blow

Forest Music

GAMES
Pass a Sound,
Action
Conducting

Year group 2–5

As dawn breaks, around 5 o'clock in the morning, the Forest starts coming back to life after a night's sleep. Tiny sounds are heard at first, sounds that can hardly be heard. At 6 o'clock a few more creatures have woken up – rustling and crunching. By 7 o'clock nearly everyone has woken up; more and more creatures are moving around looking for food so that by 8 o'clock the whole forest is teeming with life:

> What sort of sounds might you hear in a forest at night?
> (*For example: Owls, badgers, wind in the trees*).
> What sort of sounds might you hear as the forest wakes up?
> (*For example: Birds singing, twigs breaking, leaves scrunching, footsteps*).
> How do the sounds begin?
> (*Answer: Quietly with occasional sounds*).
> What happens as more and more creatures wake up?
> (*Answer: The sounds become louder and more cluttered*).

Focus 1: Timbre

🎲 Make up forest sounds on instruments:

- Place the tuned percussion and other instruments (shakers, scrapers, tappers and blowers) in two circles as shown:

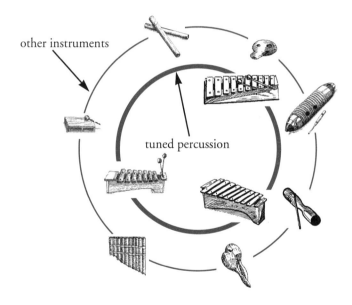

other instruments

tuned percussion

- Allow the children time to experiment on their instrument, finding a number of different sounds. If children are sharing an instrument they should take it in turns to play.

- Ask children with shakers, scrapers or tappers to play a short pattern alternating two different sounds (e.g. stroking the skin of a drum then tapping with fingers).
- Ask children with blowers to make bird call sounds.
- Ask children with tuned percussion to find ways of playing a continuous sound by repeating any note using two beaters. (This technique is called **tremolo**).

🎵 Play the individual forest sounds:

- The outer circle play their forest sounds in turn. If the children are sharing, swap instruments and repeat round the circle.
- Then the tuned percussion play their tremolo creating an overlapping chain of sound:

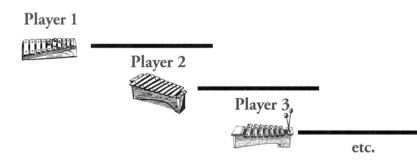

Player 1

Player 2

Player 3

etc.

RESOURCES

Focus 1

None

INSTRUMENTS

Focus 1

A selection of tuned percussion plus a selection of other instruments forming four distinct types: shakers, scrapers, tappers and blowers (e.g. pen tops, ocarina, tops of recorders) one between two

RESOURCES
Focus 2
None
Focus 3
Worksheet 1 👓
Worksheet 2 🗒

INSTRUMENTS
Focuses 2 & 3
A selection of
tuned percussion
plus a selection
of other
instruments
forming four
distinct types:
shakers,
scrapers,
tappers and
blowers (e.g. pen
tops, ocarina,
tops of
recorders)
one between two

Focus 2: Structure – sounds in sequence

♫ Practise playing the shaking, scraping, tapping and blowing forest sounds with a conductor (the tuned percussion players listen during this practice session):

- Still sitting in the same positions in the circles, select the children with the same type of instrument (e.g. scrapers).
- Choose a conductor to stand in the circle.
- The conductor signals the scrapers to play by pointing slowly round the circle, stretching his/her arm out like the minute hand of a clock.
- For the first turn of the minute hand, the children with scrapers play when the hand reaches them and then stop when it has gone past. There should be periods of silence!
- Select another type of instrument group to play (e.g. tappers). The minute hand conductor points round the circle for a second turn and the skin instruments play. Repeat the above for the shakers and blowers.

Focus 3: Texture – sounds in layers

♫ Perform the forest sounds with the tuned percussion to make forest music:

- The tuned percussion players begin by playing the background 'chain of sound' which continues throughout the piece.
- The shakers, scrapers, tappers and blowers join in on each turn of the minute hand conductor.
- The conductor decides which type of instrument plays on each turn. (Each complete turn is equivalent to the passing of one hour). For example:

Background music:
tuned percussion
Turn 1 (5 o'clock):
tuned and scrapers
Turn 2 (6 o'clock):
tuned, scrapers and shakers
Turn 3 (7 o'clock):
tuned, scrapers, shakers and blowers
Turn 4 (8 o'clock):
tuned, scrapers, shakers, blowers and tappers

- The players of each instrument type should remember whether they join in on turn 1, 2, 3 or 4.
- Perform the piece twice so that children sharing have an opportunity to play an instrument.
- Record the performances of *Forest Music.*

Listen to the class's recording of *Forest Music* and complete the picture score on worksheet 2 (see example on worksheet 1):

- Work out with the children pictures or symbols to represent the sounds of the instruments used (i.e. shakers, scrapers, tappers, blowers). For example:

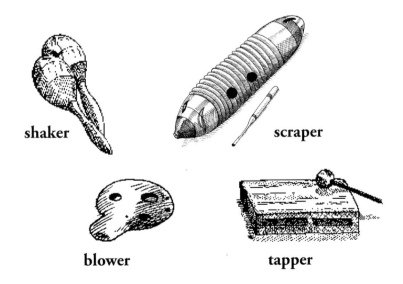

shaker

scraper

blower

tapper

- Remind the children which type played on each turn and where the instruments were placed.
- Ask the children to draw pictures for each instrument in the approximate positions for each turn of the minute hand on the blank score, worksheet 2. (See the completed example on worksheet 1).
- Play the children the recording of their *Forest Music* composition while they follow the sounds on the score.

Now listen to the recording of *Forest Music* on A53:

Can you work out which group is playing at 5 o'clock (turn 1 of the minute hand) and then 6 o'clock (turn 2), 7 o'clock (turn 3) and 8 o'clock (turn 4) ?
(Answer: turn 1– scrapers, 2 – blowers, 3 – shakers, 4 – tappers).

- Look at the picture score on worksheet 1. Listen to A53 again and ask the children to follow the symbols as they hear the different forest sounds.

Forest Music – completed picture score (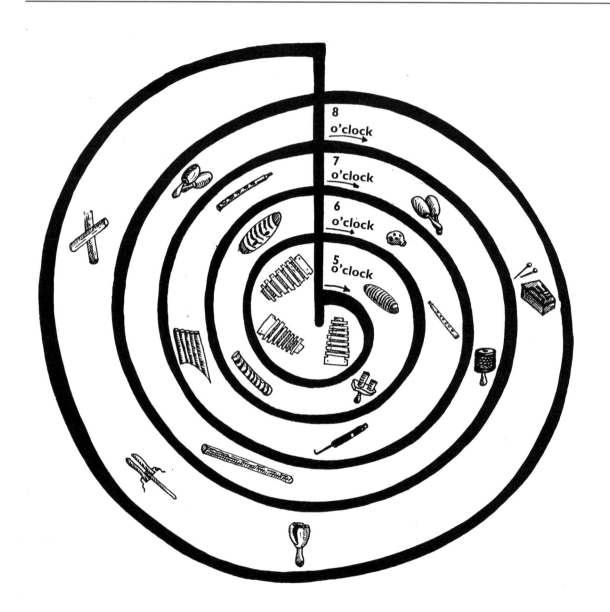 A53)

The music gradually builds up, starting with background music: **tuned percussion**

then adding at each hour:

Turn 1 (5 o'clock instruments):

scrapers

Turn 2 (6 o'clock instruments):

blowers

Turn 3 (7 o'clock instruments):

shakers

Turn 4 (8 o'clock instruments):

tappers

Forest Music – blank picture score

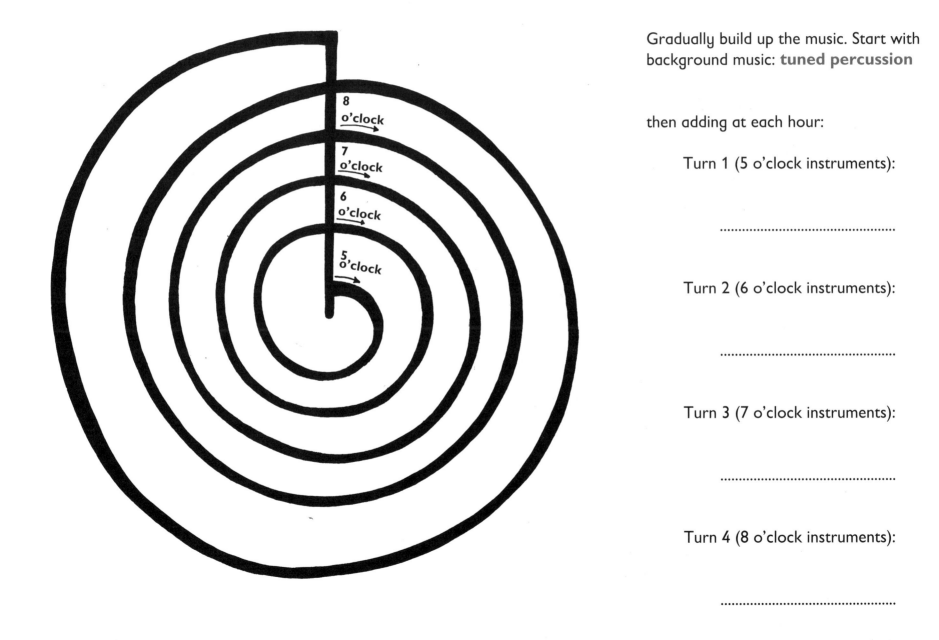

Gradually build up the music. Start with background music: **tuned percussion**

then adding at each hour:

Turn 1 (5 o'clock instruments):

....

Turn 2 (6 o'clock instruments):

....

Turn 3 (7 o'clock instruments):

....

Turn 4 (8 o'clock instruments):

....

DINOSAURS

GAMES
High and Low
Join In

RESOURCES
Focus 1
Worksheets 1 & 2
(optional) 👀

INSTRUMENTS
Focus 1
A xylophone

Year group: 2–5

No one knows for sure the reason why dinosaurs became extinct. The song linked to this project suggests that they could still be alive in hiding somewhere. If this is true, the musical activities will help the children discover the type of place they could be hiding.

Focus 1: Pitch – high and low

🎵 Sing the song *Dinosaur* on worksheets 1 or 2 (💿 B1, 2).

🎲 Compose note patterns using the word rhythm *dinosaur* from the song:

- Choose a player to make up a note pattern for a **large** dinosaur using one or more of the lowest three notes on a xylophone.
- Then ask the player to make up a note pattern for a **small** dinosaur using one or more of the highest three notes on a xylophone.

👂 Listening game:

- Unseen by the rest of the class ask one child to play his/her large or small dinosaur sound.

Which dinosaur is being played – large or small?

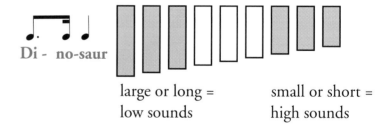

Di - no-saur

large or long =
low sounds

small or short =
high sounds

Dinosaur – music ( B1, 2)

Dinosaur – words (⊚ B1, 2)

Chorus:

Dinosaur so tall and wide,
Not an easy thing to hide.
I have tried to find just one,
But they seem to all have left and gone.

Verse 1:

In the past, upon the world,
A meteorite with force was hurled.
Dust and smoke blot out the sun,
For dinosaurs their time had come,
But some survive and stay alive, I'm sure.

Chorus:

Dinosaur so tall...

Verse 2:

Fossilised within a rock,
A skeleton we tap and knock.
Skull or thigh or tooth or toe,
It's all we've got to put on show,
But some survive and stay alive, I'm sure.

Chorus:

Dinosaur so tall...

Verse 3:

In my sleep I thought I saw
A very large pink dinosaur.
Dreamt of things pre-history,
That when I woke could no more see,
But some survive and stay alive, I'm sure.

Chorus:

Dinosaur so tall...

Focus 2: Timbre – instrumental sounds

Make up music for several types of habitat:

> In what type of places (habitats) could dinosaurs be hiding?
> What type of instruments could you use to represent each habitat?

- Choose one player for each of the habitats and one by one ask them to make up music on their related instrument. For example:

Habitat	Instruments/suggestions for music
Land	Tambour/steady beats
Sea	Glockenspiel/up and down patterns
Sky	Wind instrument/long blows or maracas /long shakes
Forest	Claves/groups of fast tapping with pauses
Mountain	Tambourine/getting louder then fading away or xylophone/going up then down
Mud pool	Water rattle (plastic bottle half filled with water)/slow steady beat

Listening game 1 – Habitats:

- With the habitat players unseen by the rest of the class, ask one of them to play their instrument.

> Which habitat is being played?

Listening game 2 – Find out where the dinosaurs have gone:

- Out of sight from the rest of the class ask a dinosaur player and a habitat player to play at the same time.

> Where is the dinosaur (is it in the sea or in the sky, etc.)?
> Is it a large or small dinosaur (did the player play on high or low notes)?

RESOURCES
Focus 2
None

INSTRUMENTS
Focus 2
A xylophone plus a selection of other tuned and untuned

♪ Perform the dinosaur and habitat music together to make a musical journey:

- Choose a conductor to signal the dinosaur player to begin repeating the *dinosaur* rhythm on high or low notes.
- Then, in any order the conductor points to each habitat player to begin playing.
- When the conductor points to another habitat player the previous player should stop.
- When the conductor gives the stop signal to the dinosaur player the journey piece ends.

👂 After the performance ask the following questions:

What was the first and last place (habitat) the dinosaur went to?
Can you remember the order of the habitats?

TRAIN GAME

Year group 2–6

In this musical train journey the driver improvises rhythms and directs the class using a series of musical signals.

Focus 1: Rhythm

👂 Listen to the three rhythm signals (shown opposite) on 💿 B3:

> Which two signals have the same rhythm?
> (*Answer:* **Start the train** *and* **Stop the train**).

🎵 As a class, chant the words while clapping the rhythm of the three signals.

Start   the   train

Stop   the   train

Change   sta -   tions

GAMES
Plug the Gap
Stop/Start

RESOURCES
Focus 1
None

INSTRUMENTS
Focus 1
A selection of untuned percussion (one per child or one between two) including a cowbell

Improvise rhythms in the train game:

- Ask the children to sit in a circle and give out the untuned percussion instruments.
- Choose a 'train driver' to play the cowbell (or similar sounding instrument).
- The train game begins with the train driver improvising a short solo rhythm as a repeating pattern (ostinato). For example:

(repeating)

Eu-ro-star ex-press

- The train driver, after playing solo four or five times, plays the signal **Start the train** making sure there is no gap between the end of the solo and the signal (see example below).

- The train driver continues repeating the rhythm (in this example 'Eurostar express') and the class joins in by copying the rhythm.
- After a short time, the train driver plays the signal **Stop the train** and everyone stops playing. (The class must watch as well as listen).
- Immediately after the stop signal, the train driver plays the signal **Change stations** and all the instruments are passed one place round the circle.
- The new train driver improvises a solo rhythm and the game continues. Allow as many children as possible to have a turn as the train driver.

Train driver 1 plays solo	plays signal	Everyone	Train driver 1 plays signal	plays signal	Train driver 2 plays solo
Eu-ro-star ex- press (repeating)	Start the train	Eu-ro-star ex-press (repeating)	Stop the train	Change sta-tions	Dir-ty die- sel en- gine (repeating)

etc.

Focus 2: Pitch

Transfer the three signals onto tuned percussion:

- The train driver composes note patterns for the three signals on the largest tuned percussion instrument. For example:

Start the train   **Stop the train**   **Change sta-tions**

- Play the Train Game again with the train driver improvising a solo repeating pattern on one or two notes.
- As before, after the signal **Start the train**, the class joins in by copying the train driver's rhythm. The players of tuned instruments play the rhythm using any note pattern from the pentatonic scale – C D E G A.

Focus 3: Rhythm and pitch

Listen to and follow the six signals in box 1 on the worksheet (B4).

Chant the words while clapping the rhythm of the six signals in box 1 on the worksheet.

Play a new version of the train game using all six signals:

- As before, the train driver improvises a short repeating solo rhythm which the class joins in with after the signal **Start the train**.
- The train driver plays **Stop the train** as before and then the following sequence of signals:

Instruments down	Place instruments on the floor.
Stand up	Everyone stands up.
Change stations	Move one place round the circle.
Sit down	Everyone sits down.

(N.B. There is no signal for picking up instruments. The children should pick up the instruments when given the signal to start the train).

- The game continues as before with the new train driver in place.

RESOURSES

Focus 2
None
Focus 3
Worksheet

INSTRUMENTS
Focuses 2 & 3
A selection of tuned and untuned percussion.
Tuned percussion use the pentatonic scale C D E G A (removing F and B notes)

Signals (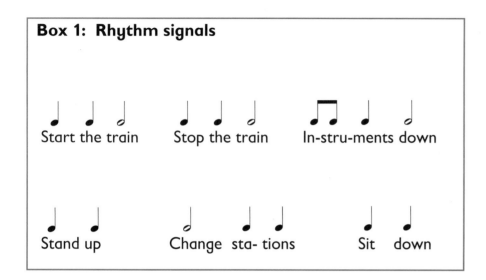 B4, 5)

Box 1: Rhythm signals

Start the train   Stop the train   In-stru-ments down

Stand up   Change sta- tions   Sit down

Box 2: Pitch signals

Start the train   Stop the train   In-stru-ments down

Stand up   Change sta-tions   Sit down

Listen to the six signals on B5 played on a tuned instrument. Follow the up and down shapes in box 2 on the worksheet.

Choose a train driver to compose note patterns on a large tuned percussion instrument following the shapes in box 2 on the worksheet. Any notes can be used as long as they follow the pitch direction. For example, this signal:

could be played using

D G A   or   C E B

The class listens to the train driver's signals and responds with the corresponding movements.

Play the Train Game using the train driver's six signals. For this version, after the signal **Start the train**, the class joins in by copying the train driver's repeating rhythm or improvising their own patterns to fit in the same length of time.

CHATTER WITH THE ANGELS

GAME
Round and Round

RESOURCES
Focuses 1 & 2
Worksheet 1 👓

INSTRUMENTS
Focuses 1 & 2
None

Year group 3–5

The melody of this Spiritual uses a pentatonic scale which gives plenty of scope for improvising and creating accompaniments.

Focus 1: Melody

♫ Sing the song *Chatter with the Angels* (💿 B6) on worksheet 1 (optional) in the following ways:

- Sing the complete song (parts one and two).
- Then divide the class into two groups; group 1 sings part one followed by group 2 singing part two.
- Sing the song with both groups starting at the same time (parts 1 and 2 together as shown worksheet 1).
- Sing the song as a two part round, for example:

Group 1 *Chatter with the angels, soon in the morning,*

etc.

Group 2 *Chatter with the angels,*

etc.

Focus 2: Rhythm – body sounds

♫ As a class, accompany the song with word rhythms and body sounds:

- Sing the song and clap the word rhythm 'join that band' only when it is sung .
- Throughout the song, clap the rhythm 'join that band' as an ostinato (i.e. repeating pattern).
- Perform a sequence of body sounds with the song using the rhythm 'join that band'. For example:

Sing	Body sound to the rhythm:		
	Join	*that*	*band*
Chatter with the angels	click	click	click
soon in the morning	clap	clap	clap
Chatter with the angels	pat	pat	pat
in that land	stamp	stamp	stamp

- Choose other word rhythms from the song and repeat the above activities.

Chatter with the Angels – words and music ( B6)

RESOURCES
Focuses 3 & 4
Worksheet 1 👓

INSTRUMENTS
Focuses 3 & 4
A selection of tuned and untuned percussion, ideally one per child or one between two. Tuned instruments use the pentatonic scale D E G A B (remove the C and F notes)

Focus 3: Rhythm – instrumental sounds

♫ Transfer the body rhythms from focus 2 onto tuned and untuned percussion:

- Give several children (or pairs of children sharing) a tuned percussion instrument. Ask them to play the word rhythm 'join that band' using the notes B A G or D E G:

Join	that	band
♩	♩	♩
B	A	G
D	E	G

- The other children select suitable untuned percussion instruments to play the word rhythm 'Chatter with the angels' or another word rhythm of their choice.
- Sing the song and ask the children to play only when the words of their rhythm are sung.
- Then sing the song again playing the word rhythms throughout as ostinati (repeating patterns). If the sound is too loud divide the class into two; group 1 plays during the first part and group 2 during the second part of the song.

Focus 4: Pitch

🎲 Improvise note patterns on tuned percussion to make an instrumental section:

- Choose several children to play the tuned percussion instruments.
- The class sings the song keeping a steady beat on their knees.
- After the song, continue the steady beat. Over this the players improvise note patterns one after another playing the word rhythm 'join that band' with any of these notes – D E G A B.
- When the last player finishes improvising sing the song again (see example on worksheet 1).
- Repeat the activity choosing a different word rhythm from the song, for example: 'soon in the morning' and choose other children to improvise note patterns.

Focus 5: Pitch and rhythm

Improvise rhythms and note patterns in part 2 of the song:

- Choose two children to play a slow steady beat on D and G, preferably on a bass xylophone:

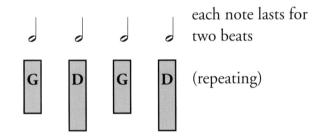

each note lasts for two beats

G **D** **G** **D** (repeating)

- Choose another child (player 1) to improvise on a tuned instrument.
- The class sings part 1 of the song accompanied by the D and G pattern. In part 2 of the song, the singing stops (but encourage the children to sing part 2 in their heads). Meanwhile player 1 improvises notes patterns and rhythms over the accompaniment (see diagram opposite).
- Sing part 1 of the song again and choose another player to improvise during part 2, etc.

SONG **part 1** sing	SONG **part 2** don't sing	SONG **part 1** sing
G **D** x4	Player 1 improvises **G** **D** x4	**G** **D** x4

Focus 6: Form

In groups of 4–5 compose accompaniments to the song and instrumental sections by following instructions on worksheet 2.

Perform the pieces to the class.

Listen to and discuss each performance:

> Which word rhythms did the group use for their accompaniment sections?
> Which word rhythms did the group use for their instrumental sections?
> Did the instruments balance or were some too loud?

RESOURCES
Focus 5
Worksheet 1
Focus 6
Worksheet 2
per group of 4–5

INSTRUMENTS
Focus 5
A selection of tuned and untuned percussion, ideally one per child or one between two. Tuned instruments use the pentatonic scale D E G A B (remove the C and F notes)
Focus 6
3– 4 untuned percussion and one tuned percussion per group of 4–5

Chatter with the Angels – accompaniments and instrumentals

In groups of 4-5 compose accompaniments and instrumental sections:

- Choose word rhythms from the song *Chatter with the Angels* and play them using body percussion and instruments.
- Decide how many times you will sing the song and how many instrumental sections to play.

- Build up your accompaniments and instrumental sections using these ideas:

  1 One player plays a steady beat all the time.
  2 Start with one player and add one player at a time.
  3 All play the same rhythm or different rhythms.
  4 Play together or one after another.
  5 Start on body percussion and then change to instruments.

- In which order will you play your ideas? There are many choices, for example:

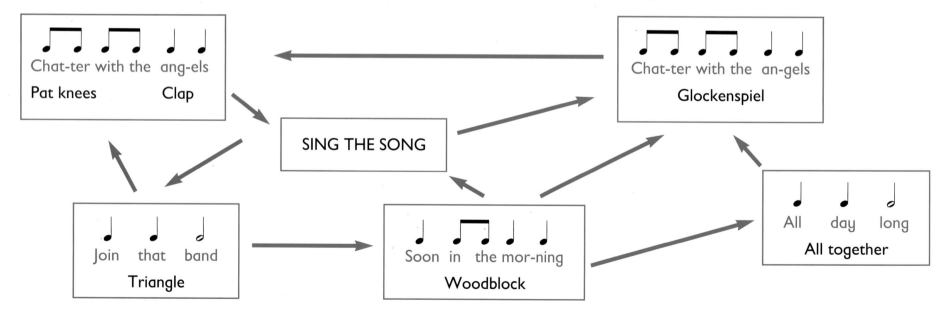

BIRD CALLS

Year group 3–6

The material in this project is mainly related to Saint-Saëns' *Carnival of the Animals* , but many composers throughout the ages have tried to imitate bird calls in their music – from simple cuckoo calls to intricate song-thrush 'melodies'. Some composers just try to capture the mood and character while others try to copy them exactly.

Focus 1: Pitch and rhythm

Bird calls can be quite complex and you can only hear the true detail by slowing them down. Listen to the following examples of bird call played at the correct speed and then slowed down:

- B7a is a hen clucking.
- B7b is a blackbird call.
- B7c is a song-thrush call.

Compare the following bird calls with their instrumental imitations:

- Cuckoos are quite easy to imitate. The second cuckoo call on B8a is made by a cuckoo whistle.

- B8b gives a slowed down version of the clucking hen followed by an instrumental imitation on xylophone. Listen to this example several times.

> Do you think the imitation matches the sound of the clucking hen? *(Answer: Yes, it matches the sound in pitch and rhythm although the sound quality is different).*

- The blackbird call on B9 even when slowed down sounds very complex, but the instrumental, imitation on metallophone that follows it does try to capture the general mood and atmosphere.

The six shapes on worksheet 1 show examples of bird call sounds. Follow these shapes as they are played on whistles and tuned percussion B10.

Interpret and perform each bird call shape on worksheet 1 using a variety of tuned instruments:

- Either choose volunteers to demonstrate or let the class work in groups of 4 –5 with instruments.

> Which instruments do you think best suit each bird call shape?

GAMES
Change a Sound, Stand Up/Sit Down

RESOURCES
Focus 1
Worksheet 1 plus recording of *Carnival of the Animals* by Saint-Saëns

INSTRUMENTS
Focus 1
A selection of tuned instruments (especially wind) Also use bird and slide whistles obtainable from charity or games shops

👂 Listening game – Bird call shapes:

- Ask a child to play one of the bird call shapes on worksheet 1 keeping his/her choice a secret.

Which bird call shape (1–6) was played?

👂 Identify bird call shapes from worksheet 1 used in three of the movements from Saint-Saëns' *Carnival of the Animals* (*Cocks and Hens, The Cuckoo in the Wood* and *The Aviary*):

- In turn listen to each movement and ask the children to listen out for the shapes given in the table on the right:

Title of the movement	Bird call shapes from worksheet 1	Instruments used to play the shapes
Cocks and Hens	1 and 2	Pianos and violins
	4	Piano
	5 (played going up only)	Violins
Cuckoo in the Wood	6	Clarinet
Aviary	1 fast and quiet	Violins
	4 and 5 (played going up only)	Flute
	4 and 5 (played going up only) and 3	Pianos

Can you hear any other type of sound or feature that gives the impression of bird sounds or activities? For example, how are dynamics (loud and quiet) used?
(*Answer: To emphasise swooping effects*).

Bird Call Shapes

B10:

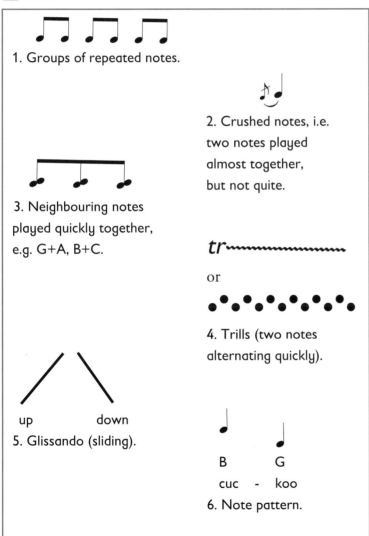

1. Groups of repeated notes.

2. Crushed notes, i.e. two notes played almost together, but not quite.

3. Neighbouring notes played quickly together, e.g. G+A, B+C.

tr ~~~~~~~~~~~~~~

or

• • • • • • • • • • • • •

4. Trills (two notes alternating quickly).

up   down

5. Glissando (sliding).

B   G

cuc - koo

6. Note pattern.

This is an example of a bird call piece (a sequence of bird call shapes)

B11:

RESOURCES
Focus 2
Worksheet 1
Worksheet 2
per child
plus recording of
Carnival of the Animals by
Saint-Saëns

INSTRUMENTS
Focus 2
A selection of tuned instruments (especially wind) Also use bird and slide whistles obtainable from charity or games shops

Focus 2: Structure – sounds in sequence

Listen to the sequence of shapes that make up the bird call piece in the example on worksheet 1 (B11):

> Thinking about the quality of the sound what type of bird do think could make this call? *(For example: Is it big or little, fierce or friendly, etc.?)* Can you spot any pattern in the way these shapes are ordered (sequenced)? *(Answer: The two lines i.e. / / alternate with other shapes).*

Compose bird call pieces by completing worksheet 2 using tuned instruments or bird whistles:

- Divide the children into groups of 3-4 and give each group one or two tuned instruments and/or bird whistles (if available).
- The children in each group should share the instruments available, but work individually.

Perform a selection of the bird call pieces.

Listening game – Bird call pieces:

- Choose a child to play his/her bird call piece (stating the type of bird) and over several playings ask the class to answer the following questions:

> Which was the first and/or last shape used?
> Which bird call shapes (1–6) were used?
> Could you hear a pattern in the way the shapes were ordered?
> How did the piece use dynamics (loud and quiet) and tempo (speed)?
> Did you feel the piece captured the mood and character of the bird?

Bird Call Pieces

Compose a bird call piece using a tuned instrument or bird whistle:

- Think of a bird – imaginary or real.
- Decide which bird call shapes to use from worksheet 1 and how you will play them on the instrument. For example, for a large bird you may choose to play the shapes on the lowest notes or sounds.
- Play and repeat the shapes in a sequence one after another in any order you like. Don't make it too long.
- To give your bird call more character think about using dynamics (loud and quiet), varying the tempo (speed) and perhaps adding pauses or rests.
- When you have composed your piece write down the sequence of shapes in the box below. See the example on worksheet 1.

Draw a picture of the bird that makes the sounds in your bird call piece:

(title) ....

RESOURCES
Focus 3
Worksheets 1
and 3 👓 per
group of 4–5

INSTRUMENTS
Focus 3
A selection of
tuned plus
bird whistles
(if available).
Several untuned
percussion
instruments that
make shaking or
scraping sounds

Focus 3: Structure and texture

👂 Listen to the example of Aviary music on worksheet 3 (💿 B12). The diagram (score) shows how the four bird calls (cuckoo, hen, blackbird and song-thrush) are played together.

🎲 In groups of 4–5 compose a piece of Aviary music by following the instructions on worksheet 3. (In turn, each group will need to choose a selection of tuned and untuned instruments).

🎵 Perform the Aviary music compositions.

👂 Listen to and discuss each performance:

> What type of aviary did the music suggest? For example was it a busy noisy aviary or a more tranquil and peaceful aviary?
> Did the music balance or did one of the bird calls seem too loud or quiet or out of place?

Aviary Music

Worksheet 3

Listen to this example of Aviary music which uses real bird calls (B12):

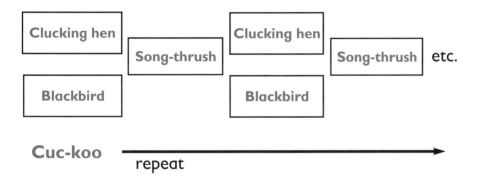

Cuc-koo ———————————————→
repeat

The cuckoo begins and repeats continually. Over this the hen and blackbird make their sounds together and alternate with the song-thrush in a kind of question and answer pattern.

In groups of 4–5 compose your own Aviary music using a variety of sounds:

- Choose instruments or use vocal sounds and make up short bird calls (alternatively use the bird call shapes from worksheet 1).
- What type of birds do your bird calls sound like? For example, a bird call played on a small glockenspiel may give the impression of a sparrow.
- If you are using an untuned instrument you won't be able to play shapes that go up and down, but you can still make sounds that resemble bird calls. For example, duck quack sounds can be made on scrapers and goose hiss sounds can be made on shakers.
- Decide how to play your bird call sounds together. Look at the example opposite and the diagram below for ideas.

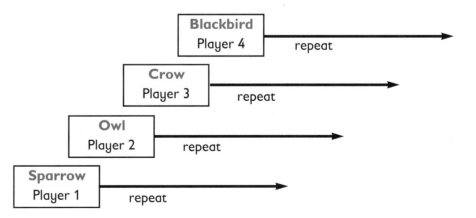

The players enter one by one and drop out one by one.

THE CARNIVAL OF ANIMAL LIFE

GAMES
Conversations
Eights

RESOURCES
Focus 1
Worksheet 1 🐾
(optional)
Worksheet 2 🐾
and a recording
of the *Carnival of
the Animals* by
Saint-Saëns
Focus 2
Worksheet 2 🐾

INSTRUMENTS
Focuses 1 & 2
None

Year group: 3–6

The song *The Carnival of Animal Life* provides an
introduction to themes and ideas used in Saint-Saëns'
Carnival of the Animals: (a series of short movements
featuring caricatures of birds, animals and musicians).
However, the words of the song also develop a more
contemporary theme relevant to our wild life –
conservation!

Focus 1: Melody and timbre

♫ Sing the song *The Carnival of Animal Life* (🔊 B13,
14), which uses melodies and ideas from Saint-Saëns'
Carnival of the Animals.

👂 Worksheet 2 shows which melodies have been taken
from Saint-Saëns' *Carnival of the Animals* and used in
the song. Look at worksheet 2 and listen to the
following three excerpts several times (🔊 B15, 16, 17):

> Which words in the song would you sing to the
> tune of each excerpt? *(Answers:*
> 🔊 *B15 is used in the verse 'Try to feed, try to rest,
> etc. and is from the Introduction.*
> 🔊 *B16 is used in the chorus 'In the water
> plankton soup,' etc. and is from the Aquarium.*

> 🔊 *B17 is used in the chorus – 'Care we must then
> take,' etc. and is from the Fossils).*
> Which instruments are playing the tune for each
> excerpt? *(Answers:*
> 🔊 *B15 Introduction – Strings, i.e. violins, violas,
> cellos and double basses.*
> 🔊 *B16 Aquarium – Strings mainly but you may
> also hear a flute and glockenspiel.*
> 🔊 *B17 Fossils – Xylophone).*

👂 Listen to the riff (repeating pattern) from the *Royal
March of the Lion* (🔊 B18) which uses two alternating
notes. These notes (slightly varied) are used for the
melody and accompaniment of the song in lines 1, 2 , 5
and 6 of the verse.

Focus 2: Links with English and Art

Use the words of the song to stimulate the writing
of poems or stories about the struggle for survival of a
particular animal or bird featured in Saint-Saëns'
Carnival of the Animals. Verses 2 and 3 can be used for
developing links with colour and shape.

The Carnival of Animal Life – words and music (B13, 14)

© 1995 Middle Eight Music Ltd. Published by Cramer Music Ltd.

The Carnival of Animal Life – words (🔊 B13, 14)

Melodies and riffs
from Saint-Saëns'
*Carnival of the
Animals*

Verse 1:

Royal March riff

The carnival of animal life,
Dramatic scenes of struggle and strife.

Introduction

Try to feed, try to rest,
Try to drink, nature's time to test.

Royal March riff

The carnival of animal life,
It walks the sharpened edge of a knife.

Introduction

Keeping fit, keeping warm,
Keeping safe, shelter from the storm.

Chorus:

Aquarium

In the water plankton soup
Will set the food chain on its loop.
From the coral to the whale,
They all exist on balanced scale.
Evolution started here,
It's where the world got into gear.
From amoeba to mankind,
A billion species all entwined.

Fossils

Care we must then take,
Not to terminate,
Not to crush all life into fossils.

Verse 2:

The carnival of animal tone,
Parade of signals in full colour shown.
Colours warn, colours hide,
Colours say will you be my bride.
The carnival of animal sound,
Primeval music to tell all around.
Tell of love, tell of fear,
Tell the world freedom you hold dear.

Chorus:

Verse 3:

The carnival of animal shape,
Processional from the ant to the ape.
Shaped for strength, shaped for speed,
Shaped to suit every single need.
The carnival of animal skill,
Astounding movement is set to thrill.
Skill of limb, skill of eye,
Skills in life needed to get by.

Chorus:

Coda:

The carnival of animal life,
The carnival of animal life,
The carnival of animal, animal, animal life.

Focus 3: Mood and character

👂 Listen to the following sections (movements) from the *Carnival of the Animals* and discuss the questions:

Royal March of the Lions:

> Can you describe the rhythm in the *Royal March of the Lions*? (*Answer: Proud, strong and steady*). Which instrument gives a roaring effect in the music? (*Answer: Piano played low down, going up and down quickly*).

Compare the *Wild Asses* with the *Kangaroos*:

> How would you describe the shape of the music in each movement? (*Answer: Up and down note patterns played on pianos. In Wild Asses they are played very quickly, but in Kangaroos slowly*). What words could you use to describe the mood of each movement? (*Answer: Wild Asses – wild, rushing, out of control. Kangaroos – comical, dotty, has a feeling of running up to a jump*).

Persons with Long Ears:

> How is the 'Hee-haw' sound and the idea of long ears portrayed in the music? (*Answer: Long sounds and large leaps*)

Compare the *Tortoises* with *Elephants*:

> What do the melodies have in common? (*Answer: Both melodies are played by low sounding stringed instruments. The Tortoises tune is played low down by all the strings and the Elephants tune is played on the double bass.*
> What words could you use to describe the mood of each movement? (*Answer: Tortoises – yawning, sleepy, lazy, relaxed. Elephants – comical, silly, clumsy*). What dance rhythm does the *Elephant* use? (*Answer: a waltz – 1 2 3 1 2 3 etc.*).

RESOURCES

Focus 3
Recording of Saint-Saëns' *Carnival of the Animals*

INSTRUMENTS

Focus 3
None

RESOURCES
Focus 4
Worksheet 3 🐛

INSTRUMENTS
Focus 4
A large tuned
instrument

Compare the *Aquarium* with *The Swan*:

> How is the effect of flowing water created in both movements? *(Answer: By rippling note patterns played on the two pianos).*

Cuckoo in the Woods:

> What type of wood does the cuckoo live in? *(Answer: Peaceful, dark, mysterious).*

Focus 4: Pulse and accompaniment

♪ Perform *The Carnival of Animal Life* chant and *Royal March Riff* accompaniment, see worksheet 3. (An example is given on (🔊 B19):

- As a class, practise keeping a steady beat using body sounds to a count of 4 as shown:

count: 1   2   3   4 (repeating)
              clap lap lap lap

- Keep the beat again using the body sounds, but, instead of counting the beats, chant the phrase *The Carnival of Animal Life* twice (see worksheet 3).

- At the end of the chant keep the beat going by repeating the pattern of body sounds four times (i.e. 4 x 4 beats). This will eventually form the instrumental section of the musical procession in focus 5.

- Repeat the chant and then the body sounds for the instrumental section several times without pause.

- Choose two children to accompany the chant by playing the *Royal March Riff* on a large tuned instrument. The children should stop playing during the instrumental section (see worksheet 3).

The Carnival of Animal Life – musical procession (B19)

Chant	Instrumental section
The car-ni-val of an-i-mal life. The car-nival of an-i-mal life.	
1 2 3 4 clap lap lap lap →repeat	**1 2 3 4** clap lap lap lap Repeat the clap and lap pattern 4 times

Royal March Riff (repeating pattern):

Count	1	2	3	4	Repeat this riff with the chant
Player 1 rh	G	G	A	A	
Player 1 lh	E	E	E	E	
Player 2	C	C	A	A	

Make a Carnival of Animal Life musical procession:

- Improvise music to represent an animal or bird in the instrumental section after the chant.
- Repeat the chant and then improvise music to represent a different type of animal or bird, and so on.

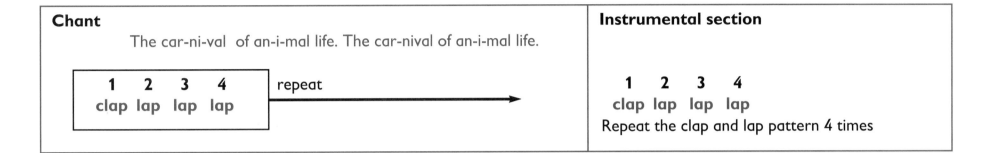

RESOURCES
Focus 5
Worksheet 3 👓

INSTRUMENTS
Focus 5
A large tuned
instrument
plus a selection
of tuned and
untuned

Focus 5: Mood and character

👂 Listen to *The Carnival of Animal Life* musical procession (💿 B19). One animal is imitated in each of the instrumental sections between the chant:

> What type of animals do you think are in the procession?

🎲 Make a *Carnival of Animal Life* musical procession:

- Choose several children to improvise animal or bird music. Ask each child to decide which animal or bird they would like to be.
- Thinking about pitch (high and low) and timbre (sound quality) each child selects an instrument to represent their animal or bird. For example, a large tambour could represent the sound of an elephant.
- Decide an order for the children to improvise and then ask the class to perform *The Carnival of Animal Life* chant.
- In the instrumental sections between the repetitions of the chant each child improvises in turn and tries to capture the character of their animal or bird. For example, an improvisation of a snake using shakers could consist of a sequence of long and short sounds, representing hissing.

👂 Listen to and discuss each performance:

> Did you agree with the choice of instrument used for each animal or bird?
> Did you think the way the players were making the sounds for each animal or bird was effective, or could they be improved in some way?

Repeat the whole activity with another group of players.

SATELLITE SONG

Year group: 3–6

The satellite is a very important part of today's communication network and this project focuses on the way messages are sent and received. In a world full of transmissions and interference, many of the problems satellites have to overcome are not so far removed from the problems we face when trying to listen to different parts in a piece of music.

Focus 1: Melody and structure – call and response

♪ Sing the *Satellite Song* on worksheets 1 and 2 (💿 B20).

The melody is the same for each line of the verse, but the melody that 'plugs the gap' in-between each line is varied each time by using a different order of notes or a slightly different rhythm. Each line of the verse could be thought of as a kind of *call* with the 'plug the gap' tune providing a *response*. (see worksheet 2).

👂 Listening game:

- Listen to the four instruments – glockenspiel, saxophone, flute and synthesiser – which 'plug the gap' between each line of the verse 1 (💿 B20).

> In which order do the four instruments play? *(Answer: After line 1 – flute, after line 2 – glockenspiel, after line 3 – saxophone, after line 4 – synthesizer).*

♪ As a class, practise keeping a steady beat to the verse of the song using 💿 B20:

- Gently pat the beats on the palm of your hand in time with the music. Count the beats in groups of 4 and slightly accent the first of each group (see worksheet 2).
- Repeat the activity, but alternate a pat of four beats on your palms with four rest beats ('patting the air'). The rest beats should coincide with the gaps between each line of the words.

🎲 Improvise rhythms and note patterns to 'plug the gaps' in each verse using 💿 B21 (the instrumental version of the song which also has 'unplugged' gaps):

- To warm up, ask all the children to 'plug the gap' at the same time, clapping their own rhythms. The rhythms may be similar to the *call* rhythm (the melody rhythm of each line) or something as simple as four steady beats.
- Then choose several children to clap solos during one or two verses.

GAMES
Conversations
Name Game
Plug the Gap

RESOURCES
Focus 1
Worksheet 1 🎭
(optional)
Worksheet 2 🎭

INSTRUMENTS
Focus 1
One tuned instrument per group of three children
If not enough tuned instruments are available some groups could use untuned percussion

Satellite Song – music (⊚ B20, 21)

Satellite Song – words and melody (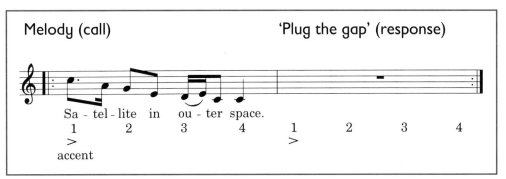 B20, 21)

1. **Satellite in outer space,**
    Whirling round with ease and grace,
    Bouncing messages we send,
    Back towards their journey's end.

    Chorus:

    One day soon,
    You'll fall to earth,
    But till that time my
    Satellite
    Spins the world,
    Once a day,
    Comes your way.

2. **Folding out to left and right,**
    Solar panels capture light.
    Turn it into energy,
    Powering the circuitry.

    Chorus:

3. **Electronic wizardry,**
    Eating signals we can't see.
    Pictures, words and numbers too,
    Processed all inside of you.

    Chorus:

    Coda:

    Satellite in outer space.

Melody (call)   'Plug the gap' (response)

Sa - tel - lite   in   ou - ter space.
1   2   3   4   1   2   3   4
>   >
accent

In the verse after each line of words, 'plug the gap' by following the directions in each box to play up, down, high or low:

1. going up   2. high   3. going down   4. low

RESOURCES
Focus 2
Worksheet 1 📖
(optional)
Worksheet 2 📖

INSTRUMENTS
Focus 2
One tuned
instrument per
group of three
children
If not enough
tuned
instruments are
available
some groups
could use
untuned
percussion

- Next, divide the class into groups of three and number each group member 1-3.
- Give each group one tuned instrument (or alternatively one untuned if not enough tuned instruments are available). Ask the children with tuned instruments to remove the B and F notes to leave the pentatonic scale C D E G A (i.e. a group of notes with only five different letter names, see worksheet 2):

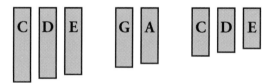

- In verse 1, the number 1 players in each group 'plug the gap' at the same time. (Players with tuned instruments can use any combination of notes). Immediately after verse 1, player number 1 passes the beaters (or their untuned instrument) to player number 2 who then 'plugs the gap' for verse 2 and so on. The members of each group who are not playing at any one time should sing the song.

Focus 2: Pitch

🎵 Plug the gaps in each verse following the up and down directions shown in the four boxes on worksheet 2:

- Organise the children into the same groups with their instruments as for focus 1.
- Explain which notes are high or low in relation to a tuned instrument (see worksheet 2).
- Groups with a tuned instrument play the pitch shape shown in each box for each 'gap' in the verse. Although the players are following the same pitch shape at the same time, they can improvise their own rhythm and decide which notes to play as they go up or down, etc.
- Groups with an untuned instrument 'plug the gap' as normal. Later, ask groups with tuned instruments to swap with groups using untuned instruments and repeat the activity.

👂 Identify the direction of a melody (up or down etc.):

- Listen to the verse melody (the notes sung to the words) on 💿 B20 and look at the boxes on worksheet 2.

Which box matches the general direction of notes in the melody? *(Answer: Box 3. The melody notes go from high to low).*

Focus 3: Pulse

Before beaming information, a transmitter (e.g. satellite) will ask the receiver (e.g. earth station) for an acknowledgement that it is ready and working. In computer communications 'speak' this is called a 'hand shake'.

Listening game – Recognise and acknowledge 'hand shake' signals sent to receiving stations on different planets:

- As a class, practise clapping the rhythm of the 'hand shake' signal *Satellite in outer space*:

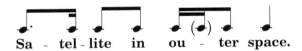

Sa – tel – lite in ou – ter space.

- Sit nine players with instruments in a line. (Tuned instruments use the pentatonic scale C D E G A). Name each player after a planet and number the planets relative to their distance from the sun:

Mercury	= 1	Saturn	= 6
Venus -	= 2	Uranus	= 7
Earth	= 3	Neptune	= 8
Mars	= 4	Pluto	= 9
Jupiter	= 5		

- Choose another player to be the satellite.
- The remaining members of the class chant quietly a steady repeating count of nine.
- Over this the satellite plays the *Satellite in outer space* rhythm (the 'hand shake' signal) once only, beginning on one of the chanted numbers.
- The planet corresponding to that number responds immediately at the end of the satellite's rhythm by copying the rhythm and completing the 'hand shake'. For example:

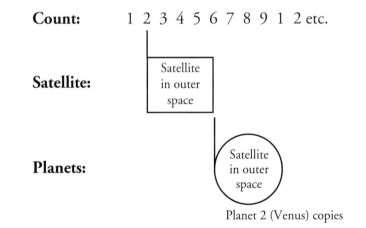

Planet 2 (Venus) copies

RESOURCES
Focus 3
None

INSTRUMENTS
Focus 3
A selection of tuned and untuned

RESOURCES
Focus 4
None

INSTRUMENTS
Focus 4
A selection of
untuned

- Meanwhile the satellite plays the *Satellite in outer space* rhythm on another number and so the next planet responds accordingly. For example:

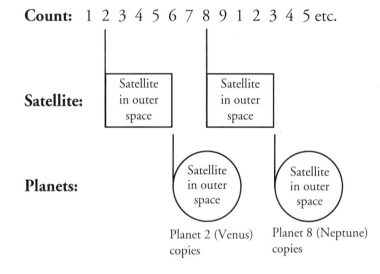

Count: 1 2 3 4 5 6 7 8 9 1 2 3 4 5 etc.

Satellite:

Planets:

Planet 2 (Venus) copies   Planet 8 (Neptune) copies

- Repeat the game with new players.

Focus 4: Rhythm and texture – sounds in layers

Space is full of transmissions from all sorts of radio and TV stations, but satellites still manage to bypass this interference and 'tune-in' to signals directed at them.

👂 Listening game – 'Tune-in' to the satellite rhythm:

- Choose several players and give each one an untuned instrument. The rest of the class are satellites (i.e. listeners waiting to 'tune-in' to a message from earth).
- Unknown to the listeners, one player chooses to play the *Satellite in outer space* rhythm from the song.

Sa - tel - lite   in   ou - ter space.

- The other players improvise interference rhythms (play anything apart from the *Satellite in outer space* rhythm).
- The players start together after a count of four and repeat their rhythms several times.

Can you 'tune-in' to (identify) which player is sending the *Satellite in outer space* word rhythm?

THESEUS AND THE MINOTAUR

Year group 3–6

The ancient Greek legend of *Theseus and the Minotaur* is the basis for this music-drama. The children need to be familiar with the story and be able to tell it in their own words:

Every year Aegeus must send a group of men to the Minotaur's maze in Crete, but they never return as the Minotaur kills them. Theseus, Aegeus's son, volunteers to go with the group and sets sail for Crete. Theseus enters the maze, where he fights and kills the Minotaur. He finds his way out of the maze thanks to Ariadne (the King of Crete's daughter) who had given him a ball of string to follow and they return to Greece to a tumultuous welcome.

Each focus concentrates on a particular part of the story though they are not introduced in the correct order. Focus 5 places the story in sequence.

Focus 1: Pitch and rhythm

Musical signals instead of string help Theseus find his way in and out of the maze. In this version of the story he is blindfolded and listens to the musical signals which indicate whether he should walk forwards, backwards, to the left or to the right.

What sounds are used as signals in everyday life? *(Answer: whistle/bell for end of playtime, doorbell, telephone, ice cream van, TV theme music).*
How do we recognise them? *(Answer: they have a particular quality of sound or use a note pattern which we find easy to remember).*
What is a signal preparing us for? *(Answer: a command to do something or warning that something is about to happen).*

In 4 groups compose musical signals:

- Each group makes up note patterns and/or rhythm for one of the following directions including a stop signal:

WALK FORWARDS – STOP

WALK BACKWARDS – STOP

WALK SIDEWAYS TO THE LEFT – STOP

WALK SIDEWAYS TO THE RIGHT – STOP

- Each group's stop signal should be distinctive. For example, two taps on a cow bell or a fast drum roll.

GAMES
Shadowing
Conversations
Stop/Start

RESOURCES
Focus 1
Approx 20 large sheets of scrap paper or newspaper

INSTRUMENTS
Focus 1
One tuned and several untuned per group of 7 to 8.

♫ Guide Theseus through a maze to the Minotaur by playing the four signals:

- Choose a child to be Theseus.
- Ask each group to play their signals one after another, repeating them several times. As a practice, Theseus walks (with eyes shut or blindfolded) in the corresponding directions, stopping on the stop signals. (NB. Theseus should always be facing the same direction).
- Make a maze by laying large sheets of paper on the floor, making sure that all four directions are included (i.e. forwards, backwards, to the left, to the right). Theseus should not see the maze being set out.
- Choose a child to be the Minotaur and ask him or her to sit in the centre of the maze.
- The four groups then guide Theseus through the maze by playing their signals (including the stop signal) at the appropriate time, keeping him/her on the sheets of paper.
- Choose other children to be Theseus and the Minotaur and repeat the activity.

Focus 2: Mood and character

In groups of 4–5 compose music for Theseus' sea journeys (see worksheet 1 or use other pictures as a visual stimulus):

> Can you think of contrasting words which describe the different moods of the sea?
> (*Answer: Calm/stormy; crashing waves/gentle ripples; dark and foreboding/light and sparkling*).

- Each group should decide on one type of sea mood and select appropriate instruments. For example: glockenspiel, triangle, Indian bells for a light and sparkling sea or drums, cymbals and vibraslap for a stormy, violent sea.

- This is one example of a stormy sea mood:

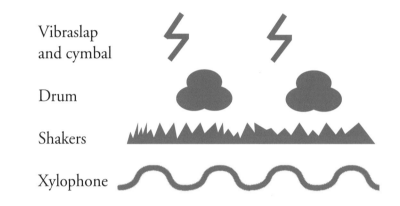

Vibraslap and cymbal

Drum

Shakers

Xylophone

Perform the sea pieces to the class.

Listen to and discuss each group's performance:

> How would you describe the mood of the sea piece?
> Which instruments helped most to capture the atmosphere of the sea piece?
> Could the group use dynamics (loud and quiet) or tempo (speed) more effectively?

RESOURCES
Focus 2
Worksheet 1 or pictures of stormy and calm seas

INSTRUMENTS
Focus 2
A selection of tuned and untuned

Sea Moods

Focus 3: Rhythm

In pairs improvise music for the battle between Theseus and the Minotaur:

- Choose two children to play two drums and two children to be Theseus and the Minotaur.
- In a simulated fight in slow motion (like a TV action replay) Drum A plays a drum pattern which Theseus mirrors with movement. Drum B copies drum A's pattern which the Minotaur mirrors with movement. For example:

Drum A
(Theseus) ●●●●   ●●●●●
Drum B
(Minotaur)   ●●●●   ●●●●●

- The drummers should vary the way they play using contrasting dynamics (louder/quieter) and tempo (faster/ slower) to make the musical fight more exciting.
- Drum B indicates defeat by improvising a drum sound or rhythm to signal the end of the fight. For example a fast drum roll. The Minotaur falls to the floor and Theseus acknowledges his victory.
- Choose other pairs of children and repeat the activity.

RESOURCES

Focus 3

None

INSTRUMENTS

Focus 3

Two drums or tambours

RESOURCES
Focus 4
Worksheet 2 👓
(optional)
Photocopy and
enlarge
Worksheet 3 and
cut out the four
boxes to make
flashcards

INSTRUMENTS
Focus 4
Tuned percussion
with the notes

Focus 4: Pitch and rhythm

Fanfares are used to announce the arrival and departure of important people.

♫ Sing *Theseus' Fanfare* on worksheet 2 (🔊 B22) to welcome Theseus back from his journey. Then sing the fanfare as a round.

♫ As a class, perform the fanfare as a round using different body sounds:

● The children sing the fanfare in their heads and clap, slap, tap and stamp the rhythm of the words of each line. For example:

Theseus, young and brave,	*clap*
Travelled through the maze.	*slap thighs left/right*
Killed the Minotaur,	*tap shoulders*
Rotten to the core!	*stamp*

● Divide the children into two groups. Group 1 sings the fanfare while group 2 claps the rhythm of one line as an ostinato accompaniment. For example:

Group 2 Thes-e - us   young and brave   (repeating)

● Use the rhythm of other lines to accompany the fanfare.

♫ As a class, perform the rhythms of the fanfare from notation using the rhythm flashcards on worksheet 3:

● Sing the fanfare and follow the flashcards in the original sequence.
● Following the flashcards again, the class claps the fanfare while singing in their heads.

Which two rhythms are the same?
(Answer: Lines 2 and 4).

● Mix up the cards and ask the children to clap the rhythms in a different order.

👂 Listen to the note pattern of each line of the fanfare played separately:

What do you notice about the shape of the melody of line 4?
(Answer: It stays on the same note).
What do you notice about the shape of the melody of line 2?
(Answer: It goes up and down using two notes).

Theseus' Fanfare (💿 B22)

The - se - us, young and brave,

Tra-velled through the maze.

Killed the Min- o - taur,

Rot- ten to the core!

© 1995 Middle Eight Music Ltd. Published by Cramer Music Ltd.

♪ Play the note patterns of the fanfare on tuned percussion by ear:

- Ask several children to accompany the fanfare by playing the note pattern of any line as a repeating pattern (ostinato). Allow many children to have a turn on the instruments while the others sing and use body percussion.
- Sing the fanfare again with the players playing their line once in the correct place (i.e. not all the way through).

Compose fanfares for Theseus' departure:

- One child improvises a fanfare phrase using these notes:

For the rhythm use phrases from the *Theseus' Fanfare* or other word rhythms connected with the story. For example:

C   C   F   F   A   C'
Wel-come back to   A - thens

- Those children with tuned instruments copy the note pattern on their instruments while the rest of the class sings it. Ask the children to play and sing the new fanfare several times as a 'follow my leader'. For example:

Fanfare 1	All copy	Fanfare 1	All copy
C C F F A C'	C C F F A C'	C C F F A C'	C C F F A C'

- Ask the children with tuned instruments to take turns improvising fanfares. For example:

Fanfare 1	All copy	Fanfare 2	All copy	
C C F F A C'	C C F F A C'	A C C A F F	A C C A A F	etc.

Rhythm Flashcards

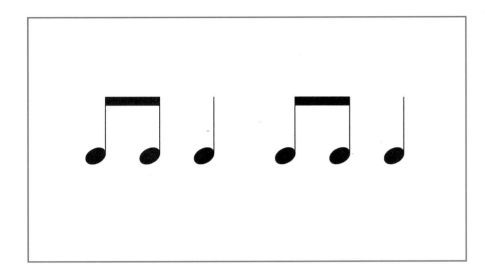

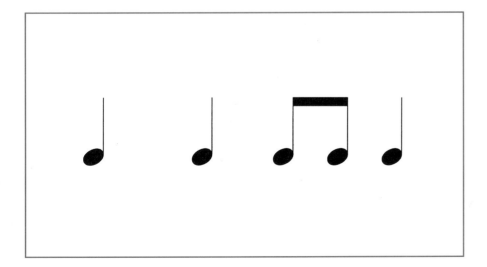

RESOURCES
Focus 5
As for
Focuses 1–4

INSTRUMENTS
Focus 5
As for
Focuses 1–4

Focus 5: Form

♪ Tell the story of *Theseus and the Minotaur* by ordering the sections as shown below:

- Choose children to be Aegeus, Theseus, the sailors, Ariadne and the Minotaur.
- Decide who will play the opening fanfares, sea music, signals and the drums for the fight.
- The whole class should sing *Theseus' Fanfare*. Use a narrator to link the musical sections.

Section A	Section B	Section C	Section D	Section C	Section B	Section A
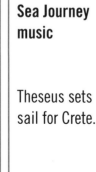						
Fanfares	**Sea Journey music**	**Maze musical signals**	**Fight music**	**Maze musical signals**	**Sea Journey music**	**Theseus' fanfare**
King Aegeus calls for Theseus to depart.	Theseus sets sail for Crete.	Theseus enters the maze and finds the Minotaur.	Theseus fights and kills the Minotaur.	Theseus comes out of the maze.	Theseus and Ariadne sail to Athens.	Theseus and Ariadne are welcomed home.

The form of the music (the order of the sections) is a palindrome, i.e. after section D the sections are played in the reverse order.

WELCOME TO THE PARTY

The song *Welcome to the Party* has a Scottish feel, both in the rhythm of the melody and the drone-like accompaniment, which develops co-ordination and improvisation skills.

Focus 1: Accompaniment – pulse and chords

♪ Sing the song *Welcome to the Party* on the worksheet (⊙B23, 24). The song is sung three times with instrumental sections in-between.

♪ As a class, accompany the song with a steady beat:

- With both hands, pat knees as shown on the worksheet, i.e. four times on right, four times on left, etc.
- Choose children to play tuned percussion using the following set of notes:

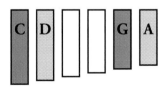

Two children can play on the same instrument if the range is wide enough to provide two sets of notes:

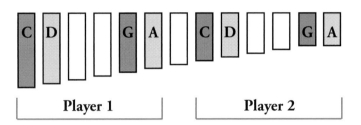

- Imitating the movement from left knee to right knee, the players play the notes D and A together as a chord followed by C and G together as a chord (see worksheet). This creates a Scottish sounding drone accompaniment.

GAMES
Conversations
Favourites

RESOURCES
Worksheet 👓
(optional)

INSTRUMENTS
Tuned percussion
use the
pentatonic scale
C D F G A
(removing the E
and B notes)

Welcome to the Party – words, music and accompaniment (◉B23, 24)

Focus 2: Melody and form

👂 Listen to the song *Welcome to the Party* (🔊 B23). In-between the repeats of the song, the accompaniment (chord sequence) is played on its own over which a player improvises a melody – first the viola, then the harp.

🎲 Improvise melodies over the chord sequence of the song:

- At the end of the song the tuned percussion players repeat the chord sequence while the rest of the class 'sings' silently in their heads. This will help the children measure the length of the song.
- On another tuned instrument choose a child to improvise a melody over this chord sequence making up his/her own rhythms or using word rhythms from the song.
- At the end of the improvisation the class sings the song again while the beaters are passed to another child who is ready to improvise the next melody and so on.

- This musical form is called a **Rondo**. The song section is labelled A with each of the solos labelled B C D successively. For example:

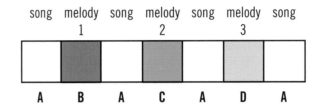

Focus 3: Structure – question and answer

🎲 Improvise question and answer melodies over the chord sequence of the song:

- Choose two players to improvise melodies while the other players continue with the alternating D and A followed by C and G as before.
- Player 1 plays a short melody (the question) over the D and A chord. In response to the question, player 2 plays a short melody (the answer) over the C and G chord. Repeat this pattern throughout.
- After doing this as a whole class activity, groups of three children using 2 tuned percussion instruments can work independently in the music corner. They should take it in turns to play the chords or improvise note patterns.

WIDE AWAKE

GAME
Eights

RESOURCES
Worksheet 🐸
and one sheet of
plain paper per
group of 4–5

INSTRUMENTS
A selection of
untuned
percussion
(optional drum
machine or
electronic
keyboard)

Year group 3–6

Most people go through a sequence of activities to get
them wide awake and ready for a day's work or play:

> What do you do in the mornings before going to
> school?
> What's the first thing you hear in the morning?
> In which order do you put on your clothes?
> Do you brush your hair before or after breakfast?

Focus 1: Rhythm

♫ As a class, perform the *Wide Awake* sequence on the
worksheet:

- Work out how to clap each word rhythm (there are
  many different ways to clap each word but decide
  on one that feels natural).
- Choose one child to play a steady beat on a
  woodblock or other untuned percussion
  instrument.
- Over this, the children chant the word rhythms one
  after another like a rap as shown on the worksheet.
- Choose several children to play the word rhythms
  on the corresponding instruments while the class
  chants.

- When this is secure the class performs the actions
  with the word rhythms.

🎲 In groups of 4–5 compose *Wide Awake* sequences
following the instructions on the worksheet.

♫ Perform the sequences following the instructions on
the worksheet.

👂 Listen to and discuss each performance:

> Did the group keep a steady beat while rapping
> the rhythm of the words?
> Was the rap slow or fast? Did it make you feel like
> getting up quickly or taking your time?

♫ Choose one group's sequence to teach to the whole
class and perform it with a strong steady beat
accompaniment. (Alternatively, provide a repeating
accompaniment using a drum machine, drum pattern on
an electronic keyboard or the drum track on 💿 B25).

Wide Awake Sequence   Worksheet

An example of a *Wide Awake* sequence:

Word rhythms:	Alarm ringing, wake up and stretch	Get dressed, eat breakfast	Brush my teeth, brush my hair
Instruments:			
Actions:			

Compose your own *Wide Awake* sequence:

- Think up a sequence of words that describes getting up in the morning.
- Decide how many times to repeat each phrase.
- Select untuned instruments to play with the word rhythms. Choose a different instrument for each rhythm. See example above.

Perform your sequence:

- Choose one person to play a steady beat.
- Chant the words like a rap over the steady beat and play the rhythm on the instruments.

Make up actions to go with the words.

Make a score to show the *Wide Awake* sequence of sounds and actions:

- On a sheet of paper draw a grid with enough boxes to write down the word rhythms.
- Draw the instruments and your own pictures or instructions for the actions below the word rhythms.

Focus 2: Texture – sounds in layers

♫ Perform a *Wide Awake* sequence as a round:

- Teach one of the *Wide Awake* sequences composed in focus 1 to the whole class or use the example on the worksheet.
- Divide the class into three groups.
- Over a strong steady beat accompaniment group 1 starts the sequence. Group 2 joins in after group 1 has finished the first box and so on. See example below.
- Perform the *Wide Awake* sequence through several times with instruments and/or actions.

	x2	x2	x2
Group 1:	Alarm ringing, wake up and stretch	Get dressed, eat breakfast	Brush my teeth, brush my hair

	x2	x2	x2
Group 2:	Alarm ringing, wake up and stretch	Get dressed, eat breakfast	Brush my teeth, brush my hair

	x2	x2	
Group 3:	Alarm ringing, wake up and stretch	Get dressed, eat breakfast	Brush my teeth, **etc.**

AFRICAN MUSIC

Year group: 5–6

Music in Africa is a very important part of daily life. It forms a major part of all ceremonies, but is also used in the telling of historical events or stories and to break the monotony of jobs like minding the cattle. Three important features of African music are included in this project: rhythm, percussion instruments and call and response patterns.

Focus 1: Rhythm and accompaniment

🎧 Listen to *Tongoyo,* a dance which originated among the Zulus of South Africa performed by Adzido (a pan-African dance ensemble), 💿 B26. The singers are accompanied by several different rhythms which are played together and repeated over and over.

🎵 As a class, practise clapping each of the 'African' rhythms on worksheet 1 to a count of eight:

- Give a 7–8 count in to start everyone together.
- Clap only on boxes containing a circle and repeat the whole rhythm without pause. When repeating the **odd** numbered rhythms a hiccup will occur as

the last unit is incomplete and therefore interrupts the flow of the pattern. For example:

- Accent (clap louder) the shaded circles to make the rhythms even more interesting.

🎲 In groups of 4–5 compose African rhythmic accompaniments by following the instructions on worksheet 1.

🎵 Practise the African rhythmic accompaniments by following the instructions on worksheet 1. Then perform to the class.

🎧 Listen to the *African Rhythmic Accompaniment* on 💿 B27. Entering one by one and repeating their rhythms over and over, the first instrument uses rhythm A and the second instrument uses rhythm E.

Which rhythm does the third instrument use?
(Answer: Rhythm D)

GAMES

Clock Gone Wrong!, Conversations, One to Eight

RESOURCES

Focus 1

Two copies of Worksheet 1 👓 per group of 4–5 children

INSTRUMENTS

Focus 1

None

African Rhythms

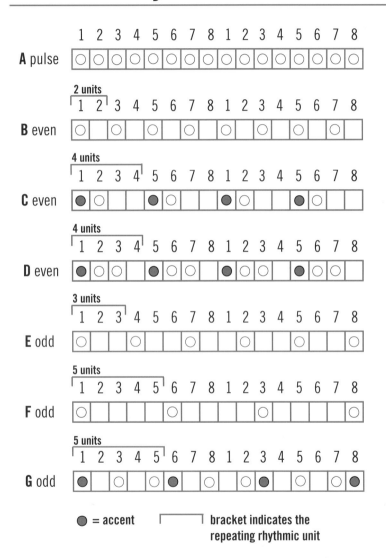

= accent   bracket indicates the
                repeating rhythmic unit

In groups of 4-5 compose an African rhythmic accompaniment:

- As a group choose three or four rhythms to clap from the box. They may be all **even** or a mixture of **odd** and **even.** (The same rhythm may be used by two or three players).
- If you use a mixture of odd and even unit rhythms the music may have a feeling of syncopation (which means 'off the beat'). This is because the repeating patterns made by the odd and even units do not fit together.

Practise clapping the rhythms together:

- After a 7–8 count-in chant the numbers while clapping and repeat your rhythms several times.
- Try to increase the tempo (speed of counting).
- Eventually, try to clap the rhythms without counting aloud.

Focus 2: Timbre

👂 Listen to *Tongoyo* again (🎵B26):

> What type of instruments can you hear playing?
> (*Answer: Mainly skinned instruments, but also shakers and rattles*).

🎲 Select untuned percussion instruments to play the rhythms on worksheet 1:

- Place a selection of untuned percussion instruments in a performance area (space) and choose volunteers to demonstrate each rhythm on several of the instruments.
- Some African drums slightly change in pitch as they are played. To do this on classroom skinned instruments, ask children to press the skin lightly (varying the pressure) with one hand while beating the rhythm with the other hand.

> Which rhythms work best on each instrument?
> (*For example, the pulse rhythm may not be suitable on a large drum as it may tend to sound clumsy*).

🎵 Perform the African rhythmic accompaniments (composed in focus 1) on untuned percussion instruments:

- Divide the class into the same groups of 4–5 as for focus 1.
- In turn, allow each group a short period of rehearsal in the performance area using the instruments before they perform to the class.

> Which instruments will your group use?
> (*For example, for a heavier sound use several different sized skinned instruments, or for a lighter sound use a mixture of shakers, rattles and wooden instruments*).

- While one group is rehearsing with the instruments the other groups should practise clapping their rhythms.

👂 Listen to and discuss each performance:

> What kind of activity or ceremony could you imagine the music accompanying? (*For example, minding the cattle, washing clothes, wedding, etc.*). Could you tell which groups were using a mixture of odd and even unit rhythms? Can you pick out the players who were using the odd unit rhythms?

RESOURCES

Focus 2

Two copies of Worksheet 1 👓 per group of 4–5

INSTRUMENTS

Focus 2

A selection of untuned percussion (wooden, skins, shakers, rattles)

RESOURCES

Focus 3

Worksheet 2 ✎
one between two

INSTRUMENTS

Focus 3

Drum

Focus 3: Structure – call and response

Listen out for a solo singer alternating with a large group of singers in *Tongoyo* on B26. This is known as call and response. In *Tongoyo* the singer is commenting on social issues and living conditions. It is a good example of how music in Africa forms a very important part of daily life.

Compose a call:

- Ask each child to make up a short phrase (the call) to do with an everyday activity. For example:

Call

Lining up at dinner time

1 2 3 4 5 6 7 8

Pulse ○○○○○○○○

- Over a quick but steady count of eight given by a partner the children chant and clap the rhythm of their calls. The words need to fit within the time it takes to chant one count of eight.

Chant and echo the calls in sequence:

- Choose a child to chant a count of eight and play a steady beat on a drum.
- Over the first count of eight a child chants a call.
- The class echoes (copies) the call over the next count of eight. For example:

Call	Echo (response)
Lining up at dinner time	Lining up at dinner time

1 2 3 4 5 6 7 8 1 2 3 4 5 6 7 8

Pulse ○○○○○○○○○○○○○○○○

- Without pause another child chants his/her call which is then echoed by the class and so on.
- Perform several of the calls with echoes over an African rhythmic accompaniment played by one of the groups from focus 2.

Listen to the two line call and response example given on worksheet 2 (B28). The call is played and sung by player 1 and the response by player 2.

In pairs compose a call and response phrase by completing worksheet 2.

Call and Response

In pairs compose a two line call and response:

For each line write the call in the box below player 1 and the response in the box below player 2. For example, 🔊 B28:

Call: Player 1	Response: Player 2
Washing up at home,	Rub-a-dub-a dub-ing

Line 1

1 2 3 4 5 6 7 8 1 2 3 4 5 6 7 8

Pulse ○○○○○○○○○○○○○○○○

Call: Player 1	Response: Player 2
Washing up at home,	Bubbles they are cleaning

Line 2

1 2 3 4 5 6 7 8 1 2 3 4 5 6 7 8

Pulse ○○○○○○○○○○○○○○○○

Perform the two line call and response:

- Over a steady count of **8** beats given by your partner practise chanting and clapping the rhythm of each phrase (the words in each box) separately.
- The words for each phrase need to fit within the time it takes to chant one count of eight.
- Decide who will clap the call phrases and who will clap the response phrases, then perform them in order.

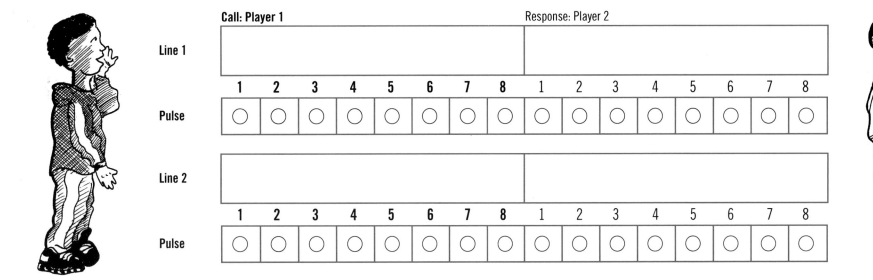

RESOURCES
Focus 4
Completed
Worksheet 2s

INSTRUMENTS
Focus 4
Drum and two
xylophones

Focus 4: Melody

Improvise melodies (note patterns) to the call and response phrases composed on worksheet 2:

- After the children have had time to practise clapping their call and response phrases, choose a pair to play them on two xylophones using the pentatonic (five note) scale:

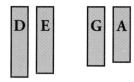

Pentatonic scales like this one are used to make melodies in many types of African music.

- Choose another child to keep a steady beat (pulse) on a drum and chant the count of eight.
- Using any combination or number of different notes from the pentatonic scale, the **caller** (player 1) improvises note patterns to the rhythm of each call over the first and third count of eight. The **responder** (player 2) improvises note patterns to the rhythm of each response over the second and fourth count of eight.

- The players should chant the words as they play and try to memorise the note patterns improvised for each line.

Repeat the activity with other pairs.

Teach the class to sing one of the call and response phrases composed on worksheet 2:

- Choose a pair to play their call and response on xylophones.
- Divide the class into two groups: Group 1 sings the call, group 2 sings the response.
- Ask the caller to play and sing his/her phrase for line 1 and ask the corresponding group of singers to echo back the words to the tune. Repeat the same procedure for each phrase.
- Perform the call and response pattern as normal, without repeats, over a steady beat or alternatively over a group playing an African rhythmic accompaniment from focus 2.

COTOPAXI AND THE PEOPLE OF THE ANDES

Year group: 5–6

Cotopaxi in Ecuador was formerly the world's highest active volcano. During the Aztec and Inca periods volcanos had a special religious significance and we learn of the people's fear of the volcano through the song *Cotopaxi*.

Focus 1: Melody

♪ Sing the song *Cotopaxi* on worksheet 1 (⊚ B29, 30).

♪ Learn to play the five motives (or segments) that make up the melody and *chuta chuta* of the verse shown on worksheet 2. (A motive is a short note pattern and/or rhythm):

- Choose a child to play a steady beat on a drum. Over this, as a class, sing or chant the words of each motive separately and clap the rhythm. Repeat each motive several times. (Alternatively as a follow-my-leader use ⊚ B31. The panpipes play each motive, leaving a gap in-between for the children to chant and clap).
- Divide the class into five groups and give each group one of the five motives. Then over a steady beat ask the groups to sing and clap their given motives in order to form the melody (see worksheet 2).

- Give each group a tuned instrument with these notes:

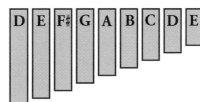

The players in each group take turns learning to play their given motive.

- Choose one child to play from each group. Then, ask the same children to play their motives in order one after another to make the melody. The members of each group who are not playing should sing or chant the words to help each player to come in at the right place and keep in time.
- Swap players in each group and repeat the activity.

👂 Listening game:

- Ask a volunteer to choose and clap any one of the five motives:

Which motive was clapped?

GAMES
Add a Beat
One Step Behind
Plug the Gap

RESOURCES
Focus 1
Worksheets
1 & 2 👥

INSTRUMENTS
Focus 1
Five tuned percussion ideally with the range of notes
D E F G A B C D E
plus a tambour or drum

Cotopaxi – words and music (⊛ B29, 30)

Cotopaxi Motives (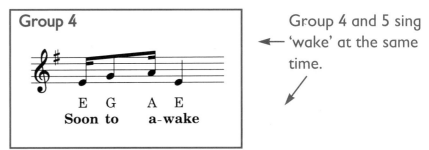 B31)

To make the tune for the verse, each group plays their motive (or segment) in order without pause:

Group 1

E B A D
Co - to - pax - i

Group 2

E B B A D
I feel your trem - or

Group 3

E F# G A B A G F#
Warn-ing of the force with-in you

Group 4

E G A E
Soon to a-wake

Group 4 and 5 sing 'wake' at the same time.

Group 5

E E B E B E
(wake from ve - ry deep sleep)

This motive is used to end the tune and is called a **Chuta Chuta**. Although these notes do not have words in the song, chant them to help you remember the rhythm.

RESOURCES

Focus 2

Worksheet 2 👓

Focus 3

Worksheet 3 👓

INSTRUMENTS

Focus 2

Five tuned percussion ideally with the range of notes D E F G A B C D E plus a tambour or drum

Focus 3

Several tuned percussion (or chime bars) with the notes D E A B and 1 tuned with the notes C D E F

Focus 2: Pitch

Musicians from the Andes compose new melodies by varying and reordering existing melodies, adding only one or two new ideas. However, over a long period of time these small variations can gradually transform the melody into something quite different.

🎲 Vary the *Cotopaxi* melody on worksheet 2:

- Following on from focus 1, the groups play their motives in order, but this time the player from group 1 composes a new note pattern for their motive, i.e. Co - to - pax - i. For example:

Original motive:	Example of changed motive using different notes:
E B A D	**E D D D**
Co-to-pax-i	Co-to-pax- i

- Do this for each group's motive in turn and the original melody will, over five stages, gradually transform into a new melody.
- Swap players in each group and repeat the activity.

👂 Listen to the *Cotopaxi* melody played six times on ⊙ B32. Each time the melody is repeated one of the

motives is varied. On the sixth playing all the motives have been varied, gradually transforming the melody into a new melody.

Focus 3: Melody

🎵 Sing the song *People of the Andes* on worksheet 3 (⊙ B33). The melody is split between two groups:

- Sit the class in a circle and choose 10 children to form group 1 with the rest of the class forming group 2.
- Group 1 begins by singing the four letter names E B A D and group 2 follows by singing the words. The two groups alternate throughout the song.

🎵 While singing the song, play the melody on instruments:

- Give as many children as possible in group 1 a tuned instrument (or four chime bars) for their part of the melody E B A D.
- Give one child in group 2 a tuned instrument with notes C D E F♯ for this group's part of the melody:

Play: C   C   D   D   E   E   F   F   E

Sing: Us - ing on - ly four notes try to make,

etc.

Focus 4: Accompaniment

👂 Listen to the four accompaniment rhythms on worksheet 3 as they enter one by one (🔊 B34). The rhythms are really steady beat patterns which double in speed. The cymbal begins and has the slowest beat; the bombo is twice as fast as the cymbal; the dull drum is twice as fast as the bombo; the low tuned instrument is twice as fast as the dull drum.

🎵 Perform the accompaniment rhythms on worksheet 3:

- As a class, clap each rhythm four times one after another over a steady beat. Start with the cymbal rhythm and count the numbers below each rhythm to keep in time.
- With the children in the same groups as for focus 3, choose four players from group 2 to play the accompaniment rhythms on instruments. For the dull drum and bombo use drums or tambours covered with material to mimic the unshaven skins (animal fur) of Andean drums.

🎵 Sing and perform the song again using both melody instruments from focus 3 and the accompaniment instruments.

RESOURCES

Focus 4

Worksheet 3 👀

INSTRUMENTS

Focus 4

In addition to focus 3, one large tuned with the notes C E G B plus a cymbal, two drums or large tambours and pieces of material to cover the skin of each drum

People of the Andes ( B33, 34)

*The drums of the Andes tend to have a very distinctive dull sound. The reason for this is that the animal drum skin is unshaven and the hairs dampen the sound. You can get the same effect by placing material over the skin of your drum.

Focus 5: Rhythm and pitch

When an Andean musician plays a new rhythm or note pattern to a group of players, they sit in a circle with their instruments and listen. If the other players like what they hear, they join in playing the same idea or a variation which they think is an improvement.

Listen to (B35). In-between the repeats of the song *(People of the Andes)* you will hear an instrumental section. The first instrument to begin improvises a short note pattern and then other instruments gradually join in by imitating the pattern or changing it in some way.

In-between repeats of the song improvise rhythm or note patterns to share with others:

- Organise the instruments and children into the same groups as for focuses 3 and 4. In addition give the children without instruments in group 1 an untuned percussion instrument to use in the instrumental section.
- Then sing and perform the song *People of the Andes* (worksheet 3).
- At the end of the song, the player of the dull drum rhythm should keep playing the steady beat.

- Over this beat one player from group 1 makes up a short rhythm plus (if using a tuned instrument with notes D E A B) a note pattern and repeats it continuously.
- Other players from group 1 listen and join in when they think they can play the rhythm or note pattern. Alternatively they can play a variation of the rhythm or note pattern (i.e. play anything that fits with the beat).
- When everyone in group 1 has joined in, the cymbal player gives a cue to sing the song again by playing four steady beats:

Cymbal:

    ♩   ♩   ♩   ♩

    1   **2**   **3**   **4**

- Choose another child in group 1 to lead (improvise a rhythm or note pattern) and choose other children to play the melody and accompaniment in group 2. Then repeat the activity.

RESOURCES

Focus 5

Worksheet 3

INSTRUMENTS

Focus 5

As for focuses 3 & 4 plus selection of light untuned percussion (i.e. claves, shakers etc.)

RESOURCES
Focus 6
Worksheet 4 👀

INSTRUMENTS
Focus 6
Several pairs of
tuned – one with
the notes C E G B
and the other
with the notes
D F♯ A (see
worksheet 4)

Focus 6: Melody

Panpipes are probably the best known instrument from South America. Most sets of panpipes are usually divided into two groups of notes, one group for each player. This means that the notes of a melody will be split between the two players as shown on worksheet 4. Playing a melody like this is known as **hocket** technique and both players need a great deal of skill and concentration in order to play their notes in the right place.

👂 Listen to and follow the melodies on worksheet 4 (💿 B36, 37) as they are played by panpipes in hocket. (NB. This will only be obvious if a stereo player is used, i.e. one set of notes will come out of the left speaker and the other set from the right).

🎵 As a class, sing the melodies on worksheet 4 in hocket:

- Choose two children to hocket one of the melodies on a pair of tuned instruments. The class slowly sings the complete melody to help the players keep in time.
- Then divide the class into two groups and ask the class to sing the complete melody in hocket, each group following one of the players.

🎵 In groups of 4 or 6 perform the melodies in hocket on instruments:

- Give each group a pair of tuned instruments or chime bar sets.
- Pairs of children in each group should take it in turns to practise playing the melodies in hocket with the rest of the group slowly singing the words.

Hocket Technique (B36, 37)

Panpipes are one type of instrument used to play melodies in hocket (dividing the notes between two players).

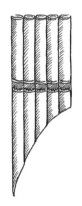 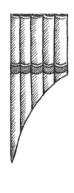

Play the melodies on this page in hocket:

- Player 1 will need these notes: C E G B

- Player 2 will need these notes: D F# A

- Both players should sing or chant all the words but only play the notes along their row.
- Each box equals one steady beat.

People of the Andes

Player 1	E		B						C	C			E	E			E	
(sing)	E		B		A		D		us-	ing	on-	ly	four	notes	try	to	make	
Player 2					A		D				D	D			F#	F#		

Cotopaxi

Player 1	E		B						E	B		B				
(sing)	Co-		to-		pax-		i		I	feel		your	tre-		mor	
Player 2					A		D						A		D	

E		G		B		G		E	G			E			
Warn-	ing	of	the	force	with-	in	you	soon	to		a-	wake			
	F#		A		A		F#				A				

NIGHT MUSIC

Year group 5–6

In this project two types of night music are created: spooky and tranquil. The stimulus for the night moods comes from Ravel's *Prelude to the Night* (*Prélude á la nuit* from *Rapsodie Espagnole*) which is played to the children after they have completed all the activities.

Focus 1: Timbre

As a class create a night time mood using words:

- Ask the children to think of words which describe sounds heard or things felt in the night.
- Say them in unusual and exaggerated voices (whispers, rolling 'Rs', squeaks, repeated consonants, suddenly loud, etc.). See examples on worksheet 1.

♪ Perform the night words with the accompaniment:

- Choose two words or phrases and ask a small group to whisper or chant them quietly as a repeating pattern accompaniment (ostinato). For example:

♩   ♩   ♫ ♩   (repeating)
dark sounds, sca-ry sounds

- While the accompaniment group chants, other children take it in turn to speak (or whisper, etc.) their words. Leave gaps between words.

Divide into groups of 4 –5 and compose night moods with words and instruments by following the instructions on worksheet 1. Each group will need to select several instruments.

♪ Perform the night mood compositions over a repeating chant accompaniment given by the rest of the class as shown above.

Listen to and discuss each performance:

> Did the group manage to create a night mood? If not, how could it be improved? (*For example, by playing more slowly or by leaving longer gaps between the sounds*).

Focus 2: Pitch and pulse

♪ Choose a group of 4 –5 children to play the night mood – spooky ostinati by following the instructions on worksheet 2.

Night Mood – words

In groups of 4–5 compose your own *Night Mood*:

- Each person in the group thinks up their own night word or chooses one from the list above and works out a way of saying it.
- Then, choose an instrument to go with the night word.
- Play your instrument **after** the word, for example:

speak:
scurrrrrrrrrying

play (guiro):
∧∧∧∧∧∧

or **with** the word, for example:

speak: dark .... 'k' ....'k' ....'k'

and play (drum):

- As a group, decide the order in which to play your night words.

Night Mood – spooky ostinato

Perform the spooky ostinato (repeating note pattern):

- Each player needs this set of notes:

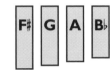

- Play the notes in this order to a steady beat:

- Take it in turns to play the ostinato still keeping a steady beat to make sure there are no gaps:

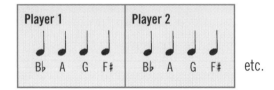

etc.

- Play the ostinato a number of times using a mixture of solos and playing together. For example:

All play together x4	Player 1 solo	Player 2 solo	All play together x4	Player 3 solo
B♭ A G F♯	B♭ A G F♯	B♭ A G F♯	B♭ A G F♯	B♭ A G F♯

etc.

Focus 3: Pitch – scale patterns

[dice/C icon] Choose pairs of children to improvise night mood - tranquil scale patterns by following the instructions on worksheet 3.

Focus 4: Form

[dice/C icon] Make a *Night Music* piece combining all three night moods:

- As a class, decide an order for the three types of night mood - words, spooky ostinato and tranquil scale patterns.
- The night moods can be repeated and played together to make a longer piece of music as shown on worksheet 4.
- With suggestions from the children, use pictures or symbols to make a graphic score (see worksheet 4).

[note icon] Perform the *Night Music*:

- Choose one or more groups of 4-5 children to perform the night mood – words section and another group for the spooky ostinato. Choose one or two pairs to perform the tranquil scale patterns.

- Choose a conductor to direct the performance, using signals to show when each group begins and ends.
- Make a tape recording of the *Night Music* piece to play back for the listening activity in focus 5.

Focus 5: Mood and character

[ear icon] Listen to the short extract from Ravel's *Prelude to the Night* ([CD icon] B38) and answer the following:

> How is the night mood created?
> (Answer: By quiet sounds and use of ostinato - repeating note pattern).
> What is played all the way through the first section?
> (Answer: The spooky ostinato from focus 2).
> What happens towards the end of this extract?
> (Answer: The ostinato stops and two instruments play scale patterns on their own)

Listen to the tape recording of the class's own *Night Music* piece and compare it with Ravel's.

RESOURCES

Focus 3
Worksheet 3 [icon]
Focus 4
Worksheets 1–4 [icon]
Focus 5
None

INSTRUMENTS
Focus 3
Pair of tuned instruments (e.g. two glockenspiels, two recorders etc.)
Focus 4
A selection of untuned, 4–5 tuned percussion with the notes F# G A B♭, pairs of glockenspiels, recorders etc.
Focus 5
None

Night Mood – tranquil scale patterns

Make up tranquil scale patterns in pairs:

- Play a scale pattern by playing notes in order, going from low to high then high to low.
- As you play your scale pattern try to capture the mood of a tranquil (peaceful and relaxing) night time scene. Don't play too loudly or quickly.

- To play as a pair sit in the positions shown below:

Player 1   Player 2

- Player 1 leads and player 2 copies the shape of the up and down scale pattern but starting on a different note. For example:

Player 1:

Player 2:

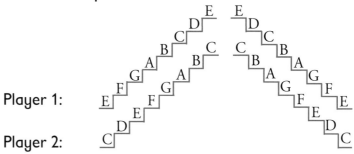

- Now try repeating some of the notes or making them longer. For example:

Player 1:

Player 2:

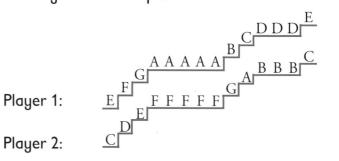

Night Music – form

This graphic score shows how the night music words, spooky ostinato and tranquil scale patterns can be put together. Each type of night music can be repeated several times within each section.

| Section A | Section B | Section C | Section B | Section C | Section A |

PAN GU – CREATION STORY

Year group: 5–6

In this creation story from China, Pan Gu is born from an egg and brings life to the world. In his efforts to separate the earth from the sky he dies; his breath becomes the wind and clouds, his blood becomes the seas, his hair becomes the trees and his eyes become the sun and moon. The children tell the story in mime and movement and from this develop musical ideas.

Focus 1: Timbre – instrumental sounds

♫ Sing the song *Pan Gu* on worksheet 2 (🎵 B39, 40).

♫ Accompany the song with untuned percussion:

- Choose 2 children to play for each verse. Select a different type of instrument for each verse (e.g. **verse 1** – metal, **verse 2** – skin, **verse 3** – wood, verse 4 – shakers and scrapers).
- The children play these word rhythms from the song as ostinati (repeating patterns) throughout the first four lines of each verse:

Verse 1
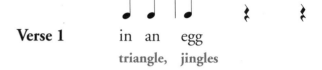
in an egg
triangle, jingles

Verse 2

deep, deep sleep
tambour, drum

Verse 3

he could do no more
woodblock, wooden agogo

Verse 4

wind and clouds
guiro, maracas

Pan Gu – music (🔊 B39, 40)

Pan Gu – words (🅑 B39, 40)

Introduction:

No birds, no bees, no sun, no breeze,
No hills, no trees, no light, no seas.

Verse 1:

Pan Gu slept for a long, long time
In an egg, dreaming of the light.
Pan Gu waited as the years went by
In his egg: all he knew was night.
   Pan Gu!
What are you waiting for?
   Pan Gu!
It's time to break the door
And let the world take flight.

Verse 3:

Pan Gu stopped when his job was done
And the land was miles from the sky.
Pan Gu knew he could do no more,
Then he fell, knowing he would die.
   Pan Gu!
Now you have done your task.
   Pan Gu!
What more could anyone ask?
It's time to say good-bye!

Verse 2:

Pan Gu woke from his deep, deep sleep
In his egg and couldn't see the light.
Pan Gu shouted but no one heard
In his egg, so he began to fight.
   Pan Gu!
It's time to break the shell!
   Pan Gu!
It's time to leave your cell
And let the world take flight!

Pan Gu pushed with all his heart!
Pan Gu pushed the world apart!

Verse 4:

Pan Gu's breath gave us wind and clouds
And his blood flowed into the seas.
Pan Gu died, but he gave us life
And his hair grew into the trees.
   Pan Gu!
He died for everyone.
   Pan Gu!
His eyes became the sun
That shines upon the breeze.

Coda:

Stars and gold and hills and streams
Started with old Pan Gu's dreams.

Focus 2: Links with movement

♪ As a class tell the story in words and mime:

- **Verse 1** Pan Gu is sleeping inside the egg: a small group of children make a dome shape with their bodies to represent the egg. Pan Gu is curled up asleep inside.
- **Verse 2** Pan Gu wakes and pushes his way out of the shell, parting the land and sky: as the egg cracks little by little the dome disintegrates and Pan Gu shows the struggle by pushing his way out in different directions.
- **Verses 3-4** Pan Gu's body gives life to the earth and brings light to the world with the Sun and Moon: other children imitating creatures and plants come to life one at a time as Pan Gu touches them. At the same time, two children hold an imaginary sun and moon and place them high up over their heads on either side of the performance area.
- **Verse 4 and coda** Pan Gu dies: he runs around looking at his work, getting gradually slower and more exhausted before he curls up and dies.

RESOURCES
Focus 2
Worksheet 1
(optional)
Worksheet 2

INSTRUMENTS
Focus 2
None

RESOURCES
Focus 3
Worksheet 3 👓
per group of 4-5

INSTRUMENTS
Focus 3
One tuned per
group of 4-5

Focus 3: Melody and accompaniment

🎲 Compose a lullaby to show Pan Gu sleeping (see the example on worksheet 3):

> What sort of sounds would you play when Pan Gu is sleeping? (*Answer: gentle, quiet, long and smooth*).
> What is the name for songs which are to do with sleeping? (*Answer: lullabies*).
> What type of note pattern and rhythm would you use to accompany a lullaby? (*Answer: a rocking pattern to a slow, steady beat*).

- Choose a pair of children to demonstrate the following, playing one tuned instrument using the notes of the pentatonic scale C D E G A: One player plays a two note rocking pattern accompaniment. Over this the other player improvises a lullaby melody using a word rhythm played on 3 or 4 notes.
- In groups of 4 –5 with one tuned instrument per group, the children take it in turns to improvise lullabies in pairs.

🎵 Choose several lullabies from each group to perform.

👂 Listen to and discuss each performance:

> Did the lullaby sound peaceful?
> If not, why not? For example, was it too loud or too fast?
> Did the player of the rocking pattern keep a steady beat?

Pan Gu – Lullaby and Waking music

Compose a lullaby to show Pan Gu sleeping:

- Take off the Fs and Bs leaving the notes of a pentatonic scale (C D E G A). This scale is a common feature of Chinese music:

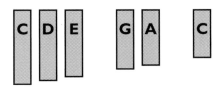

- Player 1 plays a steady beat rocking pattern. For example, alternating C and E. Player 2 improvises a melody over the rocking pattern using a word rhythm. For example, *softly sleeping*:

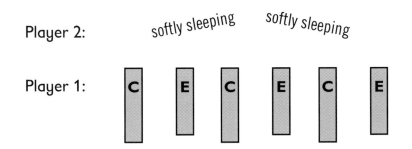

Compose waking music for Pan Gu, using sounds that get louder and quieter:

- Follow the conductor's arm movements to get louder and quieter. The term for getting louder is **crescendo,** for getting quieter **diminuendo**:

- In this example the conductor directs the instruments to play separately then altogether for one last crescendo:

RESOURCES
Focus 4
Worksheet 3 👓
Focus 5
Worksheet 4 👓

INSTRUMENTS
Focuses 4 & 5
A selection of
untuned

Focus 4: Dynamics

🎲 Compose music to show Pan Gu waking up:

> How could you use loud and quiet to show Pan Gu gradually waking up? (*Answer: It could start quietly and gradually get louder*).

- Give an untuned percussion instrument for each pair of children to share. They should take it in turns to play.
- Explain the terms and symbols which indicate getting louder/quieter on worksheet 3.
- Choose a conductor to indicate which instruments play using a start/stop signal and when to get louder/quieter using arm movements. For example see the suggestions on worksheet 3.
- Responding to the conductor's directions, the children play sounds to create the feeling of waking.

Focus 5: Rhythm and timbre

🎲 Compose a sequence of sounds to show Pan Gu pushing his way out of the shell:

> What sort of sounds does a chick make when it pecks its way out of a shell? (*Answer: groups of short, sharp, tapping sounds*).

- Choose a small group to demonstrate. Ask each player to select an untuned percussion instrument which can make short sharp sounds.
- Choose one player in the group to be the leader. The leader improvises short pecking rhythms which are echoed by the other players in turn (see worksheet 4).
- Repeat the above activity in groups of 4-5 with a selection of untuned instruments per group.

🎵 Perform the sequences.

👂 Listen to and discuss each performance:

> Were the instruments suitable for pecking sounds? Could the playing of the instruments be improved to make the pecking sounds more effective? (*For example, by hitting the instrument in a different place or making the sounds shorter*).

Getting out of the Shell

Compose music for getting out of a shell:

- Select untuned percussion instruments which make short sharp sounds. For example:

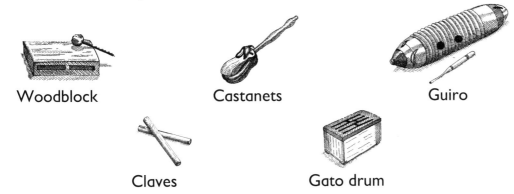

Woodblock   Castanets   Guiro

Claves   Gato drum

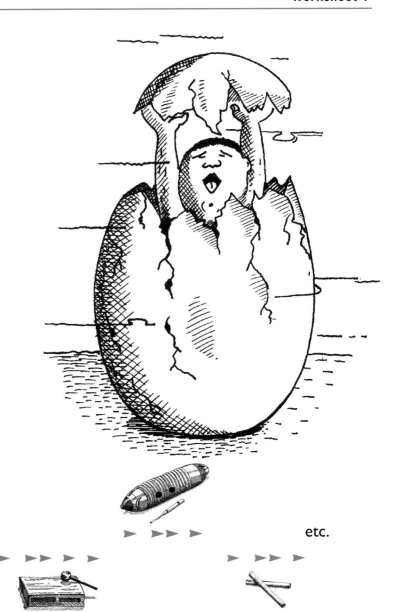

- Choose a leader to improvise short pecking rhythms which the other players echo.
- Work out an order for the echo instruments to play, sometimes separately, sometimes together.
- The leader's rhythms become more frantic as Pan Gu makes his way out of the egg. For example:

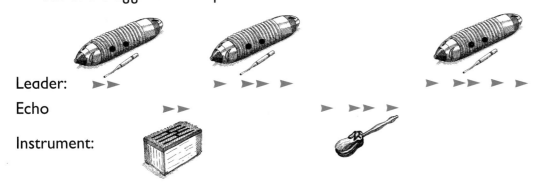

Leader: ►►   ► ► ►   ► ►► ► ►   ► ►► ►   etc.

Echo

Instrument:

RESOURCES
Focus 6
Worksheet 5

INSTRUMENTS
Focus 6
One tuned per
group of 4–5

Focus 6: Pitch

Compose note patterns which show creatures or plants coming to life (see the examples on worksheet 5):

- Demonstrate a growing shape on a tuned instrument by playing every note from low to high in a variety of ways. For example, playing slowly or quickly, using a rhythm and repeating notes or groups of notes.

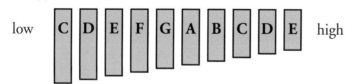

low   C D E F G A B C D E   high

- In groups of 4–5 with one tuned instrument per group, the children take it in turns to improvise growing music playing from low to high.

Choose individual children to perform their growing music.

Listen to and discuss each performance:

What sort of creatures or plants did the music make you think of?
How did the music show them coming to life?
(For example, by growing slowly and then faster?)

Compose a growing piece using several of the children's compositions:

- Choose a conductor and one child from each group to play.
- The conductor directs individual players to stop and start. Each player repeats their growing music until signalled to stop.

Growing Music – ideas for plants and creatures coming to life

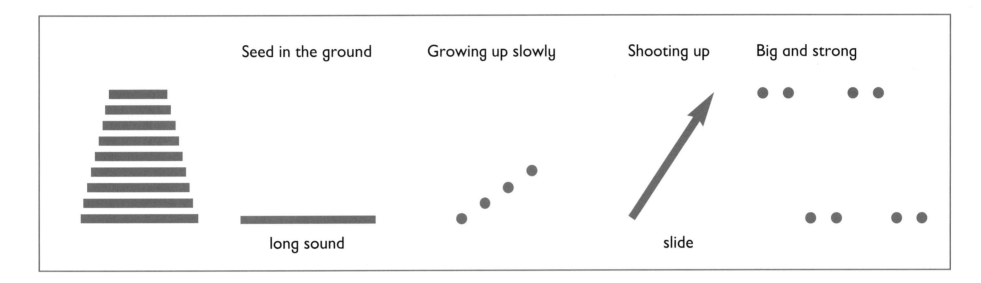

Seed in the ground   Growing up slowly   Shooting up   Big and strong

long sound

slide

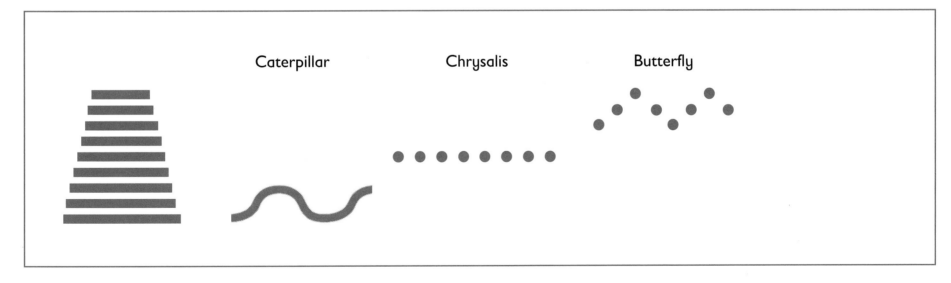

Caterpillar   Chrysalis   Butterfly

RESOURCES
Focus 7
None
Focus 8
Worksheets
1–5

INSTRUMENTS
Focus 7
One tuned per
group of 4–5
Focus 8
A selection of
tuned and
untuned

Focus 7: Melody and accompaniment

Compose laments for Pan Gu's death:

- Choose a pair of children to demonstrate on one tuned instrument using the pentatonic scale:

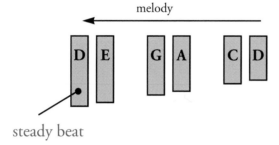

melody

steady beat

One player plays a slow steady beat accompaniment on the low note D. Over this the other player improvises a sad slow melody which starts high and ends low.

- In groups of 4–5 with one tuned instrument per group, the children take it in turns to improvise laments in pairs.

Perform one lament from each group.

Listen to and discuss each performance:

Did the lament sound sad?
If not, why not? For example, was it too fast or was the rhythm of the melody too busy?

Focus 8: Form

Tell the story of Pan Gu with words, music and mime:

- Choose groups or pairs of players to accompany the song and to perform the music for each section of the story.
- Choose other children to provide the mime.
- Sing the song at the beginning and end of the story.

TROIKA

Year group 5–6

The words of the song *On the Ski Slope* are set to an arrangement of Prokofiev's *Troika* (from *Lieutenant Kije*) originally written for orchestra. The *Troika* (meaning three-horse sleigh) depicts a fast sleigh ride in the snow. Similarly the song uses images of snow and ice, but from the point of view of someone learning to ski.

Focus 1: Form

♩ Sing the song *On the Ski Slope* on worksheet 2 (🔊 B41, 42). Make sure the children know which sections of the song are called introduction, chorus, verse and rap before attempting the following listening activity.

👂 Listen to the orchestral recording of Prokofiev's *Troika* (🔊 B43):

> Can you recognise the chorus, verse and rap music of the song in the *Troika* ?

● Play (🔊 B43) again and ask the children to follow the sections of the ***Troika* Form** (A, B, etc.) given on worksheet 2. Each section is linked to either the chorus, verse or rap melodies (apart from section D which is not used in the song).

> Given that the music is depicting a sleigh ride why do you think the composer uses the 'car horn' and rushing violin effects indicated in several sections of the chart?
> (*Answer: To give the impression of a fast hair-raising journey*).
> What other instruments in the music help give the feel of a sleigh ride?
> (*Answer: Percussion – jingle bells*).

GAMES

Add a Beat

One to Eight

RESOURCES

Focus 1

Worksheet 1 👀 (optional)

Worksheet 2 👀

On the Ski Slope: Troika – music (B41, 42)

© Copyright 1936 by Hawkes & Son (London) Ltd. This arrangement © Copyright 1996 by Hawkes & Son (London) Ltd.
Reproduced by permission of Boosey & Hawkes Music Publishers Ltd.

On the Ski Slope – words and *Troika* form (⊚ B41, 42, 43)

Introduction (instrumental)

Chorus:

Just go out on the ski slope looking cool,
Designer togs say I'm no fool.
Over moguls, ski jumps, down the black ice run,
Look out folks, danger here I come.

Verse 1:

My legs, one going left and one going right,
I bend zee knees, and try to straighten skis, – but I've lost
the fight.

Rap:

Now there's no need to despair, I'll just get back upon
the lift,
'Cos with practice on the snow one day I'll soon be
skiing swift.

Chorus:

Verse 2:

Somehow I've got on to the ski jumping track,
I think, in flight, I'm really much too young - for a
heart attack.

Rap:

Chorus:

Verse 3:

I am magnetic'lly attracted to trees,
They say, it's all, because I like to drink - many
'Jaeger'* teas.

Rap:

Chorus:

Coda:

Over moguls, ski jumps, down the black ice run,
Look out folks, danger here I come.

*Alpine alcoholic drink (Yager – 'a' as in 'say').

Troika Form

This chart shows how the song relates to the **form** of Troika. **Form** is the series of contrasting sections which make up a piece of music. Sections which use the same tune and/or instruments are given the same letter name.

Troika sections	A	A	B	C	A	B	D	A	B	C	D	A
Song sections	Introduction	Chorus	Verse	Rap	Chorus	Verse	(not used in the song)	Chorus	Verse	Rap	(not used in the song)	Chorus
Troika instrumental effects							Saxophone solo	Violins rushing up down quickly	'Car horn' effect		Saxophone solo	Violins rushing up down quickly

RESOURCES
Focus 2
Worksheet 3 👓
plus
Worksheet 4 ✏
per group of 4-5

INSTRUMENTS
Focus 2
Bells, tambourine,
triangle and
glockenspiel

Focus 2: Rhythm

👂 Listen to 💿 B44 and look at the three rhythms on worksheet 3 played separately, then together. These rhythms, repeated over and over again, are used to provide the jingle and jangle sleigh ride accompaniment in section A of the *Troika* and chorus of *On the Ski Slope*. Repeating rhythms and note patterns are called **riffs** or **ostinati**.

🎵 As a class, practise clapping the number rhythms on worksheet 3:

- Chant the numbers slowly and clap each rhythm several times without pause. Give a count-in of 7-8 to start everyone together.
- Slightly accent (clap louder) the numbers with thicker circles.
- Next, try to clap the rhythms at a faster tempo (speed).
- Clap the three rhythms together by dividing the class into three groups. Group 1 claps the bell and tambourine rhythm, group 2 the triangle rhythm and group 3 the violin rhythm.

🎵 Choose one player from each group to perform the rhythms using the instruments suggested on worksheet 3. Use a glockenspiel to play the D and A violin part.

🎲 In groups of 4-5 compose 'sleigh ride/skiing' accompaniment rhythms following the instructions on worksheet 4.

🎵 Practise clapping the rhythms following the instructions on worksheet 4, then clap them to the class.

Troika – accompaniment rhythms ( B44)

In the accompaniment for section A of the *Troika* and chorus of the song, the three rhythms below are repeated over and over again. Repeating rhythms and note patterns are called **riffs** or **ostinati.**

Perform the number rhythms:

- To a steady beat chant the numbers 1–8 quietly.
- Clap only on circled numbers.
- Slightly accent (clap louder) numbers with thicker circles.

Jingle bells Tambourine	① 2 ③ 4 ⑤ 6 ⑦ 8
Triangle	1 ② 3 ④ 5 ⑥ ⑦ ⑧
Violins (use glockenspiel)	C G C G C G C G ① ② ③ ④ ⑤ ⑥ ⑦ ⑧

Sleigh Ride / Skiing accompaniments

Compose 'sleigh ride/skiing' accompaniment rhythms:

- Each player in the group composes a rhythm by clapping on one or more numbers over a steady count of eight.
- Write the rhythm down by circling the numbers.

Player 1							
1	2	3	4	5	6	7	8
Player 2							
1	2	3	4	5	6	7	8
Player 3							
1	2	3	4	5	6	7	8
Player 4							
1	2	3	4	5	6	7	8
Player 5							
1	2	3	4	5	6	7	8

Perform the accompaniment rhythms:

- Practise clapping your own rhythm as a riff by repeating it over and over without pause:
- Next, practise clapping all the riffs together. One player gives a count-in of 7-8 and chants the repeating count of eight throughout.
- Which instruments in your class do you think make wintry type sounds?
- Which instruments will you use to play your rhythms?

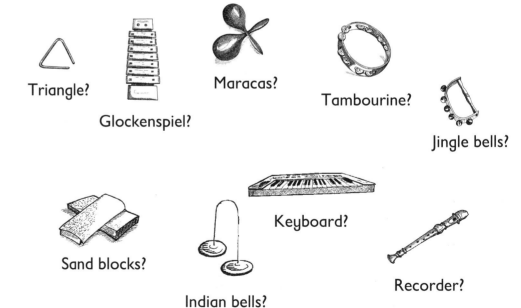

Triangle? Glockenspiel? Maracas? Tambourine? Jingle bells?

Sand blocks? Indian bells? Keyboard? Recorder?

Focus 3: Timbre – instrumental sounds

👂 Ask the class to sort wintry type sounds from your selection of instruments:

- Choose several children to demonstrate and explore the sound quality (timbre) of each instrument.
- Place the instruments chosen in a performance area (e.g. in a space at the front of the class).

🎵 Transfer the sleigh ride/skiing accompaniment rhythms composed on worksheet 4 onto instruments:

- Choose one of the groups to perform their accompaniment rhythms using the instruments in the performance area.
- Players with tuned instruments play their rhythms using notes C and G and repeat them in any order. For example:

C   C   G   C   C   G
①   ②   ③   4   ⑤   ⑥   ⑦   8

- Sing the song with one group playing their accompaniment rhythms as riffs on instruments throughout the chorus.

Focus 4: Dynamics

🎵 Using the accompaniment rhythms composed on worksheet 4, create the impression of a skier or sleigh coming closer and then going past into the distance:

- Each group practises clapping their rhythms by gradually getting louder and then quieter. To do this repeat the rhythms quite a few times.
- In turn, the groups transfer this onto instruments selected from the performance area (see focus 3). Allow each group a short period of rehearsal before they perform to the class.
- While one group is rehearsing on the instruments, other groups continue to practise clapping their accompaniments.

👂 Listen to and discuss each performance:

Did the piece capture the atmosphere of the skier or sleigh ride going by? *Discuss the choice of instruments, rhythms used, tempo (speed) and dynamics (loud and quiet).*
Did the group manage to keep the same speed (tempo) throughout? Did all the instruments balance? Were some too loud?

RESOURCES
Focuses 3 & 4
Worksheets 2 & 3
👓 plus completed
Worksheet 4 ✎

INSTRUMENTS
Focuses 3 & 4
A selection of tuned and untuned including wintry weather sounding instruments plus the bells, tambourine, triangle and glockenspiel from focus 2

Glossary of musical terms

Accent	an individual sound which is emphasised (made louder than other neighbouring sounds)
Accompaniment	background layer of sound supporting the main part of the music
Antiphonal	music for two or more alternating groups
Bar	a grouping of beats shown by bar lines in staff notation
Beat	the underlying pulse
Binary	a two part form in which the second section is different from the first; the first section is usually labelled A and the second section B
Chord	two or more notes sounding together
Chord sequence	a series of chords played in order, one after another
Cue	an aural or visual start to a section of music
Drone	continuous or repeated note/s often used to accompany a melody
Duration	the length of sounds or the length of time between sounds
Dynamics	levels of volume (loud/quiet)
Elements	the fundamental components of music (e.g. pitch, rhythm, etc.)
Flat	a musical symbol (♭) showing the lowering of pitch in relation to a letter name, e.g. B♭ is lower in pitch than B
Form	how the sections of a piece of music are ordered
Graphic notation	an approximate way of writing down music using dots, lines and other symbols
Improvising	creating music by performing 'on the spot'
Melody	a succession of notes sung or played often forming a phrase
Metre	groupings of steady beats; the first of each group is often accented; the most common metres are beat groupings of 2, 3 and 4
Mood and character	the 'feel' of a piece of music, achieved through such elements as dynamics, timbre, texture, tempo, etc.
Ostinato	a rhythm or note pattern which is repeated over and over (riff has the same meaning)
Pentatonic scale	a selection of five different notes or letter names (e.g. CDEGA)
Phrase	the divisions within a section of music analogous to the groupings of words made by commas or full stops

Pitch	high or low sounds heard in relation to each other
Pulse	steady beat
Rhythm	the sequencing of long and short sounds/durations (e.g. pattern)
Rest	a silent beat
Riff	a rhythm or note pattern which is repeated over and over (ostinato has the same meaning)
Rondo	a form in which a recurring section is alternated with contrasting sections. The recurring section is usually labelled A and the contrasting sections B, C, D, etc. For example: A B A C A D A
Round	the same tune is sung or played by two or more groups starting one after the other (e.g. *Frère Jacques*)
Scale	a succession of adjacent notes going higher or lower
Score	a written record of a piece of music
Sharp	a musical symbol (♯) showing the raising of pitch in relation to a letter name, e.g. F♯ is higher in pitch than F
Structure	the different ways sounds are organised often involving repetition and contrast
Sustained	held sound
Ternary	a three part form in which the third section is a repeat of the first. The first and third sections are usually labelled A and the contrasting second section B, i.e. A B A
Tempo	speed (fast/slow)
Texture	sounds in one or more layers
Timbre	quality of sound (the differences in tone colour, e.g. instruments made from different materials usually produce different timbres)
Tremolo	rapid repetition of the same sound or note
Trill	rapid alternation of two different notes
Tuned instrument	one which can play precise note patterns, e.g. xylophones, recorders
Untuned instrument	one which cannot play precise note patterns, e.g. wooden agogo, claves, drum
Variation	an altered version of a musical idea

Glossary of musical instruments (N.B. Illustrations are not drawn to scale)

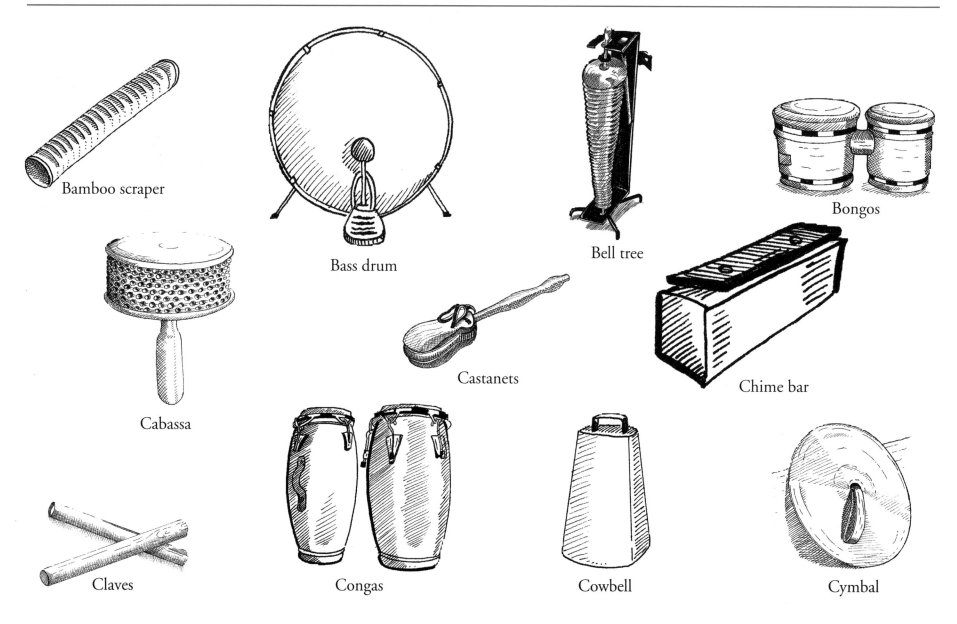

Bamboo scraper

Bass drum

Bell tree

Bongos

Cabassa

Castanets

Chime bar

Claves

Congas

Cowbell

Cymbal

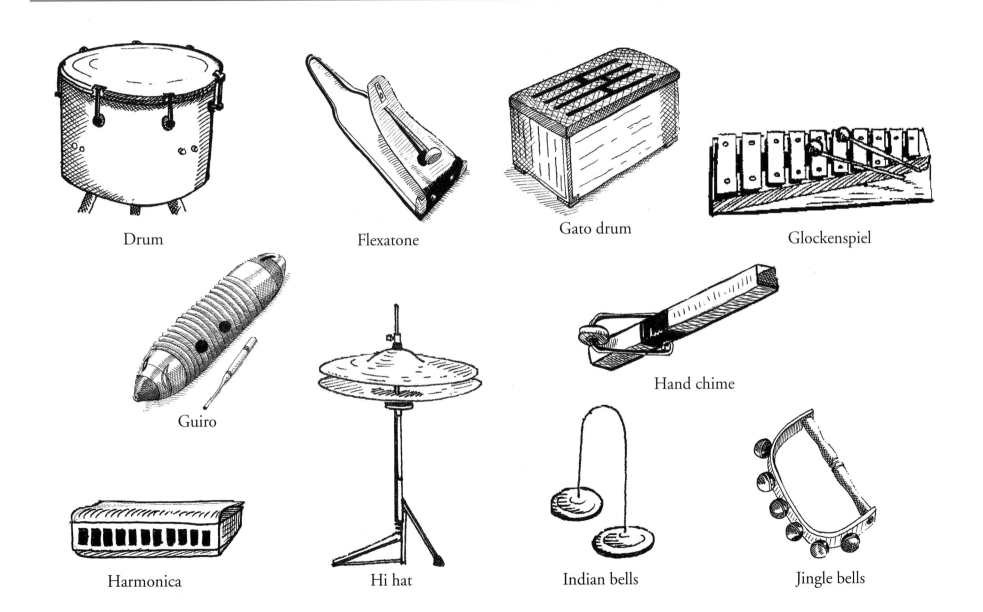

Drum

Flexatone

Gato drum

Glockenspiel

Guiro

Hi hat

Hand chime

Harmonica

Indian bells

Jingle bells

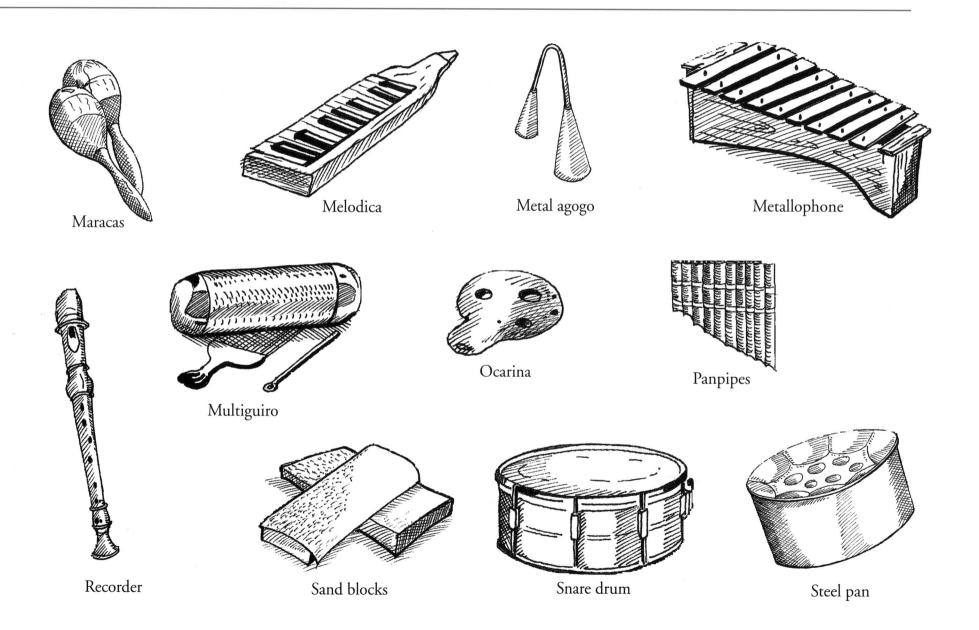

Maracas

Melodica

Metal agogo

Metallophone

Recorder

Multiguiro

Ocarina

Panpipes

Sand blocks

Snare drum

Steel pan

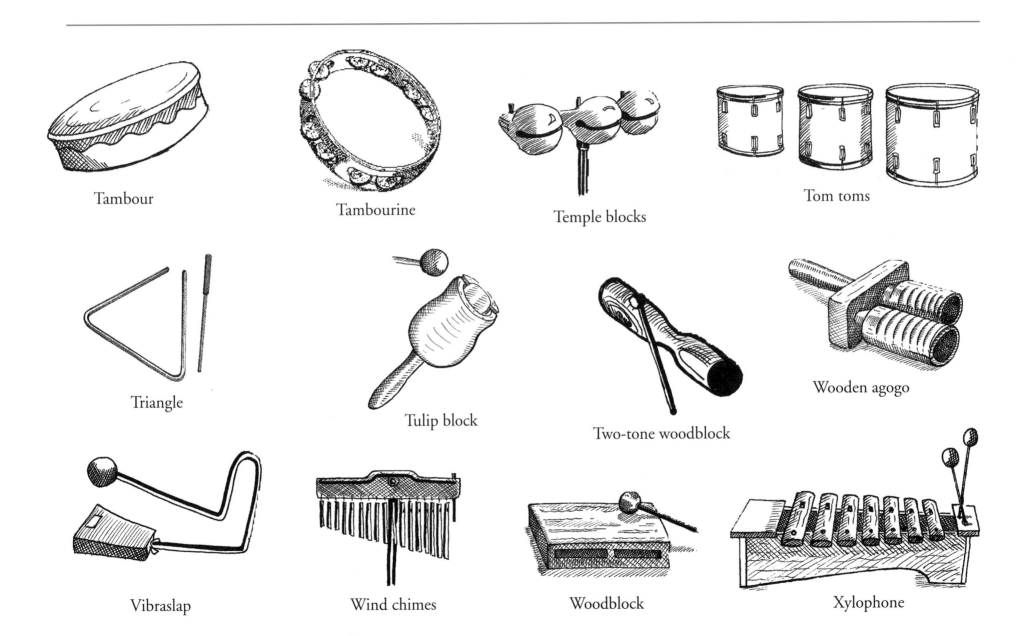

Tambour

Tambourine

Temple blocks

Tom toms

Triangle

Tulip block

Two-tone woodblock

Wooden agogo

Vibraslap

Wind chimes

Woodblock

Xylophone

Music in the National Curriculum

Programme of Study

The Programme of Study for music in the National Curriculum in England comprises a framework of activities for **Performing and Composing, Listening and Appraising** (abbreviated here for the purpose of the book):

Performing and Composing

- **a** Controlling sounds
- **b** Performing
- **c** Composing, exploring & improvising
- **d** Communicating & recording

Listening and Appraising

- **e** Developing understanding
- **f** Responding & evaluating

The National Curriculum states:

*Pupils' understanding and enjoyment of music should be developed through activities that bring together requirements from both **Performing and Composing** and **Listening and Appraising** wherever possible.*

Key Stages 1 and 2 of the *National Curriculum for Music*
(January 1995)

Music Connections meets this requirement by constantly intertwining performing, composing, listening and appraising activities to provide a balanced approach for teaching music. The National Curriculum Cross Reference Tables on pages 293-300 show the **main emphasis** of activity for each part of the book.

Musical elements

The National Curriculum highlights the following musical elements which are used as focuses throughout **Music Connections**:

Elements	KSI	KS2
a Pitch	High/low	Gradations of pitch *e.g. sliding up/down, moving by step/leap; names for pitch such as C, G, doh, soh*
b Duration	Long/short; pulse or beat; rhythm	Groups of beats, *e.g. 2s, 3s, 4s, 5s; rhythm*
c Dynamics	Loud/quiet/ silence	Different levels of volume; accent
d Tempo	Fast/slow	Different speeds, *e.g. lively/calm, slower/faster than*
e Timbre	Quality of sound, *e.g. tinkling, rattling, smooth, ringing*	Different qualities, *e.g. harsh, mellow, hollow, bright*
f Texture	Several sounds played or sung at the same time /one sound on its own	Different ways sounds are put together, *e.g. rhythm on rhythm; melody and accompaniment; parts that weave; blocks of sound, chords*

and the use of the above within

g Structure	Different sections e.g. beginning, middle, end; repetition, *e.g. repeated patterns, melody, rhythm*	Different ways sounds are organised in simple forms, *e.g. question and answer; round; phrase; repetition; ostinato (a musical pattern that is repeated many times); melody*

The National Curriculum Cross Reference Tables on pages 293-300 identify the focus of musical elements for each part of the book.

Planning schemes of work

Plan a scheme of work for several weeks by selecting material from **Games**, **Basics** and **Projects**:

- Use one or more of the following tables or indexes to find material which relates to specific musical elements and ties in with the class topic or theme:

  National Curriculum Cross Reference Tables, pp. 293-300
  Focus Index, p. 301
  Topic Index, pp. 302-303

- Remember that in general one or two focuses last one lesson (apart from those in the **Games** which are shorter warm-up activities).

- As an example, you may decide to adopt one or other of the following approaches:

  1. Spend the majority of time on a **Project**, using the **Games** and **Basics** to reinforce skills related to specific musical elements.
  2. Use one section of the **Basics** (e.g. the whole of **Words**) as a progressive course of study interspersed with games and additional singing or listening material.

- To complete the sheet – **Scheme of work for music** (page 292) – copy the corresponding information for the selected **Games**, **Basics** and **Projects** from the National Curriculum Cross Reference Tables on pages 293-300.

- Additional material (for example, songs or recordings) can be shown along the fourth row.
- If required, in other boxes write:
  1. The general topic or theme for the scheme.
  2. The main musical element that is to be developed.

Over a year a balanced programme may be achieved by thinking in blocks:

Block type A – vocal work, songs and basic skill development taken from **Games** and **Basics**.
Block type B – a greater emphasis on instrumental and group creativity involving longer term projects (taken from **Basics** and **Projects**).

For example:

Autumn term 1st half – **Block type A**
Autumn term 2nd half – **Block type B**
Spring term 1st half – **Block type A**
Spring term 2nd half – **Block type B**
Summer term 1st half – **Block type B**
Summer term 2nd half – **Block type A**

Scheme of work for music

Class:	Key Stage:	Year Group:	Term:

General class topic or theme:	The Main musical element to be developed:

	Main emphasis of activity Performing & Composing / Listening & Appraising					

Material	Focuses: musical elements	a	b	c	d	e	f
GAMES							
BASICS							
PROJECTS							
Additional material							

a Controlling sounds, **b** Performing, **c** Composing, exploring & improvising, **d** Communicating & recording, **e** Developing understanding, **f** Responding & evaluating.

National Curriculum cross reference tables

GAMES I (starters)	Key Stage	Focuses: musical elements	Main emphasis of activity Performing & Composing / Listening & Appraising					
			a	b	c	d	e	f
Copy Me (p.2)	1 – 2	Timbre	●	●	●			
High or Low (p.3)	1 – 2 2	1. Pitch 2. Pitch and timbre	●				●	
Join In (p.4)	1 – 2 1 – 2 1 – 2	1. Timbre 2. Dynamics 3. Rhythm	●	●	●			
Keep Fit (p.5)	1 1 1	1. Pulse and timbre – body sounds 2. Pulse and timbre – instrumental sounds 3. Pulse and pitch	●	●				
Left and Right (p.7)	1 – 2 1 – 2 1 – 2 1 – 2	1. Pitch – up and down 2. Pitch – scales 3. Pitch – high and low 4. Pitch – scales	●	●			●	
Name Game (p.9)	1 – 2 1 – 2	1. Pulse 2. Pitch and dynamics	●	●	●			
Plug the Gap (p.10)	1 – 2 1 – 2 2 2	1. Pulse and rhythm 2. Timbre – vocal and body sounds 3. Timbre – instrumental sounds 4. Pitch	●	●	●			
Shadowing (p.12)	1	Tempo and dynamics	●	●	●	●		
Stop / Start (p.13)	1 – 2 1 – 2	1. Sound and silence 2. Structure	●	●	●		●	

a Controlling sounds, **b** Performing, **c** Composing, exploring & improvising, **d** Communicating & recording, **e** Developing understanding, **f** Responding & evaluating.

GAMES II (more demanding)	Key Stage	Focuses: musical elements	**Main emphasis of activity** Performing & Composing / Listening & Appraising					
			a	**b**	**c**	**d**	**e**	**f**
Action Conducting (p.14)	1 – 2 1 – 2	1. Texture – body sounds in layers 2. Texture – instrumental sounds in layers	●	●	●	●		
Add a Beat (p.15)	1 – 2 2 2	1. Metre 2. Timbre – body sounds 3. Timbre – instrumental sounds	●	●				
Add a Sound (p.16)	1 – 2 2	1. Pitch and timbre 2. Melody	●	●	●			
Card Signals (p.17)	1 – 2 1 – 2	1. Rhythm 2. Texture – body sounds in layers	●	●				
Change a Sound (p.19)	1 – 2 2	1. Pitch and timbre 2. Melody	●	●	●			●
Clock Gone Wrong! (p.20)	1 – 2 2	1. Pulse and metre 2. Texture – sounds in layers	●	●			●	
Conversations (p.21)	1 – 2 2	1. Mood and character 2. Melody and accompaniment	●	●	●			●
Eights (p.23)	1 – 2	Pulse and metre	●	●			●	
Favourites (p.24)	1 – 2 1 – 2	1. Structure – question and answer 2. Melody	●	●	●		●	●
Mexican Wave (p.25)	1 – 2 1 – 2	1. Timbre and links with movement 2. Timbre and links with movement	●	●				
One Step Behind (p.26)	1 – 2 1 – 2 2	1. Timbre 2. Rhythm and timbre 3. Rhythm	●	●	●			

a Controlling sounds, **b** Performing, **c** Composing, exploring & improvising, **d** Communicating & recording, **e** Developing understanding, **f** Responding & evaluating.

			Main emphasis of activity Performing & Composing / Listening & Appraising					
GAMES II (continued)	Key Stage	Focuses: musical elements	a	b	c	d	e	f
One to Eight (p.27)	2 2	1. Pulse and timbre – vocal and body sounds 2. Pulse and timbre – instrumental sounds	●	●	●		●	
Pass a Sound (p.28)	1 – 2 1 – 2 2	1. Timbre 2. Pulse 3. Texture – sounds in layers	●	●				
Round and Round (p.29)	1 – 2 2	1. Rhythm and timbre – body sounds 2. Rhythm and timbre – instrumental sounds	●	●				
Stand Up/Sit Down (p.30)	1 – 2 1 – 2 1 – 2 2	1. Pitch 2. Dynamics 3. Pulse and tempo 4. Pitch	●	●	●		●	
BASICS								
SORTING AND MATCHING								
Matching Sounds (p.33)	1 – 2 1 – 2 1 – 2	1. Timbre 2. Dynamics 3. Tempo	●	●			●	
Mirroring with Movement (p.34)	1 – 2 1 – 2	1. Duration – long and short 2. Pitch	●	●			●	
Sorting Sounds 1 (p.35)	1	Timbre	●	●			●	
Sorting Sounds 2 (p.36)	2	Duration – long and short	●	●			●	
Sorting and Sets (p.37)	2	Timbre and pitch	●	●		●	●	
Frameworks (p.38)	2	Contrast and form	●	●	●	●	●	●

a Controlling sounds, **b** Performing, **c** Composing, exploring & improvising, **d** Communicating & recording, **e** Developing understanding, **f** Responding & evaluating.

			Main emphasis of activity Performing & Composing / Listening & Appraising					
BASICS (continued)	Key Stage	Focuses: musical elements	**a**	**b**	**c**	**d**	**e**	**f**
WORDS								
Words (p.42)	1	Pulse and rhythm	●	●	●		●	
Words in Sequence 1 (p.44)	1	Structure	●	●	●	●	●	
Lyrics and Loudness (p.47)	1 – 2	Dynamics	●	●	●		●	
Words in Sequence 2 (p.50)	2	Structure	●	●	●	●	●	
Words in Layers 2 (p.52)	2	Texture	●	●	●		●	
Questions and Answers (p.55)	2	Structure	●	●	●	●		●
NUMBERS								
Numbers 1 (p.58)	1	Pulse and rhythm	●	●	●		●	
Numbers in Layers 1 (p.59)	1	Texture	●	●	●			
Numbers 2 (p.60)	2	Pulse and rhythm	●	●	●	●	●	
Numbers in Layers 2 (p.64)	2	Texture	●	●	●	●		●
Numbers and Words (p.66)	2	Rhythm	●	●	●	●	●	
Linking Numbers (p.68)	2	Duration – long and short	●	●	●	●		●
Numbers and Symbols (p.70)	2	Dynamics	●	●	●	●	●	
Numbers in Groups (p.72)	1 – 2	Metre	●	●	●	●	●	
Notes and Numbers (p.74)	2	Pitch	●	●	●	●	●	

a Controlling sounds, **b** Performing, **c** Composing, exploring & improvising, **d** Communicating & recording, **e** Developing understanding, **f** Responding & evaluating.

BASICS (continued)	Key Stage	Focuses: musical elements	Main emphasis of activity Performing & Composing / Listening & Appraising					
			a	b	c	d	e	f
PICTURES AND SYMBOLS								
Pictures and Cues 1 *(p.78)*	1	Timbre	●	●	●		●	
Pictures and Cues 2 *(p.80)*	1	Dynamics	●	●		●		●
Pictures in Sequence 1 *(p.82)*	1	Timbre and structure	●	●	●	●	●	
Pictures in Sequence 2 *(p.83)*	1	Tempo – fast and slow	●	●	●	●		●
Pictures in Sequence 3 *(p.85)*	1	Timbre, rhythm and pitch	●	●	●	●	●	
Shapes in Sequence *(p.87)*	1	Rhythm	●	●	●	●	●	
Symbols in Sequence *(p.89)*	2	Pulse and timbre	●	●	●	●	●	
Diagrams *(p.91)*	2	Pulse and dynamics	●	●	●	●		
Musical Frieze *(p.93)*	1 – 2	Structure and texture	●	●	●	●	●	
Scenes in Sound *(p.96)*	2	Texture	●	●	●	●	●	●
Grids and Boxes 1 *(p.99)*	1 – 2	Timbre and structure	●	●	●	●	●	●
Grids and Boxes 2 *(p.103)*	2	Rhythm and structure	●	●	●	●	●	
Mapping *(p.105)*	1 – 2	Form	●	●	●			●

a Controlling sounds, **b** Performing, **c** Composing, exploring & improvising, **d** Communicating & recording, **e** Developing understanding, **f** Responding & evaluating.

BASICS (continued)	Key Stage	Focuses: musical elements	Main emphasis of activity Performing & Composing / Listening & Appraising					
			a	b	c	d	e	f
DOTS, LINES AND SPACES								
Dots and Spaces 1 *(p.110)*	1 1	1. Pulse and tempo – fast and slow 2. Rhythm	●	●	●	●	●	●
Dots and Spaces 2 *(p.113)*	2	Rhythm	●	●	●	●	●	
Dots and Lines 1 *(p.116)*	1	Pitch	●	●	●		●	
Dots and Lines 2 *(p.120)*	2	Pitch	●	●	●	●	●	
Dots and Lines in Sequence 1 *(p.124)*	1	Structure	●	●	●			
Dots and Lines in Sequence 2 *(p.126)*	2	Structure	●	●	●	●	●	
Dots and Lines in Layers 1 *(p.128)*	1	Texture	●	●	●		●	
Dots and Lines in Layers 2 *(p.130)*	2	Texture	●	●	●	●		●
Dots and Lines in Sections *(p.132)*	2	Contrast and form	●	●	●	●	●	●

a Controlling sounds, **b** Performing, **c** Composing, exploring & improvising, **d** Communicating & recording, **e** Developing understanding, **f** Responding & evaluating.

PROJECTS	Year group	Focuses: musical elements	Main emphasis of activity Performing & Composing / Listening & Appraising					
			a	b	c	d	e	f
Hidden in the Jungle *(p.136)*	R – 2	1. Timbre 2. Texture 3. Timbre	●	●	●		●	●
What time is it on the Clock *(p.140)*	R – 2	1. Pulse and accompaniment 2. Pitch 3. Pitch and rhythm 4. Pulse	●	●	●		●	
Rocket *(p.143)*	R – 3	1. Timbre and dynamics 2. Pitch	●	●	●		●	●
Roof Top Cat *(p.146)*	R – 3	Melody	●	●	●	●	●	
Wash Day *(p.151)*	R – 3	1. Pulse and accompaniment 2. Timbre 3. Timbre 4. Structure	●	●	●	●	●	●
Fireworks *(p.156)*	1 – 4	1. Timbre 2. Rhythm and texture 3. Links with movement	●	●	●			●
Noisy Traffic *(p.161)*	1 – 4	1. Pulse and metre 2. Timbre and structure 3. Timbre	●	●	●	●	●	●
Top Athlete *(p.167)*	1 – 4	1. Timbre and structure 2. Texture 3. Timbre 4. Rhythm	●	●	●	●	●	●
Weather Witch *(p.177)*	1 – 4	1. Accompaniment 2. Timbre 3. Pitch 4. Timbre 5. Texture 6. Structure 7. Rhythm 8. Timbre 9. Rhythm 10. Pitch	●	●	●	●	●	●
Forest Music *(p.188)*	2 – 5	1. Timbre 2. Structure 3. Texture	●	●	●	●	●	
Dinosaurs *(p.194)*	2 – 5	1. Pitch 2. Timbre	●	●	●		●	
Train Game *(p.199)*	2 – 6	1. Rhythm 2. Pitch 3. Rhythm and Pitch	●	●	●		●	
Chatter with the Angels *(p.204)*	3 – 5	1. Melody 2. Rhythm 3. Rhythm 4. Pitch 5. Pitch and Rhythm 6. Form	●	●	●		●	●

a Controlling sounds, **b** Performing, **c** Composing, exploring & improvising, **d** Communicating & recording, **e** Developing understanding, **f** Responding & evaluating.

PROJECTS (continued)	Year group	Focuses: musical elements	Main emphasis of activity Performing & Composing / Listening & Appraising					
			a	b	c	d	e	f
Bird Calls (p.209)	3 – 6	1. Pitch and rhythm 2. Structure 3. Structure and texture	●	●	●	●	●	●
The Carnival of Animal Life (p.216)	3 – 6	1. Melody and timbre 2. Links with English and Art 3. Mood and character 4. Pulse and accompaniment 5. Mood and Character	●	●	●		●	●
Satellite Song (p.223)	3 – 6	1. Melody and structure 2. Pitch 3. Pulse 4. Rhythm and texture	●	●	●	●	●	
Theseus and the Minotaur (p.229)	3 – 6	1. Pitch and rhythm 2. Mood and character 3. Rhythm 4. Pitch and rhythm 5. Form	●	●	●		●	●
Welcome to the Party (p.239)	3 – 6	1. Accompaniment 2. Melody and form 3. Structure	●	●	●		●	
Wide Awake (p.242)	3 – 6	1. Rhythm 2. Texture	●	●	●	●	●	●
African Music (p.245)	5 – 6	1. Rhythm and accompaniment 2. Timbre 3. Structure 4. Melody	●	●	●	●	●	●
Cotopaxi and the People (p.251) of the Andes	5 – 6	1. Melody 2. Pitch 3. Melody 4. Accompaniment 5. Rhythm and pitch 6. Melody	●	●	●		●	
Night Music (p.260)	5 – 6	1. Timbre 2. Pitch and pulse 3. Pitch 4. Form 5. Mood and character	●	●	●	●	●	●
Pan Gu – Creation Story (p.266)	5 – 6	1. Timbre 2. Links with movement 3. Melody and accompaniment 4. Dynamics 5. Rhythm and timbre 6. Pitch 7. Melody and accompaniment 8. Form	●	●	●		●	●
Troika – On the Ski Slope (p.277)	5 – 6	1. Form 2. Rhythm 3. Timbre 4. Dynamics	●	●	●	●	●	●

a Controlling sounds, b Performing, c Composing, exploring & improvising, d Communicating & recording, e Developing understanding, f Responding & evaluating.

Index A: Focuses (musical elements)

Index B: Topics

Index C: CD Contents

💿 **CD B**

Dinosaurs

B1	Dinosaur (song) *2'30"*	194	clarinet, synth
B2	Dinosaur (song, instrumental version) *2'30"*	194	clarinet, synth

Train Game

B3	Three rhythm signals *30"*	199	percussion
B4	Six rhythm signals (box 1) *29"*	201	percussion
B5	Six pitch signals (box2) *30"*	203	trumpet, percussion

Chatter with the Angels

B6	Chatter with the Angels (song, parts 1 and 2) *37"*	204	flute, clarinet, violin, viola, 'cello, synth

Bird Calls

B7	a) Hen, b) Blackbird, c) Song-thrush *1'46"*	209	samples of bird call
B8	a) Cuckoo and cuckoo whistle, b) Hen and xylophone *1'03"*	209	samples of bird call, whistle, xylophone
B9	Blackbird and metallophone *39"*	209	samples of bird call, metallophone
B10	Bird call shapes *1'22"*	209	whistles, tuned percussion
B11	Bird call piece *22"*	212	bamboo whistle
B12	Aviary Music *36"*	214	samples of bird call, bird whistles

The Carnival of Animal Life

B13	The Carnival of Animal Life (song) *3'59"*	216	trumpet, harp, violin, viola, 'cello, xylophone, guitar, synth
B14	The Carnival of Animal Life (song, instrumental version) *3'59"*	216	trumpet, harp, violin, viola, 'cello, xylophone, guitar, synth
B15	Excerpt from the Introduction (from Saint-Saëns' *Carnival of the Animals*) *38"*	216	orchestra
B16	Excerpt from the Aquarium (*Carnival of the Animals*) *34"*	216	orchestra
B17	Excerpt from the Fossils (*Carnival of the Animals*) *30"*	216	orchestra
B18	Excerpt from the Royal March of the Lion (*Carnival of the Animals*) *22"*	216	orchestra
B19	The Carnival of Animal Life musical procession *1'50"*	220	xylophone, percussion

Satellite Song

B20	Satellite Song *2'33"*	223	flute, saxophone, glockenspiel, synth
B21	Satellite Song (instrumental version) *2'33"*	223	flute, saxophone, glockenspiel, synth

Theseus and the Minotaur

B22	Theseus' Fanfare *32"*	234	trumpet, percussion

Index D: Games – Basics – Projects – *Songs and Chants*